A Companion to the Works of Thomas Bernhard

Studies in German Literature, Linguistics, and Culture

Edited by James Hardin
(*South Carolina*)

The Camden House Companions provide well-informed and up-to-date critical commentary on the most significant aspects of major literary works, periods, or figures. The Companions may be read profitably by the reader with a general interest in the subject. For the benefit of student and scholar, quotations are provided in the original language.

A COMPANION TO THE WORKS OF

Thomas Bernhard

Edited by
Matthias Konzett

CAMDEN HOUSE

First published 2002 by Camden House
Reprinted in paperback and transferred to digital printing 2010

Camden House is an imprint of Boydell & Brewer Inc.
668 Mt. Hope Avenue, Rochester, NY 14620, USA
www.camden-house.com
and of Boydell & Brewer Limited
PO Box 9, Woodbridge, Suffolk IP12 3DF, UK
www.boydellandbrewer.com

Paperback ISBN-13: 978-1-57113-461-5
Paperback ISBN-10: 1-57113-461-1
Hardback ISBN-13: 978-1-57113-216-1
Hardback ISBN-10: 1-57113-216-3

Library of Congress Cataloging-in-Publication Data

A companion to the works of Thomas Bernhard / edited by Matthias Konzett.
p. cm. — (Studies in German literature, linguistics, and culture)
Includes bibliographical references and index.
ISBN 1-57113-216-3 (alk. paper)
1. Bernhard, Thomas — Criticism and interpretation. I. Konzett, Matthias, 1960– II. Studies in German literature, linguistics, and culture (Unnumbered)

PT2662.E7 Z625 2002
838'.91409—dc21

2001059854

A catalogue record for this title is available from the British Library.

This publication is printed on acid-free paper.

Cover image: Photo of Thomas Bernhard © and used by kind permission of Joseph Gallus Rittenberg.

Contents

Bernhard and Drama

Bernhard's Social Worlds

Acknowledgments

THIS VOLUME GREW OUT OF A SYMPOSIUM at Yale University held in February 1999, commemorating Thomas Bernhard's legacy on the tenth anniversary of his death. Special thanks goes to Gitta Honegger who first approached me with this idea and organized an exciting dramatic reading of Bernhard's work with the well-known actor Phil Bosco. The event was kindly sponsored by the Austrian Cultural Institute, the Department of Germanic Languages and Literatures at Yale University and Ezra Stiles College. The idea of putting together a volume of essays extending the range of the symposium was suggested by James Hardin, editor at Camden House, who has been a supportive force throughout this project. Additional thanks to James Walker and all the contributors, particulary to Wendelin Schmidt-Dengler, Dagmar Lorenz and Mark Anderson for their encouragement and advice. Marlene Streeruwitz has kindly permitted the use of two essays for this volume. The cover image is given with the kind permission of Joseph Gallus Rittenberg, the two photographs in the volume with kind permission of Erika Schmied.

M. K.
March 2002

Abbreviations

A	*Auslöschung: Ein Zerfall* (Frankfurt: Suhrkamp, 1986)
AB	"An der Baumgrenze." *An der Baumgrenze* (Reinbek bei Hamburg: Rowohlt, 1980)
B	*Beton* (Frankfurt: Suhrkamp, 1982)
DK	*Der Keller. Eine Entziehung* (Salzburg: Residenz, 1976)
DS	*Der Stimmenimitator* (Frankfurt: Suhrkamp, 1978)
E	*Die Erzählungen* (Frankfurt: Suhrkamp, 1979)
F	*Frost* (Frankfurt: Suhrkamp, 1963)
GG	*Gesammelte Gedichte.* Ed. Volker Bohn (Frankfurt: Suhrkamp, 1991)
H	*Heldenplatz* (Frankfurt: Suhrkamp, 1988)
K	*Korrektur* (Frankfurt: Suhrkamp, 1975)
U	*Der Untergeher* (Frankfurt: Suhrkamp, 1983)
UM	Ingeborg Bachmann, "Unter Mördern und Irren." *Das dreißigste Jahr. Erzählungen* (Munich: dtv, 1995; originally published 1961)
V	*Verstörung* (Frankfurt: Suhrkamp, 1967)

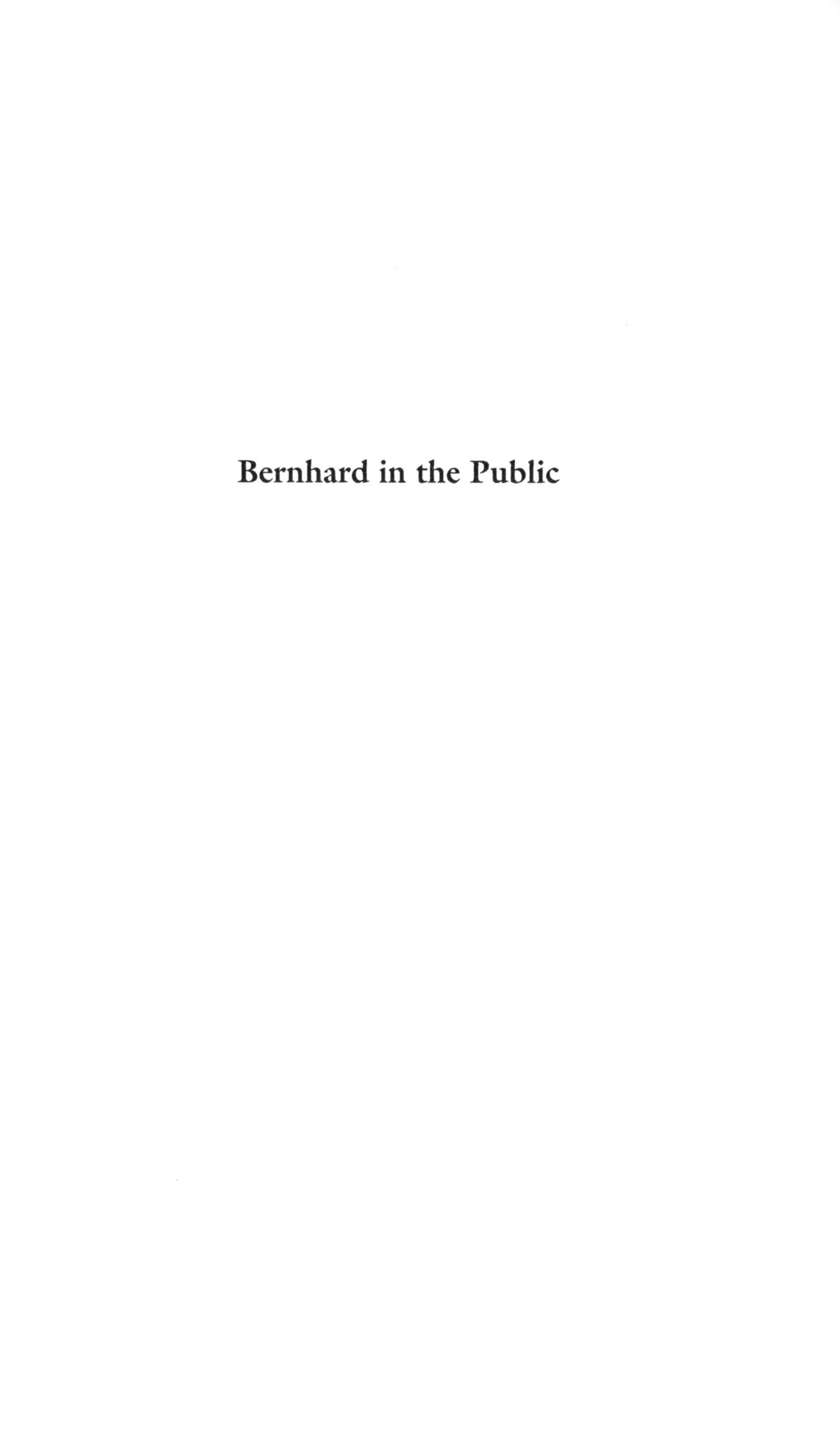

Bernhard in the Public

Matthias Konzett

Introduction
National Iconoclasm: Thomas Bernhard and the Austrian Avant-garde

THIS COLLECTION OF ESSAYS on Thomas Bernhard takes a fresh look at the author following the recent tenth anniversary of his death. Although Bernhard may have left in the eyes of some readers a rather embittered final will, prohibiting his plays to be performed in Austria for years to come, the positive reception of his works has steadily grown internationally. Bernhard's final act of self-annihilation, histrionic and ambivalent as it may be, did little to decrease or increase his already significant status as one of the most important German speaking post-war authors. Like Kafka or Becket, Bernhard has become a thoroughly canonical figure in modern literature with a bold new style that defies imitation. In Kierkegaard's sense, he may even be called a classic author, one who meets up with the defining moments of history, creating a unique and unrepeatable expression of an era. As a writer inheriting the dubious legacy of Austria's fascist past and its complicity with genocidal crimes, Bernhard has examined the violence that constitutes fascism more thoroughly and more relentlessly than most of his Austrian contemporaries. His unique style captures the xenophobic and claustrophobic atmosphere of Austria's postwar cultural homogeneity, marking the descent from an imperial transnational cultural order into the terror of a petty-bourgeois national one. Naturally, Bernhard overstates his case, idealizing at once the imperial past while denying the significant political changes that have marked Austria's democratic postwar culture. However, Bernhard's critical prose and drama serve as a steady reminder of the unease that surrounds the country's desired return to a state of normality.

The criticism of Bernhard, which this volume assembles, has also grown with the author and reached a more acute stance of self-criticism. Bernhard is no longer uncritically worshipped, as was the case when he entered the literary scene in the 1960s and 1970s. Critics have become increasingly wary of Bernhard's seductive iconoclasm, suspecting beneath it remaining symptoms of the disease the author purports to cure. Ria Endres's pathbreaking feminist study on Bernhard, *Am Ende angekommen* published in 1980, no longer comes as a shock to today's readers as it did to the many Bernhard devotees of that time. Instead, we have grown quite used to reading Bernhard against the grain while acknowledging the continuing benefit that is derived from reading his works. This volume finds its tension precisely in its balance between critical and reconstructive readings. Bernhard's work, we have gradually come to understand, embodies, expresses, dissects and celebrates the symptoms of his society. He is both a product of and a reflective agent from within his culture. Akin to Niklas Luhmann's term, he offers us "society's society," a mirror reflection of society from within itself and from no privileged vantage point. One comes to meet in Bernhard everything that he rejects in society and everything in which he is inevitably complicit and implicated. The strength of Bernhard's work is not its claim to any superior morality but its ability to reflect upon its own social pathology.

While aesthetic and ethical questions continue to preoccupy the critics of Bernhard, they have of late relaxed in applying their insights too dogmatically. After decades in which theoretical models of one kind or another have come to dominate most literary discussions, the literary text is once again at the center of focus, strangely new and reinvigorated by having traversed through various theories of signs and culture. It is only fitting therefore to include in this volume alongside the critical essays two literary pieces by the contemporary Austrian writer Marlene Streeruwitz. Her two diametrically opposed evaluations of Bernhard, spanning the time from his death and his recent anniversary, capture the tone for the entire volume, one marked by critical appreciation. The collected essays display in all their critical acuity and complexity a refreshing sense of pleasure that makes reading and literature such a vital activity in cultural communication. All essays in this volume rely heavily on the hybrid genre of literary criticism, combining both its subjective aesthetic and objective analytic tools to convey the intellectual and literary impact of Bernhard's writings. The volume also gathers an international group of scholars, thereby doing justice to the transnational significance of the author. Rather then summarizing the essays of the various contributors, I refer readers to the table of contents as the starting point of their inquiry. I hope that in doing so readers will select the essays according to their own preferences and create their own map in understanding Bernhard.

National Iconoclasm and the Austrian Avant-garde

Introducing Bernhard to readers in the new millennium requires more than a conventional summary of his work and accomplishment. These are well documented in a variety of handbooks and encyclopedia entries and shall not be repeated here. Almost unanimously they refer to Bernhard's iconoclasm, yet struggle to define the exact nature of this iconoclasm. In the following introductory essay, I would like to explore this question from a new angle, without claiming to provide final answers. Rather, I would like to focus on a somewhat overlooked relation between Thomas Bernhard and the Austrian avant-garde. Since Bernhard openly ridiculed the avant-garde in his novel *Holzfällen* (1984) and in various remarks, it is readily assumed that Bernhard cannot be located within this tradition. Contrary to the author's own claims, I would like to discuss the proximity of his work to that of the Austrian avant-garde. In doing so, a new entry into Bernhard's work will emerge, hopefully clarifying better the historical context that shapes the writer's provocative style and his sustained animosity towards the state of Austria. In fact, it will help to illustrate the political commitment of an author who despised poses of political correctness. In order to awaken postwar Austria from its historical amnesia, Bernhard made it his vocation to disturb the convenient compromise struck between art, culture and politics. In this sense, he fulfills a similar political function like that of Heinrich Böll or Günter Grass in Germany; however, Bernhard does so with an unconventional mix of avant-garde and mainstream narrative techniques that likewise disturb the literary landscape and its solidly held notions of high and low style. Bernhard's iconoclasm is in this sense extremely important from an aesthetic and political point of view, one that not only cancels the subsidiary function of art in society but also challenges its aesthetic norms from within.

In his exile memoirs *Die Welt von Gestern* (1942), Stefan Zweig describes an all-too-familiar Austria, already clichéd at the turn-of-the-century, in which political conflicts are defused and suspended in an atmosphere of harmonization and consensus:

> Man bekämpfte sich im alten Österreich chevaleresk, man beschimpfte sich zwar in den Zeitungen, im Parlament, aber dann saßen nach ihren ciceronianischen Tiraden dieselben Abgeordneten freundschaftlich beisammen beim Bier oder Kaffee und duzten einander; selbst als Lueger als Führer der antisemitischen Partei Bürgermeister der Stadt wurde, änderte sich im privaten Verkehr nicht das mindeste.[1]

The rise to power of the anti-Semitic mayor Karl Lueger, Zweig states, had no impact on the private relations between opposing political party members. Political opposition, he claims, was only practiced in parliament and suspended after hours over a beer or some coffee. Zweig has been duly questioned about his benign depiction of Vienna, one attributed to blind spots of class privilege, and the mutilations of exile. This clichéd topos of Austria's harmonized society interestingly re-appears again in Ingeborg Bachmann's postwar short story "Unter Mördern und Irren," published in 1961 but set in the mid-1950s. Once again, victims and perpetrators of racism convene over beer and have made convenient arrangements so that painful historical memories can be laid to rest through rituals of domestic conviviality. While Zweig's clichéd portrait of turn-of-the-century Austria glosses over cultural differences in an era of the imminent demise of the empire, Bachmann's clichés stand at the very beginning, the zero hour, of Austria's newly regained sovereignty.[2] Bachmann's story focuses particularly on the silent and ineffective dissent of the three Austrian Jews present at the weekly *Stammtisch*. Her sinister portrayal of Austria's postwar Jewish survivors shows them in complicit collaboration with the status quo of cultural and historical amnesia. Jewish ancestry is dismissed or belittled,[3] dissent is mostly expressed through silent glances, problematic topics are politely avoided,[4] and Nazi Austrians are even helped in their postwar social re-instatement.[5] While Bachmann's provocative depiction of the historical amnesia of the 1950s may accurately reflect the moral dilemma of Austria's Jewish community living among its murderers, it also places undue burden on the Jewish minority to force a decisive breach of the tacitly enforced consensus between victims and victimizers. The clichés of the return to civic democracy turn Bachmann's Jews into exemplary citizens who uphold the democratic institution of the public sphere just as they had done so vitally at the turn-of-the-century. This exemplary citizenship, however, is achieved only through over-assimilation and complete self-erasure, their willingness to let bygones be bygones in an era of reconstruction. Jews, it falsely appears, continue to be the problem of Austria by preserving the status quo and preventing change in their outmoded adherence to civility.

Bachmann's story eventually brings this consensus to an impasse on the very night when only three (Mahler, Friedl, and narrator) rather than the usual five Jews (Steckel, Herz) are present, when they are outnumbered by their four non-Jewish counterparts (Haderer, Bertoni, Hutter, Ranitzky): "An diesem Freitag wendete sich das Gespräch, vielleicht weil Herz und Steckel fehlten und weil Friedl, Mahler und ich keinem als Hemmnis erschienen" (UM, 81). The topic of war is openly discussed, while in an adjoining room a war veterans' meeting takes place with its members glorying in their heroic feats. A mad self-proclaimed murderer, who, as it turns out, is incapable of any military or organized violence, joins the *Stammtisch* to tell his tale and proceeds on his exit to insult the adjoining war veterans' meeting. Upon leaving the restaurant, the Jewish narrator and Mahler stumble upon the murdered murderer, who has become a victim of the insulted veterans. With the final epiphany of "Nie wieder. Nie mehr," it is surprisingly the Jewish narrator rather than the non-Jewish Austrians who is subjected to the moral lesson of war, violence and history (UM, 105). In a curious displacement of responsibility, Bachmann shows Jews rather than Austrians having to confront history.

In spite of this displaced burden of responsibility, the story nevertheless suggests the need for a social implosion in which repressed memory and crimes are brought to the surface. Originally published in 1961, the story anticipates the implosion of Austria's conspiracy of silence that was shortly to find its challenge in the works of Thomas Bernhard and the iconoclastic provocations of the Wiener Aktionismus. The story, as an example of failed accountability, a failure given not only within the story but also on the part of the writer, will serve in this essay as the measure by which I attempt to evaluate and understand the breakthroughs in Bernhard and the Austrian avant-garde's iconoclasm. To what extent was their national iconoclasm productive in challenging, suspending and canceling out convenient stereotypes of an imagined cultural consensus that obliged victims and victimizers to ongoing civic collaboration, to the myth of symbiotic co-dependence? Where did their iconoclasm fail to achieve accountability and instead rivaled with victims over the status of victimization? And finally, how do contemporary Austrian Jewish writers view their iconoclastic legacy in their own effort to secure a climate of increased historical accountability?

Bachmann is by no means a historical revisionist and is highly critical of patriarchal cults of military comradeship and the belittled crimes of the *Wehrmacht*. As I have suggested, however, she has difficulties raising the question of Austrian postwar identity and accountability in a balanced and historically objective manner. To be sure, her story exposes the war enterprise and Austria's postwar society as one of murderers and madmen. However, Jews unfairly bear the brunt of this historical responsibility and maintain an imagined over-representation in a post-genocidal Austria. Bachmann, it appears, cannot imagine Austrian postwar culture at its zero hour without its Jews. Indeed, Jewish culture and Viennese society are so fundamentally linked that an Austrian identity is posited as co-original with that of Jewish culture in Austria. In doing so, Bachmann is historically justified, as the height of Viennese culture at the turn-of-the-century is marked by the predominance of Austrian Jewish culture. Indeed, the association of culture and Jewishness in turn of-the-century Vienna, which saw all modern and progressive cultural production as Jewish, is so strong that even a non-Jewish painter like Gustav Klimt is accused of possessing a "gout juif" [Jewish taste] upon presenting his radical ceiling murals for the University of Vienna.[6] In his study *Vienna and the Jews,* Steven Beller argues that

> the Jewishness of the cultural elite in Vienna gave the capital of the Habsburg Monarchy a cultural and intellectual importance for that time which it had never known before and certainly no longer possesses. The awkward but inescapable conclusion seems to be that it was indeed the Jews which made Vienna what it was in the realm of modern culture.[7]

Similarly, Brigitte Hamann's account of Hitler's apprenticeship in Vienna attests to the city's thoroughly Jewish character. Hitler's decision to turn Berlin into the unchallenged capital of the Reich, Hamann claims, was motivated by his plans to demote Vienna, a city he detested as being the metropolis of European Jewish culture.[8]

In Bernhard's early writings and the works of the Austrian avant-garde (Wiener Gruppe, Wiener Aktionismus), Jews are absent and no longer vividly remembered as in the case of Bachmann who felt compelled to preserve their postwar presence in Austria as an anachronism. This absence may be interpreted as an example of historical amnesia on the part of a younger generation of artists raised in the era of fascism. However, Bachmann who was born in 1926 is only five years older than Bernhard, born in 1931, and was like Bernhard a teenager during the Nazi era, much like the other artists of the Austrian postwar avant-garde. One suspects therefore a change of strategy in Bernhard and the avant-garde who are more bent on confronting the Nazi legacy, bracketing the question of Jewish culture and Jewish identity in Austria altogether. Their imagined zero hour reflects more properly a post-Shoah timeline, acknowledging the absence and destruction of Jewish culture in Austria. And more importantly, Jews are no longer present to take the blame of Austria's ills as they had done so throughout history. This radical refocusing of Austria's parasitic identity, one built on envy and resentment towards its so-called exemplary Jewish citizens, now prohibits the transfer and displacement of racism onto an imagined other. Instead, the re-constituted national community is forced to confront itself as the perpetrator of genocidal crimes. Yet, as we shall see, this is a lesson that can be suppressed or forgotten, and more conveniently so, when Jews are no longer alive in the cultural memory and thus too readily imagined as dead. While Bernhard and the avant-garde were thus successful in setting out to provoke a self-recognition of the nation as a nation of murderers, they increasingly risked standing in for the victims themselves. As Robert Schindel remarks in his novel *Gebürtig* (1992): "Die Väter haben die Unsern in die Öfen geschoben, die Mütter haben den Rosenkranz gebetet, und die Söhne wollen uns großzügig eingemeinden, setzen sich darüber hinweg, wollen unbefangen selber die Opfer sein."[9] The mono-ethnic conversation among Austrians about their fascist past becomes strangely a communicative ritual in which critical dissent allows for solidarity with victims, thereby blurring the boundary of victims and victimizers beyond recognition.

This mono-ethnic scenario of confronting national guilt leads to a schizophrenic situation in which writers and artists must portray themselves in their works simultaneously as victims and victimizers. The Wiener Gruppe (1954–1960), usually seen as one of Austria's early attempts to articulate a postwar avant-garde, can also be seen as an instance of a cathartic national iconoclasm in which a second born-generation directly and indirectly purges itself of the legacy of their parents. The offensive nature of their artwork, not unlike that of its models in earlier avant-gardes such as Dadaism and Surrealism, deliberately challenges the cult of high art, one that has apparently failed to prevent a descent into barbarism. Like the emulated avant-gardes of the 1920s, the Wiener Gruppe performs mostly in a hermetic circle of insiders at various café locations (e.g. Loos Bar, on the Graben near the former cabaret Fledermaus) and ends up entertaining those who are already sympathetic to their efforts in a self-congratulatory attitude of political correctness.[10] In his late work *Holzfällen,* Bernhard parodies this self-laudatory narcissism of the Austrian avant-garde in the figure of Auersberg, an all-too-predictable enfant terrible throwing periodically his goulash around restaurants while producing compositions that last merely seconds in a radicalized post-Weberian dodecaphonic manner.[11] The circle of Bernhard's assembled characters also includes a Viennese version of Virginia Woolf and Bernhard himself who received his introduction to the avant-garde at Maria Saal where he met up with H. C. Artmann and premiered his first plays under the tutelage of Gerhard Lampersberg, the real-life Auersberg of *Holzfällen.* The cliquish self-referential narcissism parodied by Bernhard is curiously paralleled in the frequently distorted reception of the Wiener Gruppe. In the case of H. C. Artmann's bestselling volume of poetry *med ana schwoazzn dintn* (*In Black Ink*), for example, its success is ironically due to a misunderstanding, one in which subversive dialect poetry is welcomed as a new folkloric Viennese poetry, replacing earlier fascist versions of dialect poetry such as those by the widely popular Josef

Weinheber.[12] A poem like "was na ge" mocking an inbred folkloric culture marked by provincialism and its implied slow comprehension, instead was seen as a modern celebration of the Viennese idiom, an updated Weinheber so to speak.

Sensitive to fascist propaganda, many of the experiments of the Wiener Gruppe put in the foreground structural codes of language to stress arbitrariness of signification as well as visual iconographies reflecting ironically uses and abuses of mass media. The entire semantics of culture is thereby put into question and the permissive range of public utterance is provocatively expanded. Their iconoclasm targets specifically the family as a stronghold of Austria's Catholic heritage. In a poem such as "scheissen und brunzen" this seat of authority is ridiculed through conscious verbal contamination reducing the authority of parents to biologically eliminatory and excremental functions:

scheissen und brunzen
sind kunsten.
scheissvater.
scheissmutter
scheissbruder
scheisschwester
scheisskind
scheissonkel
scheisstante
scheissgrossvater
scheissgrossmutter
. . .[13]

The poem, deliberately a provocation to good taste, reveals a profound hatred towards the family as an unquestioned institution. Moreover, it reflects the difficulty of upholding family values in an ambience where families all too often sanctioned the murder of other families. Many of Bernhard's novels similarly play out grotesque gothic family scenarios, undermining this traditional source of cultural identity. Austria's postwar generation literally must commit parricide first in order to distance itself from their parents' crimes and to define itself beyond this onerous legacy.

Amras (1964), an early novella of Bernhard, can be read as a paradigmatic stock scenario for many of Bernhard's works up until his midcareer. The novella grimly opens with the failed attempt of a collective suicide by a desperate family succumbing to inherited diseases (epilepsy) and financial disaster. Of the two children that are saved by accident, the older brother eventually dies of epilepsy, leaving the younger brother, the story's narrator, in total abandonment and isolation. This imagined scenario of orphanage re-appears again and again in Bernhard's novels, producing a tale of the zero hour in which the hero has to re-invent himself along with his newly elected cultural affinities for the lack of not possessing a tradition. This gruesome scenario works to liberate the hero from unwanted dependence, sending him on the lonely path of artistic and intellectual self-discovery. Along this path, the hero often destroys the entire remaining legacy of the family, squanders the inherited estate, and sometimes even kills himself in a final act of self-cancellation. In early tales and novels of Bernhard, the inherited legacy is often construed in the biological terms of disease and madness. In *Amras*, for example, the epilepsy of the mother is depicted as a widespread disease, afflicting the entire region and therefore seen as an inescapable symptom of biological-cultural decline: "Es schien, als hätte diese jederzeit überall in Tirol entstehende Krankheit sich nach dem Tod unserer Mutter zur Gänze auf Walter geworfen."[14] This Spenglerian and de-evolutionary scenario, apart from its cancellation of parental authority, is curiously rooted in nineteenth century discourses of racial and biological determinism that had constituted the foundation of Nazi ideology. In difference to Nazi ideology, Bernhard not so much bemoans but welcomes the cultural decline of a people he has come to hate as his own kind. While Bernhard's early tales reflect the dilemma of the second-born generation and the cultural vacuum this generation inherits, they still do not clearly identify the cultural and historical reasons that have led to this decline in Austrian culture. Bernhard's early narrations remain trapped in a circular logic of self-hatred, occupying at once the role of victims and victimizers.

A growing awareness of the futility of killing off one's ancestry marks the development of Bernhard's works. For what must be overcome is not so much the ancestral generation than the already internalized and inherited ancestral ideology, turning the new postwar generation into petty bourgeois replicas of the old fascists. Enslavement to consensus on the political left or right quickly reinstates in Austria a climate of silence and conformity seemingly overcome by postwar reforms. In response to this coercive climate of consensus, Bernhard's prose increasingly aligns itself with outsiders and marginalized voices in society. Bernhard consciously stages social, cultural and intellectual difference in a hyperbolic, irritating and provocative manner. While many of his early characters succumb to their double curse of bearing a dark legacy and a marginal position in society, they also resist convenient re-integration into the postwar scenario of successful reconstruction.

Here Bernhard's work bears resemblance to the iconoclastic aesthetics of the Wiener Aktionismus that deliberately provoked the sensibility of the petty bourgeois yes-men and taunted citizens to reveal their authoritarian personalities when wishing to censor unsavory art.

Just as the Aktionisten destroy the sacrosanct confines of the painterly canvas and embark on scandalous performances that resist the demands of the bourgeois cultural sphere, Bernhard launches in his writings into a serialization of mentally diseased and socially estranged characters who are no longer compatible with Austria's regained economic and cultural confidence. In the face of increasing postwar normalization, Bernhard and the Aktionisten take on the role of reflecting society's symptoms, by staging in their works its isolated and repressed pathology. Given the different media, the methods are not identical but amount to a similar provocative gesture. In the case of the Aktionisten, society's pathology is made visible on the body through rituals of physical mutilations, mummification and staged sacrifice. "Castration (Schwarzkogler, Nitsch) and injury, wounding, crucifixion and death (Nitsch), stifling situations of helplessness, and situations where the person is reduced to the status of mere material"[15] are preferred stock scenarios in the group's performances. Frequently, these *Malaktionen* are often directly or indirectly linked to the authorities of state and church to enhance their shock impact of national iconoclasm. Hermann Nitsch's collage "the first holy communion," consisting of sanitary napkins and religious symbols, resulted in a six-month suspended sentence for offending religious sensibilities. Günter Brus likewise earned a six-month sentence and was forced to leave Austria after being indicted on charges of degrading national symbols. Allegedly he publicly defecated and urinated while singing the national anthem during one of his performances.[16] Bernhard's infamous *Staatspreisrede* of 1968 amounts to a similar verbal offense, causing the minister of education to leave the ceremony.

Apart from the superficial offense that these public scandals may have caused, they significantly altered the symbolic landscape of Austria's postwar culture. They erected a critical ambience in which the negotiation of national identity could no longer be seen apart from a pathological desire to impose a hegemonic symbolic structure as the nation's lingua franca. Bernhard's characters and the performances of the Aktionisten resist canonization in the sense of a venerable *Leitkultur* or conservative educational ideal. Granted, their works have been commercially co-opted over time and may have lost some of their vital elements of resistance. It is interesting that in both oeuvres, resistance is most often staged in a form of consciously staged self-victimization.

Breaking through the historical amnesia, they re-enact burdensome memories of the body's total disposability as in torture, mummification and physical decay. Evocations of Nazi crimes may not be intentional but always resonate in the iconography of the Aktionisten. Similarly, in Bernhard's novels outsiders are pushed to the brink of their existence in a fashion reminiscent of a well-rehearsed *Ausgrenzung* of others during the Nazi era.

In this early phase of a de-sublimation of public memory, both Bernhard and the Aktionisten return us to the scene of the forgotten crime. They intentionally inflict upon their viewers and readers an experience of suffering and disgust that surpasses conventional understanding and forms of humanistic pathos and empathy. Instead, one comes face to face with a type of dehumanization that falls outside the convenient patterns of re-integration and normalization that make up Austria's postwar history. Bernhard's novel *Frost,* published in 1963 around the time the performances of the Aktionisten came to be known, shares a similar iconographic repertoire with this group of artists. During his medical internship, the novel's narrator takes on the additional task of observing the chief surgeon's estranged brother, the painter Strauch, in a remote Alpine village. He spends twenty-six days with him and witnesses the total psychic disintegration of an individual, who shortly after his departure is missing and presumed dead. The novel opens with shocking anatomical images not unlike those evoked in Otto Muehl's performance "Versumpfung des Körpers" or Rudolf Schwarkogler's staged mutilations:

> Eine Famulatur besteht ja nicht nur aus dem Zuschauen bei komplizierten Darmoperationen, aus Bauchfellaufschneiden, Lungenflügelzuklammern und Fußabsägen, sie besteht nicht nur aus Totenaugenzudrücken und aus Kinderherausziehen in die Welt. Eine Famulatur ist nicht nur das: abgesägte und halbe Beine und Arme über die Schulter in den Emailkübel werfen.[17]

In this very opening paragraph of the novel, Bernhard presents the body in its clinical and absolutely dehumanized form as plain material to be anatomically dissected. The outrageous claim that a medical internship does not merely consist of opening up body cavities, sawing off limbs and bones and throwing them over one's shoulders into a waste bucket underscores the utterly desensitized treatment of the body in this paragraph. As the narrator eventually takes on the task of observing the surgeon's brother, one expects more human insight to be gained from this type of psychological apprenticeship. However, Bernhard's intern is instead confronted with a hopeless case of psychic disintegration.

The shock experience of cinema as described by Walter Benjamin derives from its radical change of our field of perception. Through motion, cuts and close-ups cinema fragments the human body and renders it in its most dehumanized form. Dadaism, as the most extreme expression of the avant-garde, according to Benjamin, fulfilled a similar disorienting function and prepared viewers for the shock experience of cinema: "Aus einem lockenden Augenschein oder einem überredenden Klanggebilde wurde das Kunstwerk bei den Dadaisten zu einem Geschoß. Es gewann eine taktile Qualität. Damit hat es die Nachfrage nach dem Film begünstigt."[18] The Nazi death camps had turned this simulated shock experience of physical fragmentation into a literal reality. Film footage of the horrific crimes, the camps and its mountains of dead and disposable bodies, exceed comprehension and cause a shock by far greater than cinema or Dada. For the postwar generation of visual artists, it leaves visceral and haunting images that demand to be confronted and yet defy our concepts of humanism and conventional powers of representation. As Geoffrey Hartman points out, in the post-Shoah era art "becomes suspicious of itself," particularly "of its aestheticizing drive."[19] Arguably, this legacy of an utterly destroyed confidence in the visual and the power of representation informs to a considerable degree the works of the Aktionisten and Bernhard's novel *Frost.*

In a crucial scene in *Frost,* Strauch confides in the narrator about a horrific scene of poaching that he has witnessed, evoking images of the initial anatomical setting of the novel. At this point, the initial setting of the dissecting lab has spread to the entire Alpine landscape, bearing the mark of criminal and bloody deeds. Amidst a river drenched with blood, Strauch espies the severed heads and limbs of slaughtered animals. He suspects the bloodstained river to be the source of a crime of humanity, "der Ausläufer eines Verbrechens, wie ich ganz klar erkannte, eines Menschenverbrechens" (F, 274). The blood orgy described by Strauch also calls forth associations with Hermann Nitsch's work in which the blood of slaughtered sheep is poured onto a canvas. In the novel's setting, blood similarly covers the white snow canvases ("weiße Leinwand des Schnees") of the mountain region. Strauch at one point forms red snowballs soaked with blood. In another graphic depiction, he describes the visceral impact of this grotesque spectacle:

> Köpfe, Schwänze, Gerippebrocken von Kühen. Das Weiche und Warme des frisch Geschlachteten lag noch in der Luft, der Gegensatz zwischen Kälte und Nichts und Wärme und Nichts; der Brechreiz des Grauens auf der weißen Leinwand des Schnees, ein unwiederholbares Bild: die von Himmel und Hölle zerbissene und zerschlagene und zerschnittene Anatomie der Entmenschung. (F, 275)

Bernhard's text cannot address the Holocaust directly since its description renders the reader into a passive witness facing an incomprehensible event or risks becoming an aestheticizing reduction on the author's part. The challenge for Bernhard, however, lies in evoking a visceral and moral response on the part of the reader/viewer to overcome the position of the bystander.

In her discussion of Claude Lanzmann's *Shoah*, a film documentary about the Holocaust that consciously avoids graphic depiction and original footage of the camps, Shoshana Felman shows that its structure is based instead on the performance of witnessing:

> Lanzmann's film is an exploration of the differences between heterogeneous points of view, testimonial stances. . . . Victims, bystanders and perpetrators are here differentiated not so much by what they actually see . . . as by what and how they *do not* see, by what and how they *fail to witness.*[20]

This "relation between art and witnessing"[21] similarly constitutes the core of Bernhard's works and the Aktionisten. While they may never directly address and only indirectly evoke the civilizational crime or *Zivilisationsbruch* that marks the zero hour for postwar Austria, they are very much engaged in raising civic awareness in the form of witnessing. In this sense, the act of seeing takes on an ethical dimension of accurate vision. Carold Reed's *The Third Man* (1949), a re-education film set in postwar Vienna, demonstrates in the two major protagonists that one must be able to turn in the perpetrator even if he happens to be a close friend and national compatriot. Much of the film dwells on the necessity to see and acknowledge victimization so as to become aware of a committed crime.

Bernhard, in pursuing an aesthetics of witnessing, projects the nonwitnessed and overlooked crime back onto the beloved landscape of the perpetrators, soiling their cherished Alpine region that is about to be marketed for the Winter Olympic Games of 1964 in scenic Innsbruck. Following this international event, the Alps of Austria would once again appear sanitized in the musical *Sound of Music* (1965). Bernhard's anti-*Heimatsroman* clearly opposes this tendency of rehabilitating Austria too quickly. It is interesting to note that Strauch refers to the witnessed scene as an unrepeatable image, "ein unwiederholbares Bild" as if referring to that other singularly unique event of barbarism. And like an action painter, Strauch no longer confines himself to the painterly canvas. Like Arnulf Rainer, a consociate of the Aktionisten, he practices a "Malerei, um die Malerei zu verlassen."[22] Stepping in front of the landscape and assuming responsibility for the act of witnessing, he pronounces the scene of the crime a ready-made painting: "Ich will das Bild 'Abschlachtung' nennen" (F, 276). As with Dadaism and the avant-garde, the aura of art is destroyed to provoke action rather than passive contemplation. In Bernhard's text, the act of witnessing is presented as a learning process, an internship, in which the narrator has to acquire the skill of observation in the active and interventionist sense. Naturally he fails but leaves instead a written record of Strauch's psychic disintegration. Strauch remains equally ambivalent about his lesson in the art of witnessing, telling the narrator to remain silent about the entire incident: "Eine kopflos publik gemachte Zeugenschaft," Strauch claims, "führt in den unglaublichen Ekel gestrenger Gerichtsmeierei" (F, 278–79). This statement betrays at once justified skepticism about appropriate justice where crime exceeds the scope of justice as well as resignation and withdrawal into silence.

As a writer, Bernhard adopts both the persona of the demented painter Strauch, contaminated by what he witnesses, and that of the medical intern who scrupulously records, dissects and analyses the pathology under investigation. Hartman's statement that in post-Shoah art "the reflective and the creative . . . mingle conspicuously"[23] could be well applied to Bernhard's own suspicious aesthetics, one forever tracking its own conspiracy of silence. In subsequent works, Bernhard no longer represents the act of seeing and witnessing in its immediate visual sense and interconnectedness. Instead, many of his narrators come across abandoned manuscripts from which they reconstruct the demise of the protagonist. Painting reappears one more time prominently in Bernhard's *Alte Meister* where the main protagonist is entranced by a self-portrait of the Venetian master Tintoretto. It can be argued that the visual violence depicted in Bernhard's *Frost* is increasingly imported into the medium of writing, following the rise of structuralism as mediated through the experiments of the Grazer Literaturforum and its Wittgensteinian variation of linguistic determinism. Bernhard's *Korrektur,* for example, finds in architecture an appropriate correlate for the syntactic violence that the author wishes to convey. The novel's abstract and cold narration echoes the actual designs of Wittgenstein's sterile building dedicated to his sister in the narcissistic fashion of the self-aggrandized genius. The Wittgensteinian turn in Bernhard's prose, one characterized by obsessive syntactical qualification, pushes his art further down the path of dehumanization. In spite of this aesthetic change in Bernhard's work, his social and cultural iconoclasm remains constant to the point of turning into a mannerism. As is the case with the avant-garde, Bernhard's work eventually becomes reabsorbed by the mainstream and thereby loses the edge of its iconoclastic function. Also, the topos of social victimization, as Bernhard realizes, becomes increasingly facile and needs ironic complication. By the mid-1970s, Bernhard, as is generally acknowledged, takes on a lighter tone, ironizing his self-destructive characters and their self-serving use of social marginalization. A change less frequently noted, is the cautious return of Jewish characters as in *Wittgenstein's Neffe, Der Untergeher,* and *Heldenplatz.* Although Bernhard no longer witnesses the rise of a new generation of Jewish voices in Austria in the 1990s, he anticipates their imminent return. With Bernhard's death, the self-revolving discourse of national iconoclasm and confrontation comes to an end. Austria's recent history, it becomes clear, cannot be entirely told from the point-of-view of the perpetrators or their dissenting children. *Heldenplatz, Auslöschung* and Bernhard's final will, prohibiting the performance of his plays in Austria, can be understood as the author's ironic acknowledgement of this imminent change in Austria's cultural landscape in which a new dissenting force, namely the living and present Jewish community of Austria, would occupy center stage.

At the present, we witness a return of Bachmann's zero hour scenario discussed earlier in this essay, however, with a markedly different negotiation of its position of victims and victimizers. In a critical rethinking of the issues of Nazi legacy and its confrontation, Austrian Jewish writers take a decidedly different stance from the previous generation of non-Jewish dissenters. What was once seen as the authentic outcry of moral outrage is now more soberly questioned as revealing residual self-serving and narcissistic features. After all, the staged victimization and protest of the second-generation, often earned the children of the perpetrators public recognition and rewards. Meanwhile, the return of Austrian exiles was consistently aborted and only facilitated in a few cases. Bernhard's suspicious and quasi-Foucaultian stance, in which power and violence characterize all institutions and above all language, the tool by which institutional power is maintained, may have well made him an early postmodernist in postwar Austrian literature. His ironic treatment of his perspective of suspicion added a further postmodern touch to the author who not only identifies but also celebrates his pathology. Enjoy your symptom, Lacan's catchword, becomes the motto of Bernhard's later works and its aesthetics of posthumanism. This confidence in resurrecting a negative theology of power in a posthumanist society ultimately undermines the iconoclastic impulse of Bernhard and makes him a commodity for cultural skeptics of any political conviction (left and right, and even far right). A lack of historical specificity facilitates at once his transnational appeal but also restricts his relevance for the developing discourse about Austria's past.

Doron Rabinovici's novel *Suche nach M.* (1997) restores this local specificity that is absent in Bernhard's prose. An ironic detective story, the novel narrates the destinies of a variety of interwoven biographies and generations and of crimes past and present. To complicate matters, the story provides us with a number of professional decoders such as the detective Siebert, the art historian Sina Mohn, the psychoanalyst Caro Sandner and the avant-garde painter Otto Toot, each tracking down in their own manner histories of obscured and overlooked criminal acts. The novel's entire scenario ironically plays upon films like *M.* and *The Third Man* in which elusive killers must be brought to trial with the help of the entire population. In contrast to these films, this novel's search is conducted for the most part by the victims themselves to the point where even new crimes fall under their investigation. This overcompensation on the part of the victims lends the work a dark humor. Austria's dubious past that everybody wishes to forget resurfaces with comical revenge in unexpected turns in the lives of subsequent generations as persistent symptoms that defy repression.

Dani and Arieh, the sons of Gitta and Mosche Morgenthau and Jakob and Ruth Scheinowiz, are the children of survivors from Cracow. Their youth in Vienna is both burdened by the denial of the perpetrators and the silence of the victims whose memories only erupt after decades. Dani and Arieh respond to this dilemma with mysterious symptomatic abilities. Dani always takes on the guilt incurred by other people, compulsively confessing to crimes he did not commit. He appears everywhere at scenes of crimes where confessions can be made and keeps the entire country in suspense with his revelations, becoming the elusive phantom M. Arieh boasts of a similar intuitive power and is capable of finding guilty people without knowing their identity by slowly transforming into their appearance and adopting their mannerism. This peculiar skill allows him to track down neo-Nazis and, as an agent recruited by the Mossad, enemies of the state of Israel. Not unlike Bernhard's works, the novel is wary of an obsessive preoccupation with guilt, although it proceeds from the opposite direction. For the most part, survivors and their descendants become involved in acts of denial, confession and accusation, while the remainder of the population remains untouched by its historical legacy.

In a crucial chapter, Rabinovici's novel also addresses the legacy of the Austrian avant-garde personified by the painter Otto Toot, a comical caricature of the Viennese action painters. His new show attracts the kleptomaniac art critic Sina Mohn who had an earlier run-in with Dani who confesses in her stead an act of shoplifting and becomes her temporary lover. Dani, developing skin rashes due to his sensitive response to unconfessed crimes, is covered all over his body with large bandages. He is referred to as "Mullemann" or bandage man and resembles the artwork of the Aktionist Rudolf Schwarzkogler or of the fictionalized counterpart Otto Toot who produces artwork along the lines of Schwarzkogler and his bandage performances:

> Dennoch lockte sie [Sina Mohn] zunächst, was sie von Otto Toots Bildern gehört hatte, daß er Vermummte und Einbandagierte, Schmerzensmänner in Mull malte. Sina Mohn wußte verschiedene, insbesondere heimische Traditionen der Avantgarde zu nennen, die sich ebenfalls mit der Übermalung von Potraitierten, mit der Auslöschung im Schmerz, mit Verletzungen, Wundmalen und Blutorgien, mit Verbänden und Verhüllungen beschäftigt hatten.[24]

In a humorous comedy of errors and misrecognitions, Sina Mohn comes across another painting in the gallery that appears to be a portrait of her recent lover Dani/Mullemann. It is entitled "Ahasver," provocatively referring to the legend of "the eternal wandering Jew." Another spectator, Navah Bein, a Holocaust historian from Israel and the wife of Arieh, joins Sina in front of the canvas. She claims that the painting is rather a portrait of her husband (who in his effort to track down M. has transformed into the appearance of Mulleman) and the two women soon become involved in a debate over the private and public identity of the depicted bandaged man. Navah instructs Sina that Ahasver is an anti-Semitic legend and therefore offensive as a subject matter. In a later conversation, Sina Mohn confronts the painter with this recently acquired knowledge but he claims that the painting is a self-portrait and that he was unaware of the political import of the legend of Ahasver. Toot resembles here to some degree the Viennese sculptor Alfred Hrdlicka who has been attacked for his Holocaust monument and its stereotypical representation of the Jew as victim.[25]

Rabinovici's slapstick comedy repeatedly shows its characters tripping up over a shared history of crime and violence, often due to ignorance, corrective stereotypes of philo-Semitism and awkward and self-conscious reaction towards Jews. His novel humorously qualifies the legacy of the Austrian avant-garde, pointing to its own blind spots of overlegitimation. As Navah Bein observes:

> Da stand sie, Navah Bein, eine Historikerin aus Tel-Aviv, die seit Jahren die Geschichte der jüdischen Gemeinde in Czernowitz und ihrer hunderttausendfachen Ausmordung erforschte, die durch einen Zufall in eine Bank dieses Landes, der Heimat Luegers und Schoenerers, Hitlers und Eichmanns geraten war, um Geld zu wechseln und nun stolperte sie über die Darstellung jener Mullfigur, eines Ahasver, eines ewigen Juden, einer Ghettogestalt. Gewiß hatte der Künstler mit diesem Ge-

> mälde keine böse Karikatur beabsichtigt; womöglich das Gegenteil. Irgendwo dachte es aber in ihr: "So wollten und so wollen sie uns seit jeher sehen; in Fetzen, von Wunden umkränzt, zerschlagen, eingeschnürt und verletzt. Der ewige Jude war und ist ihnen eine Ausstellung wert. Die Väter haben ihn als Untermenschen hingerichtet, die Söhne richten ihn als Heiligen her." (Rabinovici, 203)

In Rabinovici, the politics of iconoclasm has been complicated by an insistence on differentiated positions between victims and victimizers that haunt subsequent generations of descendants. In doing so, the consensus of Austrian society is challenged along different fault lines, marking the dissymmetry between its Jewish and non-Jewish history. The novel differs from Bernhard and the Aktionisten by insisting that guilt cannot be negotiated in national and ethnic isolation. Bachmann's Jews are back at the table and no longer exchange silent glances of disapproval but demand to become a part of a real discourse of agreements and disagreements. At the same time, they still appear to carry the entire burden of the country's history, as seen in the humorous parody of symptoms of compulsive confessions (Mullemann) and an equally obsessive search for culprits (Arieh). The novel ends with Arieh tracking down Dani/Mulleman; it thus rejoins the divided Jewish identity, granting it a well-deserved normalization and a rest from history.

Rabinovici's novel allows us to look at the legacy of Bernhard in a new light. While Bernhard was immensely important in extending the freedom of what can be said in Austria's public and cultural sphere, he should not be seen as the paradigmatic representative of all its cultural participants. Historically, Bernhard's role remains limited to voicing Austria's postwar dissent and its dissatisfaction with the country's rapid normalization. He does so from within a critical margin imagined from within mainstream culture. Bernhard provides a unique critical mirror to a culture of resentment that made possible enormous acts of administrative violence through a conspiracy of silence. This violence, skillfully maneuvered in the evasive mode of passive aggression, is finally brought to surface in Bernhard. Bernhard's tirades, his staging of hatred and resentment, are not so much expressions of the author's own frustration but depict the concealed language of petty-bourgeois Austria and its postwar adjustment to its new and drastically curtailed historical role. This final stage of the implosion of the Habsburg Empire represents in its last pathetic stage the ultimate deconstruction of power.

Bernhard's entire oeuvre engages history and culture in a confrontational and relentless iconoclastic manner, deserving the label avantgarde to the extent that it calls the institution of art itself into question. Bernhard's art offers no redemptive vision of society, betraying the critical stoicism of post-Shoah art. Like the avant-garde, his work is marked by a strong sense of victimization, either staged or suffered in simulation. It is here where Bernhard betrays a remaining sentimentality of the artist as society's martyr. Rabinovici's novel, as we have seen, shows us that the status of victimization can itself become an obsessive form of self-legitimation, thereby creating a rivalry between the actual victims and their self-appointed representatives in the artists of the avant-garde. Bernhard ultimately parts with the avant-garde on this matter, distrusting the iconoclasm of the son who slays the father only to become like him. In Bernhard's case, this parricide is aborted as the author increasingly turns against himself and his age in the manner Brecht once attributed to Karl Kraus: "Als das Zeitalter Hand an sich legte, war er diese Hand."[26]

Bernhard's later and more ironic works express the realization that the critical dissent of the avant-garde had become a commodity and had turned into a mannerism in his own work. By placing his art under erasure, bringing about its own extinction (*Auslöschung*), he resembles Arnulf Rainer and his ironic qualification of avant-garde iconoclasm through the gesture of *Übermalungen.* Much like Rainer's doubled portraits consisting of photographs depicting the artist in grotesque poses and of finger paints at once exposing and erasing these poses, Bernhard's later works approach the artist's narcissism in a similar self-revealing and subversive fashion. Like Karl Kraus, Bernhard increasingly comes to view nationalism as a chauvinism built on excessive love for one's own culture, a narcissism that in turn requires xenophobia to sustain itself. The cautious return of Jewish characters (Wittgenstein, Gould, the Schuster brothers) and an intensifying cosmopolitanism in Bernhard's late work can be seen as an attempt at reopening cultural borders, indicating that the era of Austria's national insularity is coming to an end. The insertion of other Austrian voices opposes nationalism's monologic and hegemonic nature, anticipating the concern with multiculturalism in the present Europe. It is in this significant gesture of clearing a space (*Holzfällen* and *Auslöschung*) for other suppressed voices to emerge that Bernhard's legacy can be remembered in both constructive and critical fashion.

Notes

[1] Stefan Zweig, *Die Welt von gestern. Erinnerungen eines Europäers* (Frankfurt: Suhrkamp, 1998), 41.

[2] "Wir sind in Wien, mehr als zehn Jahre nach dem Krieg." Ingeborg Bachmann, "Unter Mördern und Irren," *Das dreißigste Jahr. Erzählungen* (Munich: dtv, 1995), 79; hereafter quoted in text as UM.

[3] "Friedl starrte ihn verständnislos mit seinen kugeligen wäßrigen Augen an und preßte seine Hände ineinander, wohl weil er dachte, daß er doch gar kein Jude sei, und Mahler war es auch nicht, sein Vater vielleicht, sein Großvater — Friedl wußte es nicht genau" (UM, 81).

[4] "Haderer legte eine kurze Pause ein, verwarnte erst Hutter, tadelte darauf Friedl und sprach dann überaschend vom ersten Weltkrieg, um dem zweiten auszuweichen. . . . Bertoni benutzte den Augenblick, in dem Haderer durstig sein Glas an den Mund setzte, und fing unerbittlich an, eine unglaubliche und verwickelte Geschichte aus dem zweiten Weltkrieg zu erzählen. . . . Sogar Friedl schüttelte sich plötzlich vor Lachen, es wunderte mich und wunderte mich noch mehr, als er plötzlich sich bemühte, auch eingeweiht zu erscheinen in die Operationen, Chargen, Daten" (UM, 89–90). "Jetzt mußte man befürchten, daß Haderer Friedl und mir unsere mangelhaften Griechisch- und Lateinkenntnisse vorhalten würde, ungeachtet dessen, daß seinesgleichen uns daran gehindert hatte, diese Kenntnisse rechtzeitig zu erwerben. Aber ich [Jewish narrator] war nicht in der Stimmung, auf eines der von Haderer bevorzugten Themen einzugehen oder gar ihn herauszufordern, sondern beugte mich zu Mahler hinüber, als hätte ich nichts gehört" (UM, 99).

[5] "Er [Bertoni] hatte Steckel, bevor Steckel emigrieren mußte, gut gekannt, war wieder Steckels bester Freund, nicht nur weil der bald nach 1945 für ihn gebürgt und ihn ans 'Tagblatt' zurückgeholt hatte" (UM, 85).

[6] See Carl Schorske, *Fin-de-Siècle Vienna: Politics and Culture* (New York: Vintage, 1980), 239–40.

[7] Steven Beller, *Vienna and the Jews 1867–1938: A Cultural History* (New York: Cambridge UP, 1993), 244.

[8] Brigitte Hamann, *Hitler's Vienna: A Dictator's Apprenticeship* (Oxford: Oxford UP, 1999), 6, 80.

[9] Robert Schindel, *Gebürtig* (Frankfurt: Suhrkamp, 1992), 15.

[10] "der gesellig exclusive 'strohkoffer' — so hieß das neue 'artclub' — lokal unter der kärntnerbar von adolf loos, weil der fassungsraum sehr beschränkt und die wände mit schilf austapeziert waren — zog, nicht zuletzt durch einige turbulente feste, neue besucher an, fast ausschließlich jugendliche." *die*

wiener gruppe: a moment of modernity 1954–1960, ed. Peter Weibel (Vienna: Bundesverlag, 1997), 17.

[11] Thomas Bernhard, *Holzfällen. Eine Erregung* (Frankfurt: Suhrkamp, 1984).

[12] Hans Carl Artmann, *med ana schwoazzn dintn* (Salzburg: Otto Müller, 1958).

[13] Konrad Bayer and Gerhard Rühm, "scheissen und brunzen," in *die wiener gruppe: a moment of modernity 1954–1960,* 251

[14] Thomas Bernhard, *Amras, Die Erzählungen* (Frankfurt: Suhrkamp, 1979), 12.

[15] Malcolm Greene, "Introduction," *Writings of the Vienna Actionists* (London: Atlas Press, 1999), 17.

[16] *Writings of the Vienna Actionists,* 60.

[17] Thomas Bernhard, *Frost* (Frankfurt: Suhrkamp, 1972), 7.

[18] Walter Benjamin, "Das Kunstwerk im Zeitalter seiner technischen Reproduzierbarkeit," *Illuminationen. Ausgewählte Schriften 1* (Frankfurt: Suhrkamp, 1977), 164.

[19] Geoffrey Hartman, "Introduction: Darkness Visible," *Holocaust Remembrance: The Shapes of Memory,* ed. Geoffrey H. Hartman (Oxford, UK: Blackwell, 1994): 1–22; here 20.

[20] Shoshana Felman, "Film as Witness: Claude Lanzmann's *Shoah,*" *Holocaust Remembrance: The Shapes of Memory,* ed. Geoffrey H. Hartman (Oxford, UK: Blackwell, 1994), 90–103; here 93.

[21] Felman, 91.

[22] Arnulf Rainer, "Malerei, um die Malerei zu verlassen," originally written in 1952; reprinted in exhibition catalogue *Arnulf Rainer,* ed. Rudi Fuchs (Vienna: Historisches Museum der Stadt Wien, 1987).

[23] Hartman, 22.

[24] Doron Rabinovici, *Suche nach M.* (Frankfurt: Suhrkamp, 1997), 198.

[25] See James E. Young's *Holocaust Memorials and Meaning* (New Haven: Yale UP, 1993), 104–12. Young discusses here the controversial sculpture of the "streetwashing Jew" at the Albertina Square in Vienna. Hrdlicka's depiction of the Jews in the image of their humiliation is recalled in Otto Toot's portrait of Ahasver.

[26] Bertold Brecht quoted in Walter Benjamin, "Karl Kraus," *Illuminationen,* 366.

Marlene Streeruwitz

Perverted Attitudes of Mourning in the Wake of Thomas Bernhard's Death[1]

> . . . und jetzt auch schon in der Gewohnheit, selbst das Fürchterliche als eine leicht zu verarbeitende Alltäglichkeit hinter mich zu bringen, ein Meister, hatte ich alle Voraussetzungen, über das, was ich immer eindringlicher zu beobachten hatte, nachzudenken und mir sozusagen als willkommene Anschauung viele dazu geeignete Anschauungen oder Vorkommnisse zu einem lehrreichen Studiengegenstand zu machen.
>
> — Thomas Bernhard, *Der Atem,* 1978

Object of Study: Number One

A MUSIC TEACHER AT A VIENNESE HIGH SCHOOL says, he knew him, the master, very well indeed, and met him, Thomas Bernhard, frequently. In the café Bräunerhof. And took pictures, pictures that he, the master, liked very much, just as much as the poet had always enjoyed meeting him. And now he, the music teacher, was going to put together a book of these pictures. A book about the master, about Thomas Bernhard. And he, the music teacher, was going to become famous with this book. World-famous. Of course.

The work of mourning is a difficult, existential process and painful. It is a laborious undertaking, until all the internalized particles of the object of mourning have been surgically removed, and it becomes all too necessary to construe strategies for avoiding pain so as not to collapse completely under the weight of a loss.

On the other hand, one can always infer from the manner that characterizes the work of mourning of the bereft, whether the mourned person was loved and respected. Or whether the person doing the mourning is more at stake in all the laments, whatever they may be. In the case of Thomas Bernhard we are the ones left behind, and for the Austrian an additional sense accrues to belong to those people that were cut out of Bernhard's will. Relatives who are not to receive anything, and are not worthy of a share.

Objects of Study of a Mixed Nature

People, whom one may have seen portrayed in one or the other plays by Bernhard, have masses celebrated in his memory. Masses for Thomas Bernhard with young nuns of the Carmelite order reading early poems and psalms of the poet. Hopefully this helps those who attend the mass.

It may also calm those who talk now about Thomas Bernhard as if one had always been on close friendly terms, with all its shoulder-on-shoulder implications and all its syndromes of hugging, the verandas in the Salzkammergut and the hunting lodges with the many antlers on the wall. But one was not on intimate terms. One always heard: "Thomas, do you want some more noodle soup?" This retroactive intimacy with its informal mode of address may help.

As an observer one is somewhat amazed to note how mourning operates in the reverse order, how the mourned object is internalized rather than expelled. In all honesty, one has to admit that the thought "What would he have said about it?" originates in a similar strategy of avoiding pain as the lighthearted conversations of the salon. The sentences that begin with "Thomas would have . . .," "Here Thomas would . . .," "Bernhard did not . . . ."

Exegesis, substitute of God through citation, incantation of the person for the duration of a citation, recalling the cited person back among the living. Here lies the basic problem of all exegesis. In most cases, we are dealing with reported statements, and for the most part the personal opinion of the person reporting is clothed in a Thomas-Bernhard-costume.

Commemoration of the dead and incantation of the dead belong to the inventory of unchanging anthropological models. The dead person is conjured up in mass or over coffee and cake or over pork roast and beer. Everyone has to do so according to ability and belief. The salons in the Salzkammergut where Thomas Bernhard led serious conversations about the advantages of hand-tailored shoes serve just as well as the site of the Bräunerhof where Thomas Bernhard had a *Kleinen Braunen* and read the *Neue Zürcher*. And perhaps the remark "Thomas Bernhard sat here" is well intentioned. However. The old heads of state also sit in the salons grinning while shrugging their shoulders. After all, they have survived. But even the triumph of the living over the dead is rather normal in its cruelty.

The Pedagogical in All This

What turns this process of coping with loss into an object of study as given in the initial citation is the common urge to make mourning public.

The music teacher wants to become famous. World-famous. One works on remembrances. Letters are written to the dead person. In intimate terms, of course, and the publication can no longer be held back. Karl Hennetmair takes up two pages of the *Zeit* magazine. Austrian broadcasting anchors and directors of the Burgtheater document their proximity to Bernhard on pictures in which one appears together and preferably at the Heldenplatz. Former lovers appear in rumors. Widows have not yet been spotted.

If one were to place these pictures in a silver frame on the grand piano, for eternal memory, that would be a loving gesture. In the public, these pictures turn easily into a cornering, a wanting-to-be-in-the-picture of the bystanders. An index of one's friendship with him. Perhaps one should also look at this with regard to the technique of the work of mourning. But media are never that friendly.

What, for example, caused Mr. Schödel (*Die Zeit* Nr. 32, 1989), following immediately the advice of the photographer Rittenberg "Look at Hennetmair," when he, as he reports, was found by him in Switzerland, to allow Hennetmair's rather private work of commemoration turn into a public matter? Was it a question of demonstrating in exemplary fashion how one is to cope when one's former idol dies not reconciled and in irreconcilable fashion and the conflict is prolonged into eternity

The falling out between Bernhard and Hennetmair stems from a severe breach of trust. The publication of a description about a nonfunctioning TV-set from 1972 can be seen as an act of remorse and an attempt to be excused by handing it over to the public. Also the remark of Schödel "Yes. I was a guest at the *Weltverbesserer*" can be interpreted as severe breach of trust, yet an understandable case of the biographical method and again as Schödel's work of mourning. This has nothing to do with Thomas Bernhard. Rather with yellow journalism. Even sensitive and cautious sentences won't help here. And towards the end of the article in *Die Zeit,* one is drawn logically to the core of all discussions about Bernhard, the author's final will.

Here too, as in the quasi-citations à la "Thomas certainly would not have . . ." the last breach of trust that can still be committed against someone is prepared. Namely, not to respect his final decrees.

One refers to the brother. He announces a guided tour through Bernhard's estate. In doing so, one receives no longer an image of people suffering in their state of mourning. A landscape in the hills of Ohlsdorf emerges where journalists wander about and are served stories and fragments of memories. Female adepts of the master, whose love letters could not be considered during his lifetime, bathe in a post-mortal intimate "you." The man who helps out in the villa displays the blue leather jacket that the master purchased in Sicily and immediately gave away. The neighbor, from whom the master gladly accepted X-mas cookies, now offers them. For sale, naturally. We all have to make a living. And the famous publisher will one day place the manuscript of the TV-set criticisms into our hand in a deluxe facsimile edition. Ohlsdorf elevated to a site of pilgrimage. Nearby Mariazell for selected groups. Preferably from a sentimental-melodramatic spectrum. The descendants of idealistic chains of weeping.

Presently, we're still searching among pieces of memory. Perhaps somebody still owns a note where the master kept score of a game of blackjack or jotted down scribbles and malicious caricatures of the players. As is known, one can possess the remembered person by means of memorabilia — and not always in a non-malicious fashion. One should bear in mind that relics, which is what we're dealing with here, that relics are remains and originate from either corpses or instruments of torture.

In this pressing into the public, we may be dealing with the attempt to externalize the mourned object. By means of this externalization, the object can be transferred onto a larger and more remote context. The mourning person surrenders and gets rid of the surrendered. Under the pretext to make it available to everybody, yes having to do so, the single person becomes free. Perhaps also free from feelings of guilt that play a considerable role in the work of mourning. That this method may involve a form of surrender which may neither look delicate nor sensitive and may have nothing to do with the mourned person, particularly not his work, doesn't really do much damage to our somewhat dried-up yet still rather lavish baroque culture of mourning. We love our dead and celebrate them.

We do not yet know the full scope of the planned surrender. "Only selected groups," says the brother. Everything else will be revealed at upcoming book fairs. One works on the super-memorial, that much we hear from Frankfurt.

In the Austrian TV talk show "Club 2," we already had a chance to listen to the benignly smiling notary, holding forth with examples of the most incredible changes in wills witnessed in his professional career. And that only a few really mean what is actually stated. And that the true evil is that people die. And no longer have a chance to change the will. In their fashion. How they would have wanted it originally. The testators. But then nothing can be done about it anymore. And that taught him not to take wills seriously anymore. And above all. Intellectual property.

Nobody shall be embarrassed when the first play will be performed again in Austria. Redirecting arguments via a liberal discussion roundtable à la "Club 2."

One could have withdrawn after the first disclosure of the will into a corner and reflected about what had happened that made such decrees necessary and that were above all not changed anymore. Everybody would have had a reason to reflect about what it was, here in this Austrian world, which always required a superlative of atrocities. And people elsewhere and in the Federal Republic of Germany could have examined Austria, the poet and the will as a case study in what a climate of intellectual narrowness does to a person. Others too know how to repress, something we do so elegantly here. That can be done anywhere. By accident we were given a few centuries to master this art and are nowadays powerless enough to possess nothing but this art. The result: extreme cruelty, unbelievable inconsiderateness and deepest misery, in Frankfurt as well as Timbuktu. An opportunity for reflection is certainly given.

Why can't one permit a grand gesture of mourning and announce the plays of Thomas Bernhard in Austrian theaters. And then not perform anything. The audience could just sit there and simply think. There is enough to think about.

Translated by Matthias Konzett

Notes

[1] Marlene Streeruwitz, "In der Gewohnheit das Fürchterliche," *Und. Sonst. Noch. Aber. Texte.* 1989–1996 (Vienna: edition Selene, 1999), 7–13.

Dagmar Lorenz

The Established Outsider: Thomas Bernhard

WHEN THOMAS BERNHARD DIED in 1989 leaving a will stipulating that none of his works ever be performed again in Austria, critics had already established a consensus about the man and his work. Bernhard was the rebellious outsider *par excellence,* the most unrelenting Austria-critic. One paradox, however, remained. Despite his criticism of the Second Republic that had made him notorious, his writing was clearly paradigmatic of Austrian literature after 1945.[1] His rhetoric notwithstanding, Bernhard, whose works were published by the prestigious Suhrkamp publishing house, was one of the most prominent and successful authors of his generation, one of the few Austrians who had won international acclaim.[2] Often referred to as a *Nestbeschmutzer* (one who defiles his own "nest") Bernhard had a reputation based precisely on what Austrian media critics and many of his fellow citizens perceived as a perpetual defamation of their national heritage and the postwar republic. Unlike other authors critical of Austrian society Bernhard occupied an unassailable position in Austrian mainstream culture. Residing in his native country until his death in 1989 he became a legend in his time and a canonical author. His plays, awaited with anticipation over the controversy they would cause, were part of the regular fare at Austrian national theaters, most notably the Vienna Burgtheater. Media events such as the public protest of the Austrian chancellor concerning *Der Theatermacher* (1984) and the stir over *Heldenplatz* (1988), commissioned by Klaus Peymann on the occasion of the 100th anniversary of the Burgtheater, added only to Bernhard's prominence.[3]

In his staged self-exclusion from the Austrian mainstream, a reaction in part to the prevailing social and political conditions, and in part to Bernhard's own problematic socialization and life experiences, including professional conflicts and his oppositional relationship with the public, Bernhard is part of a notable line of established Austrian outsiders, including Franz Grillparzer, who withdrew from Austrian public life after the unsuccessful performance of *Weh dem der lügt* (1838) and did not allow any productions of his unpublished works on Austrian stages until his death in 1892. Like Bernhard, Grillparzer was celebrated as the foremost Austrian dramatist of his time, and there can be no question about his "mainstream" status as an author. The same is true for Johann Nestroy whose irony bordering on nihilism shows a certain affinity with Bernhard's negativism and penchant for the grotesque. Among his contemporaries Bernhard has been compared to Peter Handke, whose merciless *Publikumsbeschimpfung* (1966) appeared the same year as Bernhard's polemic "Politische Morgenandacht."[4] Insofar as Bernhard's protest was directed not only against Austria but life in general, particularly modern life, he can also be compared to Oswald Wiener and other postwar avant-garde authors such as the *Wiener Gruppe*. His eccentric style and textual strategies also call to mind Fritz von Herzmanovsky-Orlando and Heimito von Doderer, writers rooted in the declining Habsburg era.

Focusing on his flamboyant anti-Austrian tirades, scholars tended to interpret Bernhard's position as nonconformist while largely ignoring his national and international standing. Despite the fact that Bernhard's work is replete with references to recent Austrian history he was rarely read in the context of national and international debates on Nazi crimes and the Holocaust. One reason for ignoring this obvious connection may be the universality of his invectives. They are directed against Austria, the Austrians, German culture, and ultimately the human condition. In *Heldenplatz,* for example, Bernhard attacks a "total verkommener Sozialismus, total verkommenes Christentum,"[5] concluding that there are no more political alternatives left: "In diesem fürchterlichsten aller Staaten haben Sie ja nur die Wahl zwischen schwarzen und roten Schweinen" (H, 164). In addition, he maintains that the Vienna is still characterized by virulent anti-Semitism: "Die Wiener sind Judenhasser und werden Judenhasser bleiben in alle Ewigkeit" (H, 84). In *Auslöschung,* Bernhard's invectives variously decry a persistent climate of National Socialism, a burdensome Germanic cultural heritage, political opportunism and the decline of morality in general:

> Ihre katholisch-nationalsozialistische Lebensweise ertrage ich ganz einfach nicht, ihren Tonfall ertrage ich nicht" (304) . . . "die deutschen Wörter hängen wie Bleigewichte an der deutschen Sprache, sagte ich zu Gambetti" (8) . . . "Das Deutsche ist das Unerträglichste" (42) . . . "Was für scheußliche Kreaturen in diesem Österreich heute die Macht haben! Die Niedrigsten sitzen jetzt oben. Die Widerwärtigsten und die Gemeinsten haben alles in der Hand und sind drauf und daran, alles, das etwas ist, zu zerstören" (112) . . . "Wir lieben unsere Mutter natürlich, sagte ich zu Gambetti, aber wir sehen doch ihre Gemeinheit und ihren Vernichtungswillen. Das infame Element kommt zum Zuge, sagte ich zu Gambetti das Moralische wird lächerlich (104)."[6]

Examining Bernhard's writing in his larger historical environment reveals a turning point in his writing several years after the widely publicized Eichmann Trial (1960) and the Frankfurt Auschwitz Trials (1962), during both of which Austria's complicity in the Nazi genocide was exposed on an international scale.

In his early polemic "Politische Morgenandacht," published in the Austrian mainstream journal *Wort in der Zeit* as part of a larger debate on Austrian identity and the growing politicization of culture, Bernhard cursorily dismissed such a concept, deploring instead the intellectual and moral decline of which he believed such a debate was indicative. One must keep in mind that Bernhard's statement was written as a response to one of the numerous *Wort in der Zeit* opinion polls, conducted at a time when the debate over Hannah Arendt's *Eichmann in Jerusalem* (1964) was still in progress. Neither the Holocaust nor related issues were addressed in the journal. One should also consider that Peter Weiss's Auschwitz drama *Die Ermittlung* (1964), Robert Neumann's criticism of Arendt, *Der Tatbestand oder der gute Glaube der Deutschen* (1965), and Jean Améry's reflections on the concentration camp experience and the long-range effects of Nazism and anti-Semitism in *Jenseits von Schuld und Sühne* (1966) date from the same time. Given Bernhard's rather general and non-specific rhetoric of cultural decline, it reveals how much more he was in tune with the discourse of the Austrian mainstream reflected in the journals *Literatur und Kritik* and *Wort in der Zeit* than with the concurrent international debates promoted in part by formerly persecuted Austrians such as Neumann and Améry. Moreover, Bernhard's laments about the corruption and shallowness of contemporary Austrian society were nothing new since similar complaints already abound in his earlier writings. What was new was the direction they took in the 1960s.

The Eichmann trial was of particular concern for Austria. Simon Wiesenthal who had his headquarters in Vienna had played a significant role in locating and identifying the man instrumental in engineering the Holocaust. In Eichmann's career Vienna had represented an important stepping stone. It was there that in 1938 Eichmann had directed the Nazi "Office for Jewish Emigration" and with the help of the local population effected the forced emigration of approximately 150,000 Jews from Austria. Considering these historical facts leading up to the genocide, the Eichmann debate,[7] and the Eichmann trial in the German-speaking media and world-wide as well as the renewed attention to Nazi atrocities in literature, it is not surprising for the Austrians and Germans of the war and postwar generations to be sickened by their country's history. Bernhard's vehement lashing out against Austria by no means lacks motivation. As Gerald L. Posner observes in *Hitler's Children,* the sins of the father "affected a second generation of Germans [and Austrians] in ways little understood or appreciated."[8] Even though Bernhard and most of his age cohort did not have to deal with the same burden as the sons and daughters of Nazi leaders, the following observations apply also to them:

> The generation responsible for the crimes closed all discussion. They refused to be honest and forthright. This silence did not eliminate the family friction, but only submerged it, often into the child's psyche. Years after the parents' death, some of the children seek to have the public discussion about their feelings that their father denied them. Since the perpetrators remained silent, the burden of seeking the truth and acknowledging the responsibility was passed to another generation.[9]

The discontent expressed by Bernhard in elemental rather than rational terms must be considered a reaction specific to a generation of Austrians and Germans. It presupposes a youth in mainstream Austria experiencing the disillusionment with the older generation and the social structures created or endorsed by them, and the repeated embarrassment associated with being a descendent of the Nazi generation. The extraordinary resonance of Bernhard's works in the 1960s until the present time, be it approval or outrage, has different origins than the more cerebral positive or negative reception of the critical writing and films by Jewish authors, Jean Améry, Friedrich Torberg, Ruth Beckermann, Nadja Seelich, Robert Schindel, and Doron Rabinovici. The response to Bernhard's works, particularly his plays, was far more widespread and passionate. Notwithstanding the fact that the author reiterated certain core themes from one work to the next, Bernhard's writings elicited intense resonance. In the true sense of the word Bernhard was a popular writer even though much of his popularity was based on his ability to incense and arouse the public.

Two years prior to "Politische Morgenandacht" the Jewish philosopher Günther Anders, who had taken up residence in Vienna after his exile years, had explored the moral and ethical ramifications of the facts brought to light in the Eichmann trial for older and younger Germans and Austrians. In his open letter to Klaus Eichmann, *Wir Eichmannssöhne,* Anders argued that the name "Eichmann" applied to everyone who did not want to know of, had actively participated in, or knew about the Nazi crimes, and that finally the term applied to the totalitarianism of mass destruction. Anders held that there was but one viable alternative not only for Eichmann's son Klaus but all "Eichmann sons," namely to repudiate their fathers since mourning them was not an option.[10] In light of the essays and accounts by survivors connected to Austria such as Jean Améry and Simon Wiesenthal the position Bernhard assumed was one of political correctness.[11] In contrast to Klaus Eichmann and others, he did not defend the perpetrators and unlike Peter Handke in *Wunschloses Unglück* (1972) and other Austrian authors in search of the world of their mothers and fathers, like Jutta Schutting, Brigitte Schwaiger, and Gerald Szyskowitz, Bernhard refrained from empathizing with or validating the viewpoints of the generation of the perpetrators.[12] Bernhard never tired to articulate his disgust with the corruption and duplicity of the Austrian public. Thus he came to represent the righteous, the exceptional Austrian. However, with many children of less well-known Nazis and Nazi supporters Anders's message fell on deaf ears. Posner notes that especially in the case of Nazi parents who themselves deny any wrongdoing "it is not surprising that some children should forgo an aggressive search for the truth at the expense of a more benign, less threatening judgment."[13]

Bernhard's fame is based on the deliberate violation of the code of silence that Ruth Beckermann aptly describes as the way both the Austrian mainstream and the survivors of the Holocaust relied on when dealing with the past in the early years of the Second Republic.[14] Coming face to face with Austro-Fascism, Austrian National Socialism, anti-Semitism, and Austria's role in the Second World War and the Holocaust became finally unavoidable during the Waldheim scandal in 1986, the year Bernhard's novel *Auslöschung* was published. The novel is an exemplary indictment of the pervasive dishonesty and cowardice that Bernhard ascribed to his fellow countrymen. *Auslöschung* takes members of the pre- and postwar generations to task, the former for their spinelessness that made them accomplices of the engineers of the genocide as well as opportunistic turncoat supporters of the Allied occupiers, the latter for their dullness of spirit and complacency.[15] The novel exposes individuals and groups that invented and endorsed the "Geschichtslüge," the historical lie, according to which Austria was the first victim of National Socialism, overwhelmed and subjugated by Hitler's army. As in Bernhard's earlier works, the theme of cultural decline as the direct result of Austria's collective lack of integrity is central in *Auslöschung*. The effects of Austro-Fascism and the participation in the genocide are manifest in the personal and public lives of the contemporary rural gentry whose representatives are portrayed as insane, moronic, or loathsome, unworthy of Austria's rich cultural heritage, incapable of carrying it on or even comprehending it. Also the mentalities of the lower classes have been poisoned by the recent past, thus erasing liberal dreams of a social revolution from below.

The first name of Bernhard's narrator Murau, Franz-Joseph, calls to mind the Habsburg past pointing to the period *ante quem*. Bernhard's protagonist would have possibly been more at home in an Austria before the decay of the multi-nation state at a time when he and his student Gambetti might have been citizens of one state. The monarchical hierarchy as well as the existence of a private scholar in an era when the liberal arts were the prerogative of an intellectual leisure class would have suited Murau's elitist pose. The act through which Murau attempts to sever his ties with his family and their legacy, the donation of his inheritance, the castle compound of Wolfsegg and the libraries, to his "Studienkollege," his former fellow student, and "Geistesbruder," his spiritual brother, Eisenberg, to benefit the Jewish Community (Israelitische Kultusgemeinde), is also his last: his suicide is implied in the note "gestorben 1983 in Rom" (A, 212, 650–51).[16] The donation followed by the narrator's death finalize the "dissolution" and thus the stated objective of the narrative:

> *Auslöschung* werde ich diesen Bericht nennen, hatte ich zu Gambetti gesagt, denn ich lösche in diesem Bericht tatsächlich alles aus, alles, das ich in diesem Bericht aufschreibe, wird ausgelöscht, meine ganze Familie wird ausgelöscht, ihre Zeit wird darin ausgelöscht, Wolfsegg wird ausgelöscht in meinem Bericht auf meine Weise. (A, 201)

It is significant that Bernhard had no personal acquaintance either with Paul Chaim Eisenberg, the chief rabbi of Vienna, nor with his father and predecessor, Bela Akiba Eisenreich. Attributing the name of an historical person to an idealized fictitious Jewish character is indicative of Bernhard's problematic attitude toward Jews and the Jewish community. Other than the name and title, Bernhard's Eisenberg lacks Jewish cultural and religious characteristics. Not unlike the Jewish characters of postwar German authors, the Jewish characters in *Heldenplatz,* wealthy but profoundly neurotic intellectuals, are modeled after traditional Jewish stereotypes and can be read as latently anti-Semitic.

The way Bernhard positioned himself in the 1960s had anything but disadvantageous consequences for the author. Neither was he ousted by his fellow Austrians and unlike other controversial intellectuals, he felt no need to leave his native country. His career began to take off after the publication of *Frost* (1963), which, like the ensuing works, differs dramatically in tone and texture from his local patriotic early writings in *Das Demokratische Volksblatt.*[17] Apparently still unaware of Austria's role in recent history, Bernhard had begun publishing in the early fifties. The short prose pieces of that era convey the image of an intact rural Austria. As Christian Klug maintains, *Heimat* (home country) in the idyllic sense was the dominant thematic complex of Bernhard's early writing. Simple country living, rejection of modern life styles, reverence for the people in and around Salzburg, epitomized in the figure of his beloved grandfather Johannes Freumbichler, author of the novel *Philomena Ellenhub*, nature mysticism, and love of folk traditions and holidays are hallmarks of these texts.[18] All in all, they conform to the postwar Austrian literary mainstream and gloss over the Nazi years. Not unlike the legacy of Austro-fascist and *Blut-und-Boden* (blood and soil) literature, they affirm the integrity especially of rural Austria. Commenting on Bernhard's aesthetic views at the time, Klug writes: "Von der Dichtung verlangt Bernhard Einfachheit und natürliche Weihe . . Das Vorbild des wahren Dichters ist der Handwerker."[19] Equally compatible with Austria's ahistoric postwar position was Bernhard's view of history, evinced by his notion of "heutige Jugend" (in 1952) "in den Jahren nach dem Ersten, ganz besonders aber nach dem Zweiten Weltkrieg."[20] At age twenty-two Bernhard considered the postwar era, rather than Austro-Fascism and the Nazi takeover, the major historical break. Klug maintains: "Bernhard strebt offenbar eine Kontinuität mit jenen Autoren an, die erst während des Austrofaschismus und des 'Anschlusses' ihre große Zeit hatten und nach 1945 als 'Heimatdichter' rehabilitiert wurden."[21] The primary historical guilt acknowledged by Bernhard involves the wrongs suffered by Austrians of his own generation and background and does not include the Jewish victims.

In Bernhard's later writings there was little change as to the preferred settings, the Upper Austrian countryside around Salzburg and Gmunden where the author grew up and continued to reside. His literary characters were frequently modeled after individuals he knew personally. The correspondences between Bernhard's biography and his writing have often inspired autobiographical interpretations of his texts. The themes of disintegration, loss, and disavowal of self as well as the lament over the state of depravity that the protagonists attribute to their environment are intimately linked to actual sites and the places where Bernhard lived. This makes Bernhard's texts unmistakably Austrian. The combination of geography, biography, and local history calls to mind Heimito von Doderer, an author of the prewar generation. Both Bernhard and Doderer were sons of mainstream Austria, both shaped by political developments of their era. Initially taken in by the same reactionary ideology, they attempted to correct their point of view, each according to the spirit of their time. Ultimately, they assumed the position of established outsiders, Doderer in Vienna's ninth district, Bernhard in Upper Austria.

Putting the poverty and deprivation of his boyhood years behind him, the increasingly prominent Bernhard acquired several real properties in Upper Austria, including a historical farm in Ohlsdorf and a house in Ottnang.[22] In painstaking avoidance of anything apt to evoke the type of *Gemütlichkeit* associated with the Austrian lower middle class life-style, Bernhard's house in Ohlsdorf emulates the taste of the landed gentry. The stark furnishings and color schemes, whitewashed walls combined with furnishings made of dark wood and wrought iron fixtures, some self-designed, as well as the ancestral-looking portraits call to mind similar elements associated with the castle Wolfsegg in *Auslöschung* (A, 168–90). Suggesting an imperious distance to the groups and individuals who joined the masses in welcoming the Nazis at the Heldenplatz seems to be the intent of Bernhard's interior design as found also in his later writings. The tendencies and social forces denounced by the protagonist of *Auslöschung* are configured in political, medical, and aesthetic terms: "Gemeinheit und Geschmacklosigkeit," "Naturverfälschung," "Krankheit," "*der heute herrschende Sozialismus,*" "Katholizismus" and "Nationalsozialismus" (A, 116, 142, 118, 141, 292). The rhetorical gesture of superiority calls to mind the lofty perspective of Doderer's Sektionsrat Geyrenhoff, the narrator of *Die Dämonen* that dates back to the same years as Bernhard's early texts.[23]

Bernhard's protagonist Franz-Joseph Murau projects an air of intellectual superiority. He appears aloof and socially uninvolved and like Bernhard he is unmarried and hostile to the notion of procreation. With the exception of his student Gambetti he lacks positive personal attachments. In fact, his continued obsession with his own family and Austria would preclude those. It is no coincidence that the person he is closest to is an Italian male, his junior in years and intellect. Like Murau, Gambetti is the product of a former fascist society and the son of wealthy parents, whom Murau does not hesitate to overcharge for his services. Beyond the student-teacher relationship the intensity of Murau's language suggests a homoerotic bond. The exclusivity of the relationship between the student and the teacher allows for the kind of apodictic statements in which Murau not only discredits modern society and technology but also the institutions of heterosexual society:

> Der Kleinbürger und der Proletarier sind erbarmungswürdige, aber unerträgliche Produkte des Maschinenzeitlalters und wir erschrecken, wenn wir sie vor uns haben, weil wir denken müssen, was die Maschinen und die Büros aus ihnen gemacht haben. . . . Die Mütter werfen ihre Kinder in die Welt und machen die Welt dafür und für alles mit diesen Kindern Folgende verantwortlich. (A, 299–380)

Not unlike Otto Weininger, who in his endeavor to detach himself from his Jewish background considers sexual abstinence and the extinction of humanity preferable, Bernhard's protagonist seeks as well as abhors isolation.[24] The author suggests through Murau's persona that it might be possible to isolate oneself from one's contemporaries and live outside the fold. At the same time, Bernhard constructs a position of authority through the amorphous use of "we" and the appeal to like-minded readers, conceding that total isolation is synonymous with insanity. Indeed, Murau's repeatedly stated superiority over his fellow human beings and Austrians in particular are expressions of a deep-seated pathology. Ruling out debate or dialogue as an option for communicative mediation, all of his statements take the form of apodictic pronouncements. Even his imaginary exchanges with Gambetti are monologues rather than conversations.

In a society hesitant to own up to the National Socialist past, an oeuvre such as Bernhard's, even though frequently declared a nuisance, could clearly serve an alibi function. To the world on which Austria's tourist economy depends in order to flourish, Bernhard was proof that righteousness and unrelenting soul-searching went on among Austrians. His success demonstrated that critical voices were validated. Moreover, the sensationalist appeal of his publications overshadowed the intellectually more rigorous, often Jewish, critics who likewise examined their Austrian socialization in painstaking detail and with critical acumen. Founded on cutting edge theory and historical facts, their works called for informed debates while Bernhard's writings called forth impulses and attitudes. In 1988 Donald Daviau aptly observed that Bernhard's name represented "big business" for publishers, directors, actors, and critics, scholars. This, if nothing else distinguishes Bernhard from actual outsiders, who like Améry, Neumann, and Anders were never "big business" in Austria or elsewhere. Implicitly questioning the sincerity of Bernhard's rhetoric, Daviau writes: "If Bernhard were incorporated, it would behoove all of us to invest in him."[25] In contrast to other critics who cited Bernhard's own derogatory statements about Austria and the Austrians as evidence of his nonconformist status, Daviau is struck by the discrepancy between the author's literary voice and his demeanor at a reading: "He was pleasant, gregarious, outgoing, witty, and humorous."[26] The Bernhard Daviau met seems to have come across much like the man in Sepp Dreissinger's photographs taken between 1978 and 1988. Some of them show Bernhard cheerful and smiling, engaging in communicative acts such as talking or pointing at objects, some show him pensive, but certainly not bitter or despondent.[27] Posing and histrionics were clearly as much a part of Bernhard's personality as his writings.

The wider phenomenon of Bernhard appears open-ended and ambivalent not unlike the author's invectives against Austria. The public response to his supposed insults of Austria and the Austrians, similarly displays a blend of indignation, identification, and acceptance. The supposed consternation about Bernhard parallels the ambivalence with which Austrians viewed the Second Republic. This ambivalence became apparent in the presidential campaign of 1986 when the successful presidential candidate maintained that it had been his duty to serve in the Nazi German military. The popularity of this statement points to the general confusion concerning allegiance, identity, and responsibility in the Second Republic. As a result of the lies and half-truths on which postwar Austrian identity was based, ongoing secrecy about the involvement of Austrians in Nazi crimes seemed required. In order to reconcile one's personal experience with the dominant version of history claiming that Austria was the first victim of Nazi aggression, a tremendous repression of collective memory and amnesia had to be effected, leading to a consistently dishonest management of the past. The resulting anguish is expressed by a woman, apparently born after 1945, upon visiting the exhibition "Vernichtungskrieg: Verbrechen der Wehrmacht 1941–1944" in Vienna in 1995: "Aber das hier, das macht uns glauben, daß unsere Onkel, unsere Väter Mörder sind. Denn sie stellen es ja als Mord hin oder nicht? Gut, es war ein Angriffskrieg, ja. Aber es war nicht so, wie es hier dargestellt wird. Sicher nicht."[28] Bernhard's early articles in the *Demokratisches Volksblatt* with their focus on an idyllic *Heimat* and wholesome simplicity exemplify the mindset required of those who are to trust and accept Austria's historical lies and self-deceptions.

Christian Klug notes that Bernhard's relentless attacks on Austria in general and Salzburg in particular must be read with these early texts in mind as the author's polemic against himself. The radical verbal invectives reveal the desire to distance himself from his past self that had been deceived by the revisionist ideology of the 1950s: "Die Schonungslosigkeit seiner verbalen Attacken erklärt sich aus dem Verlangen, sich von einem vergangenen Selbst zu distanzieren, welches der restaurativen Ideen- und Gedankenwelt jener Jahre restlos erlegen war."[29] Yet his attacks are so extreme and so general at the same time so as to allow for multiple and contradictory readings. Without the presence of an unambiguous authoritative voice, the outpourings in Bernhard's narratives and dramas are apt to energize so called forbidden impulses and sensations. They raise unacknowledged, officially discredited, views and attitudes such as xenophobia, anti-Semitism, and ethnocentrism to the conscious level. Naming the taboo without validating it encourages a safe kind of indulgence on the part of the reader. The following passage, for example, conveys hatred as well as uncertainty:

> Die Schwestern erschienen mir ganz einfach als die lächerlichen, die sie sind. Ich zweifelte nicht an ihrer Lächerlichkeit. Aber verdienen sie, daß du sie *widerlich* nennst? sagte ich mir. In dieser Stunde? Ich schämte mich, aber gleich darauf mußte ich mir sagen, daß wir ja nicht aus unserem Kopf heraus können und ich beharrte darauf, daß meine Schwestern *lächerliche* und *widerliche* sind. (A, 106)

The speaker's initially unambiguous displeasure with his immediate family is explained as a subjective impression, the result of wishes and desires, and is thereby neutralized.

By portraying the full range of the authoritarian attitudes that anti-fascist critics such as Theodor Adorno and Wilhelm Reich ascribed to the petty bourgeoisie and the *lumpenproletariat,* by insisting that European culture is in a state of irreversible decline, Bernhard's works, including *Auslöschung* and *Heldenplatz,* can be read as an indictment of a pervasive anti-intellectualism and "wrong-thinking" the author attributes to post-Shoah Austrian and, more generally, German culture.[30] In other words, Bernhard's oeuvre could be read as leftist. Indeed, the targets of contempt and derision include precisely the social groups that traditional anti-fascist criticism had identified as the stronghold of National Socialism. Contrary to Socialist theory, however, the working class does not find favor with Bernhard. The overt anti-proletarian sentiments of his work cannot be ignored. Indeed, all segments of society are blamed for the ills of modern society. Through the eyes of Bernhard's central characters Austria appears like a breeding ground of a retarded and brutalized lower class of workers and farmers, dominated by narrow-minded, corrupt elite of aristocrats, clergy, and the bourgeoisie. Franz-Joseph Murau, who seems to agree with the notion of a wholesale death sentence for all Austrians — "alle Österreicher sind zu dieser Todesstrafe verurteilt" — considers the complete erasure of everything Austrian, including himself, the only solution (A, 648, 650). Murau appears to believe that the remedy for the misery of the present lies in expunging the remnants of the past, his own and that of his culture by donating his inheritance to the Jewish community and committing suicide.[31] The grandiosity and pathology manifest in his attitudes and actions make it impossible to take the seemingly implied social criticism seriously. This is also the case with other protagonists in Bernhard's work. Insofar as their attitudes and actions are expressions of mental and emotional suffering, they deserve attention. Inasmuch as they present themselves as a serious assessment of facts, they do not. Bernhard's protagonists are case studies of individuals and groups deeply traumatized by past guilt and historical lies. Torn between their desires and their inability to detach themselves from a past not of their making, they refuse to rebuild and reproduce and engage on a path of self-destruction.

The significance of Murau's decisions is highly ambiguous. Not only does his complete abdication as a landowner and an Austrian aristocrat call to mind the National Socialist rhetoric of totality (including the total war), but his method of extricating himself from his responsibilities is reminiscent of the actions taken by leading Nazis in the face of imminent defeat. By leaving the compromised property to his parents' intended victims, Murau rids himself of an unwanted legacy. His suicide represents the ultimate repudiation of all they stood for as well as his personal identity. Yet Murau's suicide seems a re-enactment of the solution sought by those Nazis who killed themselves in the face of defeat, Hitler, Goering, and Goebbels. In other words, the son reproduces the patterns of the parents' generation even outside fascist dictatorship on a variety of levels, as given, for example, in his Austro-German-Italian alliance with Gambetti. Likewise problematic is Murau's predilection for Rabbi Eisenberg whom he, the child of perpetrators, pronounces his soul mate and equal, as much as his parents would have considered him the subhuman. Ultimately Murau's solutions call to mind the all-or-nothing pattern of the authoritarian personality. In conjunction with the polarities suggested by juxtaposing Wolfsegg and Rome and the people of Wolfsegg and the Jewish community, the Mediterranean countries are stereotypically configured as the antidote for the North. Rabbi Eisenberg similarly is functionalized as the antidote for the Nazi past. He is cast as part of a reductive dualistic pattern that serves as the organizing principle of the entire text and is conducive to virulent but ambiguous rhetorical outbursts. The global condemnations do not speak to specific social conditions or concrete issues but rather foreground sensations like frustration, rage, and disgust, articulated by terms such as "fürchterlich" (horrible), "blödsinning" (idiotic), "unerträglich" (unbearable), "gemein und niederträchtig" (vulgar and mean-spirited), "entsetzlich" (awful).[32] The origins of and possible remedies for the traumatic states expressed through these ravings are not and possibly cannot be stated in rational language. Transcending verbal expression they cannot be resolved on the verbal plane. Consequently there is no solution, at least not in the psychoanalytical sense, since Bernhard's characters remain forever caught up in their traumas.

Whether it is the descendant of Austrian gentry and Nazi collaborators as in *Auslöschung*, or Jewish survivors and their children in *Heldenplatz*, they are inscribed with the same contempt and despair. Both in *Auslöschung* and *Heldenplatz* the death of important individuals in the protagonists' lives precede the main plot. Professor Josef Schuster in *Heldenplatz* commits suicide and Murau's parents die in an accident. However, Bernhard's protagonists suffer their own gloom and misery independent of these deaths. *Auslöschung* and *Heldenplatz* foreground predominantly Austrian issues and personal concerns, while the Shoah remains for the most part in the background. The Jewish Professor Robert Schuster, brother of the deceased Josef Schuster in *Heldenplatz* asserts:

> Die Welt ist ja schon heute nurmehr noch eine zerstörte / alles in allem unerträglich häßliche / man kann hingehen wo man will / die Welt ist heute nur noch eine häßliche / und eine durch und durch stumpfsinnige / alles verkommen wohin man schaut / alles verwahrlost wohin man schaut / am liebsten möchte man gar nicht mehr aufwachen / in den letzten fünfzig Jahren haben die Regierenden alles zerstört. (H, 87)

Assigned to a Jewish character in a play performed in Vienna fifty years after *Kristallnacht*, this pronouncement, open to numerous interpretations, is decidedly problematic. On the one hand it may signify that Nazi ideology and practices in Austria did not end with the Second World War, and that the Second Republic is an extension of the Nazi era. Another reading would imply that the German invasion of Austria was the root cause of Austria's current ills, thereby exonerating Austrians from historical responsibility. Finally, it might also be taken to mean that the world powers, the former allies, no less so than the Nazis have "destroyed everything" and that nothing has changed since the Nazi era. The openness of such statements makes Bernhard's texts accessible to readers of many different points of view as a projection for their individual and collective dissatisfaction.

The deceased in *Auslöschung* and *Heldenplatz* are portrayed both as victims and victimizers. The tyrannical traits of the Jewish professor who returns to Vienna with his family cannot be overlooked, as he oppresses his wife and rules supremely over his employees. On the other hand, Murau's father, a former Nazi, has some qualities of the victim. Betrayed and exploited by his low-class wife and his vulgar children, this pathetic man lives a life of anguish. A similar conflation of victim and victimizer is common throughout Bernhard's work. It is frequently suggested that the conduct of whoever is in power must be the cause of incurable psychosis among the socially weak and the younger generations, including Bernhard's own. This particular view of the long-range effects of authoritarianism and National Socialism was characteristic of the 1960s and 1970s when the publications of Wilhelm Reich, Theodor Adorno, but also those of Alice Miller and Klaus Theweleit, enjoyed wide acclaim.

Born in 1931, Bernhard experienced his formative years in Nazi-dominated Austria under extremely difficult circumstances. The exhibit at the Bernhard house in Obernathal/Ohlsdorf reveals the dreadful poverty, the social disenfranchisement, and pretentiousness of his closest relatives. There can be little doubt that the environment into which he was born profoundly traumatized him. However, the trauma was not Bernhard's alone. The experience of living through the demise of the society into which he was socialized, the disillusionment with his closest of kin, outrage at the dishonesty of his elders, and the process of re-socialization into a new political system was common to Austrians (and Germans) after 1945. At the age of fourteen Bernhard was hardly old enough to comprehend the formidable impact of Nazi ideology and the authoritarian structure of everyday fascism on his environment and his own life. The older generation, including the cultural and educational establishment, was not about to enlighten young people about the past and the role they had played. Hence the lack of awareness in the articles of the twenty-one to twenty-three-year-old Thomas Bernhard comes as no surprise.

The rage and pain expressed in his later writings address the collective trauma of the Austrian and German postwar generations, a great concern at the time.[33] As if compelled to re-enact the unmanageable anguish, Bernhard's texts articulate over and over the individual's inability to confront the past and make the necessary adjustments for the future. Henryk Broder observed that authors of the postwar generation in search of the National Socialist past stopped short at implicating their immediate family and their home environment, ignoring or rationalizing any evidence of past crimes.[34] Those who undertook a painstaking examination of their submerged memory and their parents' role during the war, as did Niklas Frank, the son of the Nazi General Governor of Poland, faced widespread disapproval.[35] Bernhard's work illustrates the emotional price to be paid for rebelling against the world of the parents. Without much more than hinting at the actual transgressions of the previous generation, Bernhard's works re-enact the damage incurred by the children of the Nazi generations. Their deep-seated feelings of worthlessness, coupled, as in Murau's case, with an inordinate megalomania, result from the inability to know the facts withheld by the older generation. The feelings expressed by the Jewish characters in *Heldenplatz*, most notably Professor Robert Schuster, together with their speech patterns resemble Murau's tirades in *Auslöschung*. Both Murau and Josef Schuster commit suicide to escape their inner turmoil. Indeed, Bernhard's writings suggest affinities between both Nazi "victims," the young Austrians co-opted by their parent's ideology, and the true Nazi victims. A correspondence between Jews and non-Jews of the post-Nazi generations is vividly suggested in *Die Auslöschung* through the motif of the spiritual friendship between Murau and Eisenberg as well as in the meeting of the two men, Jew and non-Jew with Maria, a character reminiscent of Ingeborg Bachmann. Gregor Hens is correct in assuming that Bernhard undertakes neither a textual recreation of experience nor a fictionalization of the real world: "Der Heldenplatz ist ein Symbol für die unausweichliche Präsenz der Geschichte."[36] The same is true for Murau's Wolfsegg and Rome. Although Bernhard's works contain countless allusions to Austro-Fascism, National Socialism, Socialism, and the Habsburg era, the rhetoric of totality de-historicizes them.[37] It is precisely the avoidance of specificity and the conflation of the experience of Nazi victims and mainstream Austrians of his generation through which Bernhard provides his Austrian readers with a comfortable, if not pleasurable, reading experience.

The fact that Bernhard reached and enraged so many of his contemporaries with his outrage (rather than meeting with indifference) indicates how well he knew his fellow Austrians' sensitive spots. His keen insights into a malaise he characterized as specifically Austrian were possible because he shared in the mainstream experience and spoke the language of average Austrians. Contrary to the equally biting criticism by actual "outsiders," for example the film *Kieselsteine* (1982) by the Prague-born Jewish film author and director Nadja Seelich or Robert Schindel's satirical portrayal of victims and perpetrators, Bernhard's aggression was one with which the majority of Austrians (and Germans) could identify.[38] They recognized the rhetoric as well as the trajectory of Bernhard's accusations, hence their effectiveness and the author's success. Bernhard's posture as arbiter in matters of taste and morality, his elitist claims of possessing superior insight may bear a superficial resemblance with similar gestures in Karl Kraus, Elias Canetti, and Elfriede Jelinek. However, the cultural experience from which Bernhard's writings emerge is fundamentally different. Bernhard's works lack the analytical quality, the personal detachment, of interwar and postwar Jewish satire and his authorial position is instead one of outrage and shame. The Jewish authors know the language and demeanor of anti-Semites and the history and facts of Nazism and neo-Nazism. Bernhard is familiar with the emotional factors from which they arise. Compared to the intellectual tradition from which Jewish satire emerged, Bernhard's writing is compulsive. His complaints and accusations are diffuse and hardly original such as the recurrent lament over past greatness lost, the misanthropic disdain of his contemporaries, and the idolization of a few exceptional individuals.

Postwar Jewish writing, on the other hand, is informed by a profound personal involvement with the Shoah, the implied textual norm being that of the victim/survivor. The memory of the destroyed Ashkenazi culture, mourning over the loss of family members and European Jewish culture are central in their texts. Bernhard, on the other hand, articulates the psychological wound of the Austrian mainstream. The target of his rebellion is his parent's generation imbued with fascist and National Socialist ideology as well as his own self, socialized under National Socialism and the recipient of the older generation's viewpoints and sentiments. Bernhard's scathing criticism stems from frustration over the inability to escape his background. The dilemma of being raised the ally and accomplice of his elders is paradigmatic of Austrians his age and younger. The traumatic process of recognizing the implications of Austria's recent history is expressed through the self- and other-directed aggression in Bernhard's writing, pointing to an outrage over having been misled and shamed by one's own gullibility. These impulses are too strong to allow for the distance and clarity that prevail in the works of post-Shoah Jewish writers such as Ruth Beckermann and Doron Rabinovici. Irene Heidelberger-Leonard formulates the difference between Bernhard's attacks on Austria and the critical but often at the same time nostalgic attitude of younger and older Jewish authors as follows:

> In seiner narzißtischen Megalomanie war es Bernhard jedenfalls nicht gegeben, der inneren Dynamik von Amérys Leidengeschichte nachzuspüren und das zu allerletzt in seinem doch in dieser Ausrichtung angelegten Roman *Auslöschung*. Ich möchte vermuten, daß auch Thomas Bernhard von den 'jüdischen Nöten' Jean Amérys und seinesgleichen absolut nichts begriffen hat(te).[39]

The form Bernhard's writing took in the 1960s has given rise to varying critical assessments. Even though Matthias Konzett characterized Bernhard's universe as one of dissent and resistance and claims that his legacy may eventually empower Austria to "re-assemble and reconstruct its ambivalent cultural heritage overshadowed by the narcissistic self-perception of its culture,"[40] Konzett also notes the lack of rational arbitration of conflicting views in Bernhard's works. He points out that Bernhard rejects theories which posit an enlightenment telos as in the case of Jürgen Habermas with its idealization of the public sphere.[41]

Indeed, Bernhard seems to despise the very notion of modern democracy, since in his works nothing but contempt is expressed for the prevailing public discourse. Gregor Hens, commenting on Bernhard's non-deliberative critical method, describes Bernhard as a fundamentally non-philosophical author. By disposing his readers to allow themselves to be inundated with words, Bernhard provides them with less with a reflective rather than a "highly satisfying reading experience."[42] Clearly, there must be something pleasurable about reading Bernhard and watching his plays, how else would one explain the sustained and far-reaching response on the part of the literary market that Konzett considers "controversial and puzzling."[43] If Bernhard were, as Konzett argues, indeed positioned "curiously both at the presumed centers and borders of the cultural public sphere whose attention [he] command[s] but whose function [he] reject[s]," the author's success would seem a mystery.[44] Yet there is nothing marginal about Bernhard, his background, his core experiences, and literary development even though the position he assumes and the oppositional ideas he expresses are designed to set him apart from the Austrian public. The majority of his Austrian and German contemporaries, however, shared his desire for cultural detachment. Similar to Doderer, Bernhard is paradigmatic of a specific age group of mainstream readers and their collective experiences and traumas, hence the resonance of his works.[45]

William Donahue convincingly argues that Bernhard's entire work is an account of that which no one knows or wants to know about. In other words, by giving voice to the repudiated collective memory, Austria's foremost writer acted as the nation's suppressed guilty conscience.[46] First and foremost, Bernhard broke taboos by denouncing the presence of former Nazis and the role of the Nazi legacy in the Second Republic. He articulated the latent anti-Semitism, and commented on the fascist and authoritarian structures in public and private life. Through compulsive and repeated articulation of these phenomena, Bernhard contributed to making these phenomena accessible and available for debate. Regardless of how they were cast, Bernhard gave the collectively repressed fascist impulses identifiable patterns of representation. His unfavorable portrayal of contemporary Austria and his assessment of Austria's role in the era of National Socialism caused controversies that helped integrate the Nazi memory into the cultural discourse. Precisely because Bernhard's harsh dissent invited objections from different quarters, more moderately phrased reactionary views often appeared in the end more convincing.

The pleasure Bernhard's works elicited was intrinsic and extrinsic: it derived from the text or dramatic production as well as from the media scandals. Since his first major literary success, the novel *Frost* (1963), Bernhard transgressed against the Austrian code of silence and debunked the *Geschichtslüge,* the historical construct according to which Austria was the first victim of Nazi Germany. By evoking protest no less so than assent, Bernhard raised the stakes of the public debates in the wake of the Waldheim scandal (1986/87) that had brought to light the widespread popular support for a presidential candidate who proclaimed his service in the Nazi military his duty at the time.[47] The election victory for Waldheim suggested an unspoken identification with the Nazi past on the part of many Austrians as did the fascination older Austrian men displayed at the exhibition *Vernichtungskrieg: Verbrechen der Wehrmacht 1941–1944.*[48] As is obvious from the increasing popularity of the FPÖ and Jörg Haider's rhetoric, there is a significant residue of cultural memory validating the developments of the 1930s and 1940s. Euphoric recall of the Austro-Fascist and Nazi eras has anything but vanished, and it came to the fore in the mid-1980s when anti-Semitism found its public expression in the media, with conservative boulevard papers such as the *Kronen-Zeitung* taking the lead role. Austria's rightwing extremist and anti-Semitic legacy continues to provide a stock house of ideas for the current generations. Until after his untimely death in 1989, Bernhard remained at the center of Austrian debates. His contribution to the public discourse of the Second Republic is no less ambiguous than the position of his officially innocent and neutral home country in the heart of Europe.

Notes

[1] In his *The Rhetoric of National Dissent in Thomas Bernhard, Peter Handke and Elfriede Jelinek* (Rochester, NY; Woodbridge, UK: Camden House, 2000), Matthias Konzett maintains that Bernhard follows the tradition of Nestroy, Hofmannsthal, Kraus and Musil, applying a "mixture of histrionic and self-conscious staging of one's public voice" against the respective climate (28). Bernhard has cast himself as "*Der Schwierige* or unappeasable participant in Austria's public sphere," Konzett writes, noting Bernhard's "discomforting, provocative and transgressive range of expression" (29).

[2] Wendelin Schmidt-Dengler, *Bruchlinien. Vorlesungen zur österreichischen Literatur 1945 bis 1900* (Salzburg: Residenz, 1995), 302. See also Konzett, who discusses Bernhard's idiosyncratically expressed social criticism, observing that his "seemingly tasteless remarks about the visible resurgence of National Socialism have unfortunately been vindicated by the recent history of neo-fascist acts of aggression and the current *Rechtsruck* in the European political arena" (48).

[3] Thomas Bernhard, *Der Theatermacher* (Frankfurt: Suhrkamp, 1984); *Heldenplatz* (Frankfurt: Suhrkamp, 1988).

[4] Peter Handke, *Publikumsbeschimpfung* (Frankfurt: Suhrkamp, 1966). Thomas Bernhard, "Politische Morgenandacht," *Wort in der Zeit* 12/1 (1966): 11–13.

[5] Thomas Bernhard, *Heldenplatz* (Frankfurt: Suhrkamp, 1988), 118; hereafter quoted in text as H.

[6] Thomas Bernhard, *Auslöschung. Ein Zerfall* (Frankfurt: Suhrkamp, 1986), 304, 8, 42, 112, 104; hereafter quoted in texts as A.

[7] Hannah Arendt, *Eichmann in Jerusalem* (Munich: Piper, 1964). The Vienna-born writer and critic Robert Neumann satirized Arendt's study of Eichmann as the embodiment of the "Banality of Evil" in *Der Tatbestand oder der gute Glaube der Deutschen* (Munich: Piper 1965). On the international scale, intellectuals such as Raul Hilberg, H. G. Adler, Gershom Scholem, Alexander Mitscherlich and many others entered the Eichmann-debate. See Dagmar C. G. Lorenz, *Verfolgung bis zum Massenmord* (New York: Lang, 1992), 341.

[8] Gerald L. Posner, *Hitler's Children. Sons and Daughters of Leaders of the Third Reich Talk About Themselves and Their Fathers* (New York: Random House, 1991), 216.

[9] Posner, 218.

[10] Günter Anders, *Wir Eichmannssöhne. Offener Brief an Klaus Eichmann* (Munich: Beck, 1964), 17, 5.

[11] Jean Améry, *Jenseits von Schuld und Sühne* (Stuttgart: Klett-Cotta, 1977). First published 1966. Simon Wiesenthal, *Ich jagte Eichmann* (Gütersloh: Mohn, 1961) and *Doch die Mörder leben* (Munich: Droemer-Knaur, 1968).

[12] Peter Handke, *Wunschloses Unglück* (Frankfurt: Suhrkamp, 1972); Jutta Schutting, *Der Vater.*(Salzburg: Residenz, 1980); Brigitte Schwaiger, *Lange Abwesenheit* (Vienna: Zsolnay, 1980); Gerald Szyskowitz, *Puntigam oder die Kunst des Vergessens* (Vienna: Zsolnay, 1988).

[13] Posner, 218.

[14] Ruth Beckermann, *Unzugehörig* (Vienna: Döcker, 1989), 108, 118.

[15] In the novel, Murau reports that his parents hid their Nazi comrades in the children's mansion while dining with the American occupational forces: "Aber über alle diese Unheimlichkeiten hatten meine Eltern immer geschwiegen und es war auch aus ihnen nichts herauszubringen, sie verweigerten jede Auskunft, nur ihre regelmäßige Korrespondenz mit allen diesen Leuten bis zu ihrem Tod war der Beweis dafür, wie eng doch ihre Verbundenheit mit allen diesen Leuten gewesen ist. Während sie mit den Amerikanern beim Nachtmahl gesessen sind und den General Eisenhower hochleben ließen schon auf den Champagnerfrühstücken, saßen die Gauleiter ein paar hundert Meter weiter in der Kindervilla wahrscheinlich nicht weniger

ausgelassen beisammen . . . Wolfsegg ist immer pervers gewesen" (A, 442). The historical amnesia is further shown in the family's reluctance to read, keeping their library merely for display purposes: "Mein Vater las kein Buch, meine Mutter blätterte nur ab und zu in alten naturwissenschaftlichen Büchern, um sich an den farbenprächtigen Stichen, die diese Bücher schmücken, zu ergötzen. Meine Schwestern betraten diese Bibliotheken überhaupt nicht, es sei denn, sie zeigten sie den Besuchern, die den Wunsch geäußert hatten, unsere Bibliotheken sehen zu wollen" (A, 23).

[16] A, 212, 650–51. Paul Chaim Eisenberg is the Rabbi of the Jewish community in Vienna. In an interview he stated that neither he nor his father were acquainted with Bernhard and their biographies did not resemble those of the spiritual brother of Bernhard's narrator. See Hans Höller, "Menschen, Geschichte(n), Orte und Landschaften," *Anti-autobiografie. Thomas Bernhards Auslöschung,* ed. Hans Höller and Irene Heidelberger-Leonard (Frankfurt: Suhrkamp, 1995), 217–34; here 212.

[17] Thomas Bernhard, *Frost* (Frankfurt: Suhrkamp, 1963); Christian Klug, "Thomas Bernhards Arbeiten für das Salzburger Demokratische Volksblatt 1952–54." *Modern Austrian Literature* 21, no. 3/4 (1988): 135–72. Klug notes that Bernhard's work for the *Demokratisches Volksblatt* was the result of his grandmother's intervention on his behalf with Josef Kaut, a Salzburg SPÖ politician and later president of the *Salzburger Festspiele* (165n 3).

[18] Klug, 140–44.

[19] Klug, 146–47.

[20] Klug, 148.

[21] Klug, 150.

[22] Donald G. Daviau, "Preface," *Modern Austrian Literature* 21, no. 3/4 (1988): iii.

[23] Heimito von Doderer, *Die Dämonen* (Munich: Biederstein, 1956).

[24] Otto Weininger, *Geschlecht und Charakter* (Vienna: Braumüller, 1906).

[25] Daviau, iii.

[26] Daviau, iii.

[27] Sepp Dreissinger, *Thomas Bernhard — Portraits — Bilder und Texte* (Weitra: Bibliothek der Provinz, 1990).

[28] Ruth Beckermann, *Jenseits des Krieges. Ehemalige Wehrmachtssoldaten erinnern sich.* (Vienna: Döcker, 1998), 71.

[29] Klug, 137.

[30] Theodor W. Adorno et al., *The Authoritarian Personality* (New York: Harper, 1950); Wilhelm Reich, *Massenpsychologie des Faschismus* (Frankfurt am Main: Fischer, 1974); Klaus Theweleit, Männerphantasien (Frankfurt: Rowohlt, 1980); Alice Miller, *Am Anfang war die Erziehung* (Frankfurt: Suhrkamp, 1980).

[31] The novel's last page cites 1934, the year of the Austro-fascist victory as the year of Murau's birth, and 1983 as the year of his death. *Auslöschung,* 651.

[32] All of these emotive intensifiers can be found in *Heldenplatz,* 61, 65, 66, 70.

[33] See, for example, Alexander and Margarete Mitscherlich, *Die Unfähigkeit zu trauern* (Munich: Piper, 1967).

[34] Henryk M. Broder, "Diese Scheißbilder trage ich mit mir rum. Henryk Broder über die Reaktionen auf Niklas Franks 'Mein Vater, der Nazi-Mörder.'" *Der Spiegel,* July 6 (1987).

[35] Niklas Frank, *Der Vater: Eine Abrechnung* (Munich: Bertelsmann, 1987).

[36] Gregor Hens, *Thomas Bernhards Trilogie der Künste: Der Untergeher, Holzfällen, Alte Meister* (Rochester, NY: Camden House, 1999), 17.

[37] Carl E. Schorske, in *Thinking with History. Explorations in the Passage to Modernism* (Princeton: U of Princeton P, 1998), ascribes thinking without history to most fields of modern intellectual and artistic culture (3). This observation applies also to Bernhard's approach to the past and his obsession with it which prevents or saves him from confronting recent history.

[38] Nadja Seelich, *Kieselsteine.* Dir. Lukas Stepanik. Cinéart. Filmverleih Hofmann, 1981. Robert Schindel, *Gebürtig* (Frankfurt: Suhrkamp, 1992).

[39] Irene Heidelberger-Leonard, "Auschwitz als Pflichtfach für Schriftsteller," *Anti-autobiografie. Thomas Bernhards Auslöschung,* ed. Hans Höller and Irene Heidelberger-Leonard (Frankfurt: Suhrkamp, 1995): 181–94; here 194.

[40] *Rhetoric of National Dissent,* 52.

[41] *Rhetoric of National Dissent,* 28.

[42] Hens, 7.

[43] *Rhetoric of National Dissent,* 2.

[44] *Rhetoric of National Dissent,* 1.

[45] Born in the Netherlands the illegitimate son of an Austrian mother in 1931, Bernhard attended a boarding school run under the auspices of National Socialism. Equally significant for his career was his chaotic family background marked by illegitimacy, poverty, abuse, and cruelty and his frequent illnesses and hospitalizations. Although Bernhard and his family were under no danger from the Nazi regime for ethnic and racial reasons, they were not part of the privileged classes before and after 1945. The alienation, confusion, and rage that pervade his work and characterize his protagonists appear to have emerged from these dismal experiences.

[46] William J. Donahue, "Zu Thomas Bernhards *Die Ursache. Eine Andeutung,*" *Modern Austrian Literature* 21, no. 3/4 (1988): 89–106; here, 92–93.

[47] See Josef Haslinger, *Die Politik der Gefühle* (Darmstadt: Luchterhand, 1987).

[48] This exhibit was shown in Vienna in 1995. In her film and book, Ruth Beckermann documents the various responses on the part of those who at-

tended the exhibition, frequently former members of the Wehrmacht. Beckermann dir., *Jenseits des Krieges* (Vienna: filmladen, 1997).

Stephen D. Dowden

A Testament Betrayed: Bernhard and His Legacy

SINCE THE END OF THE Second World War, the two figures who have risen above the welter of competitors for attention in Austrian fiction remain Peter Handke and Thomas Bernhard. Significantly, the differences between these two writers roughly correspond to the two dominant traditions of novel writing in Austria. Handke's imaginative impulse has been to strive for ascendance over historical particularity and its contingencies. His wandering way of life, recalling that of Rilke, another Austrian who sought to hover above the vicissitudes of time and place, embodies a degree of universality. One senses in his lengthy and productive stays outside of Austria in France, Germany, the United States and elsewhere not so much an active rejection of Austria as a perspective that simply transcends Austria. Even when his protagonists are distinctively Austrian figures, what interests Handke is not principally their national identity and historical contingency. The question of Austrian-ness is always only incidental to his deeper theme, even when the protagonist is his own mother. What seizes Handke's imagination is much more the desire to strip away all that is external and adventitious in order to penetrate down to the elemental strata of human experience: uniquely individual, highly volatile states of being, incarnate in rare moments of "true" feeling, perception, and experience.

Given his proclivities, Handke is naturally a highly idiosyncratic writer. Still, in his aims he belongs to a tradition that reaches back, above all, to Musil and Rilke and from them, forward to Ingeborg Bachman, Oswald Wiener, and Christoph Ransmayr. This tradition of Austrian narrative prose differs obviously from the postwar tradition of German fiction, which is characteristically preoccupied with historical and now cultural (for example, the German writer Sten Nadolny) specificity. Writers like Grass, Böll, Wolf, and Johnson, to name only the most prominent figures, have sought reality elsewhere: in fictional confrontations with the past, especially the Nazi past. To them, it is precisely the contingencies of history and morality that are most engaging.

Postwar Austrian writers have seldom gravitated toward this sort of confrontation, with one extraordinary exception. Thomas Bernhard turned confrontation into an aesthetic mode in its own right, one that is fundamentally comic despite its extreme bitterness. Bernhard's comedy draws its poisonous nourishment from his permanent rage against the moral catastrophe of Austrian history, and against postwar Austria's failure to face that history. As Austria's pre-eminent moral comedian of the postwar era, Bernhard is linked, *mutatis mutandis,* to the tradition that belongs not primarily to the Austrian novel — Broch and Musil are not his precursors — but to theater. Indeed, his novels in the widest sense are theater, a late development in the satirical tradition of Raimund, Nestroy, and Kraus. They are theater insofar as they produced histrionic national public spectacles. Bernhard was a *Theatermacher* in both literal and figurative senses. His vitriolic ridicule of Austria's artistic elite of the 1970s and 1980s in *Holzfällen* generated a hue and cry that is paradigmatic for his public reputation and tempestuous career as a whole. And Bernhard overlooked no venue, however minor. Even his letters to newspapers tend in the direction of histrionic public comedy.[1] Yet up until the late 1980s Bernhard was conventionally misunderstood as a solipsist, a disengaged philosophical writer with little "serious" interest in history or politics. Careful reading of his works, and especially those written after his memoirs (but not *only* those) reveals that Bernhard's imagination was fueled specifically by Austria's long-standing repression of its Nazi past, which in Bernhard's grotesque mockeries of Austrian life remains continuous with the present. The mode of Bernhard's seriousness is not, as is the case in German literature, reasoned critique and moral realism. Bernhard's mode is morally absolute: an unforgiving, unapologetic, venomously impassioned satire. Its profound wrath, unbounded yet simultaneously governed by a superbly mastered literary style, is the measure of its seriousness.

Especially in *Heldenplatz* and his final novel *Auslöschung* Bernhard reveled in rubbing his countrymen's noses in a past at odds with the one presented by the guardian intellectuals of Austria's official culture. *It's worse now than fifty years ago!* is the refrain of his drama *Heldenplatz* (1988), referring in particular to Austrian anti-Semitism but also to the rightward drift of political life in Austria under the amnesiac presidency of Kurt Waldheim. It is as if Austria had at some point decided to live out the motto of Johann Strauss's operetta *Die Fledermaus:* "Glücklich ist, wer vergißt, was doch nicht zu ändern ist." Then when international public opinion turned against Waldheim's disgraceful cover-up of his compromised war years, Austrian public opinion took a distinctly reactionary turn (with *ressentiment*-laden slogans such as "Wir Österreicher wählen wen wir wollen") and reverted even to traditional anti-Semitic paranoia about a conspiracy of international Jewry, this time supposedly out to revenge itself on the alpine republic for past wrongs.

An anecdote from the 1980s will illustrate the peculiarly unwholesome conditions of intellectual freedom in Austria. Peter Jankowitsch, who was Austria's foreign minister at the time of the Waldheim controversy, circulated a memo among Austrian historians urging them to rebut what he called "gross distortions" written by British historian Robert Knight and by American historian Gordon Craig. Knight had offended by publishing an article for the *Times Literary Supplement* on the limits of denazification in Austria.[2] When Craig wrote a similar essay for the *New York Review of Books* Jankowitsch raised a call to arms against what he claimed was gratuitous Austria bashing.[3] In his letter to Austrian historians, Minister Jankowitsch used his influence to pressure academics into defending Austria against outsiders seeking an "Anschluss of Austria onto a past from which our nation has long since thought itself liberated."[4] Jankowitsch's resentment and overwrought reaction to Knight and Craig, coupled with his scandalous attempt to manipulate Austrian historiography from the seat of government power, is a good indication to how ragged the nerve-endings of national identity were and remain in Austria; and it suggests that there is much work to be done toward crafting an image of the national self that is both truthful and can be lived with.

To some extent, the problem is a familiar one to Americans who come from the South. Since the Civil War, Southern intellectuals have wrestled with the irreconcilable conflict between regional pride and the historical burden of the institution of slavery.[5] This conflict stoked the imagination of William Faulkner, to name only the most important of the writers who have addressed and helped shape modern Southern identity. It was the writers who were foremost among those who worked to recast the South's modern conscience and self-consciousness in an intellectually responsible way. The situation in Austria bears comparison. It is the writers who have been asking the hardest questions about what it means to be Austrian. In Bernhard's lifetime, the Austrian government never officially acknowledged guilt on the part of Austria as a nation for the crimes of the Hitler era. Since the Republic of Austria was "invaded" in 1938 by Hitler and his forces, and since the Allies' Moscow Declaration of November 1, 1943 declared the Austrians to be the first victims of Nazi aggression, postwar Austria had settled into its comfortable reputation of having almost no political identity at all, just a cultural one.[6] Austria depicts itself as the land of Haydn, Beethoven, Mozart and Schubert, of the Vienna Boys Choir, fine skiing, good coffee, rich desserts and waltzing until dawn. Traditional anti-Semitism and Austrian participation in Nazi atrocities have been topics that seldom came up in a public setting or even in literature until recently.

No writer has done more than Thomas Bernhard to focus the attention of Austrians on the meaning of their own history. In his memoirs, collected and published in English under the title *Gathering Evidence,* Bernhard writes about his memories of Salzburg during the war, his suffering as a child there under a vindictive Nazi schoolmaster, and the toxic atmosphere of everyday life. He writes that he is continually maddened to find that the people of his contemporary Salzburg seem collectively to have expunged those seven years from their memories. Unlike them, he remains permanently tormented by the terrible things he cannot forget. The protagonist of his last major work of fiction, *Auslöschung,* which was first published in German in 1986, is a character much like Bernhard himself. Franz-Josef Murau is obsessed with his identity as an Austrian, a morally catastrophic burden he seeks to lighten by living exclusively in foreign countries and speaking foreign languages. As the novel opens he is living in Rome, speaking Italian, happily estranged from his miserable kinsmen. They live at Wolfsegg, the ancestral family estate in Upper Austria.

The metaphor that dominates this late novel of Bernhard is the idea of "family" in the widest sense. The Murau clan embodies for Bernhard, and for his voluble protagonist, the Austrian nation and its morally blighted identity, an inherited nightmare, as he calls it. The Murau genealogy reaches deep into Austria's Habsburg past. But with the modern, postwar generation, that greatness has become extinct. The family has reached a low point in its history from which no recovery will be possible. The title, its absolute and implacable tone is characteristic, refers to the obliteration of the family, of its history and identity, for the Muraus, and by extension for Austria as a whole. At his desk in Rome, Franz-Josef has received a telegram informing him that his parents and older brother have been killed in an automobile accident. He has been summoned out of his self-imposed exile to return and assume his allotted role, whether he likes it or not, as head of the Murau clan of which remains little other than his two dim-witted, grasping sisters. If Franz-Josef dies, the clan will be extinguished.

The novel comprises his thoughts into a vast, satirically heightened monologue, as is always the case in Bernhard's fiction, carried on in the voice of the lonely, melancholy protagonist. His monologue, part bitter memoir, part comic tirade, gradually reconstructs the family history: his mother's enthusiasm for the Nazis, his father's spineless acquiescence in their use of Wolfsegg for National Socialist events, his mother's brazen opportunism upon the arrival of the Americans, suddenly no longer the victorious enemy but liberators from Nazi oppression. Wolfsegg, a miniature of Austria, is always near the center of the narrator's thoughts:

> Ich bin schon zu lange Zeit in Rom, überhaupt im Ausland, ich bin ein Ausländer geworden, es ist mir unerträglich, auch nur eine Stunde ohne Widerwillen in Wolfsegg zu sein. Ich könne mir nicht vorstellen, jemals wieder auf längere Zeit in Wolfsegg zu sein. Ich habe keine Beziehung mehr zu Wolfsegg. Ich verabscheue alles, das mit Wolfsegg zusammenhängt. Die Geschichte von Wolfsegg belastet mich *in einer vernichtenden Weise,* der ich mich nicht mehr aussetzen werde.[7]

The second part of the book, though, finds Murau back on the estate with his loathsome sisters, ready to attend the funeral. Here the manic flow of words and thought continues, developing the characters and ideas with increasing insistence and incrementally gathering clarity. Most vivid of all is Murau himself: cantankerous, opinionated, and crushed by a moral burden and sense of loss he can scarcely name. By the time we arrive at the novel's finale, the funeral, and the Nazi grandees appear, it has become clear that family and history are Bernhard's deepest themes. Murau seeks and finds a gesture to express his moral sensibilities, his outrage over Austrian silence since the end of the Second World War. He makes an unconditional gift of Wolfsegg and all its dependencies to the Jewish community of Vienna. Murau then leaves Austria for Rome, where he writes a book he calls *Auslöschung* and dies.

Bernhard died in 1989, leaving something of a vacuum in Austria's literary scene. Moreover, the era of confrontation and wicked satire may have passed with the end of Waldheim's tenure. At the end of the 1980s a barrier seems to have been broken in Austria, and I suspect that Thomas Bernhard's fearless, reckless, vitriolic polemics may have had much to do with it. He smashed taboos, "opened the windows," to borrow the metaphor that Murau uses to express his intentions toward Wolfsegg. Consequently, a significant aspect of Bernhard's legacy lies in these themes, which through him have become available for other Austrian writers to explore. Much that went unspoken for decades, especially about Austrian identity and history, now can be talked about. Robert Schindel is a conspicuous example. No one has explored these topics more compellingly than he does in his novel of 1992 *Gebürtig*.

Schindel, an Austrian born in 1944, was the child of parents who were both communists and both Jews. The Nazis murdered his father in Dachau, but his mother survived Auschwitz and Ravensbrück. She returned to Austria because, as a native Austrian, she wanted to participate in rebuilding a new, socialist state. As an infant Schindel was smuggled into a Nazi welfare home and then put up with foster parents. As a young intellectual of the generation of 1968, Schindel was a Marxist who devoted little thought to his Jewish-Austrian identity. For Marxists, ethnic and national identities were supposed to be beside the point. By the 1980s, though, his political ardor had cooled and he began to doubt the doctrine of assimilation that leftist culture had insisted upon.[8] He began to explore and embrace his (emphatically secular) Jewish identity, thinking of himself less as a cosmopolitan leftist, above national and ethnic identity, and more as a Viennese Jew.[9] When asked in 1992 if he thought of himself as an Austrian writer, Schindel answered: “Ich fühle mich als Wiener Schriftsteller.” When pressed to clarify the distinction, he went on, “In Wien kann man als Jude noch relativ unbehelligt leben. Aber hinter Purkersdorf habe ich immer schon das Gefühl, daß dort das Ausland beginnt.”[10] He complains that when he is outside Vienna, no sooner does he sit down in a restaurant for a coffee, local loafers begin to regale one another with Jewish jokes as response to his distinctively Jewish looks.

The comment gives an important clue to understanding *Gebürtig*. Strangely, the novel has been widely received as a search for Jewish identity. But Schindel, like most of the Viennese Jews in his novel, does not primarily have a problem with Jewish identity. The Jews in *Gebürtig* all manage their Jewishness in different ways, but most of them are as certain of that identity as Schindel is of his own face. Jewish identity is a foregone conclusion for two reasons. First, because it is an identity they are born with and know from the inside out. Second, because it is emphatically and constantly enforced on them from the outside. No Jew in Austria or Germany can forget that he is a Jew, even if he wants to. Men demonstratively swapping Jewish jokes within earshot are as good an example as any of the ways in which Jewish identity can be enforced from without. The real issue in the novel is not Jewish identity, but *Austrian* identity. In another interview, Schindel calls attention to his lifelong struggle not to be Jewish, but to be Austrian, an identity that is also his birthright, but which has been denied him by his fellow Austrians:

> Mir wurde von Anbeginn in der Schule von den Mitschülern gesagt, daß ich nicht hierher gehöre. Deshalb versuchte ich, besonders gut Deutsch und übrigens besonders gut wienerisch zu sprechen — um zu zeigen: Als ihr noch in Böhmen wart, war meine Familie schon in Wien.[11]

The various interviews he has given almost always have a comment of this sort. He is preoccupied with his native background: not only is he a born Jew, he is also native born Austrian. The novel explores the problem of these backgrounds.

This problem of native background is likewise one of Bernhard's most urgent themes. Josef Schuster of *Heldenplatz* is a native-born Jew and a native-born Austrian. After decades as an émigré scholar in England he returns to Austria only to discover that, because he is a Jew, other Austrians will not allow him to become fully what he always has been anyway: Austrian. Franz-Josef Murau of *Auslöschung* flees from his native country, seeking refuge in foreign countries and foreign languages. Everything Austrian, embodied in Wolfsegg, has become unendurable for him because of the identity it forces upon him. He is a member of the family and there is nothing he can do about it:

> Zu allem Unglück . . . ist dann auch noch der Nationalsozialismus gekommen, für den die Meinigen die Anfälligsten gewesen waren. Der Nationalsozialismus hat ihnen in allem und jedem entsprochen, sie hatten sich in ihm sozusagen selbst entdeckt. Neben ihrem großen, größtenteils aber doch nur *lieben Gott,* hatten sie auf einmal noch den *großen Führer.* Obwohl er, als ich sozusagen in die denkenden Jahre gekommen bin, längst der Vergangenheit angehörte, hatte ich den Nationalsozialismus noch auf die schädlichste Weise zu spüren bekommen. Denn der Nationalsozialismus meiner Eltern hatte mit dem Ende des Nationalsozialismus nicht geendet, weil er ihnen angeboren war, pflegten sie ihn nach dem Ende der nationalsozialistischen Ära weiter, er, wie ihr Katholizismus, war tatsächlich nichts anderes gewesen, als ihr Lebensinhalt, ohne welchen sie gar nicht auskommen und gar nicht existieren konnten.[12]

In Bernhard's grotesque world Nazis are born, not made. It is precisely this circumstance in which Nazism figures as a congenital defect that makes a normal life morally hopeless for Franz-Josef Murau. His only release from an intolerable identity is death. Similarly, the Jewish protagonist of *Heldenplatz* chooses suicide as a way out of his identity bind. Both cases strikingly recall that of essayist and Holocaust survivor Jean Améry. Robbed of his natal identity, culture, and language by the Austrian Nazis, Hans Mayer changed his name to Jean Améry and attempted to refashion himself after the war as a Belgian. The unrelieved torment of being neither Austrian nor Belgian evidently led to his suicide in Salzburg.

Schindel, the Viennese Jew who finds it necessary to remind other Austrians that he too is Austrian, belongs to the distinctively Austrian family of writers and intellectuals that include people like Améry and

Bernhard's imaginary émigré Josef Schuster. In some sense, too, he is a descendant of Arthur Schnitzler, whose novel *Der Weg ins Freie* (1908) is centrally concerned with the seemingly insuperable difficulties of being both an Austrian and a Jew. The principle characters of *Gebürtig* are mostly Viennese Jews. Schindel presents them in their variously ramified attitudes towards their own Jewishness and their struggle to make a place for themselves in Austria. They range from the confrontational banker-turned-novelist Emanuel Katz (with his weakness for big German blondes) to the self-denying lyric poet Hirschfeld. But the two most fully realized figures in the novel are Konrad Sachs — a Gentile German struggling with his family's Nazi past — and Herrmann Gebirtig — a camp survivor living as an émigré in New York City.

Sachs is a successful cultural journalist who writes for a national weekly in Hamburg. For years he has kept to himself the shame of a dark family secret. His father was the brutal governor-general of Poland during the Second World War, and he himself was known as the Prince of Poland in his early childhood. The father has long since been tried and executed for his war crimes, yet Sachs, who has changed his birth name in order to conceal his identity, feels immensely burdened by a guilt he did not earn but (like his Austrian cousin Franz-Josef Murau) inherited by birth. The weight of this burden is crushing his spirit. He will not tell anyone, not even his wife, for fear that if he does, something terrible will happen. The truth is unbearable and will, he thinks, ruin his life, destroy his reputation, reveal him for what he is. The secret breaks up his marriage, costs him his job, and isolates him entirely from his friends. Gradually he suffers a nervous breakdown and decides that he must confess the truth to Katz, the Austrian Jew he once met in the company of a big German blonde vacationing fashionably on an island in the North Sea. Katz refers him to Danny Demant, a Jew who is willing to hear him out. The effect for Sachs is cathartic, and more. Demant, an editor with a Viennese publishing house, knows a good story when he hears one and so encourages Sachs to write his confession for publication. Sachs does so, regains his sense of self-worth and becomes a national celebrity in Germany.

More than one facet of this episode is noteworthy. First is the fact, much remarked by critics and book reviewers, that Schindel based his Konrad Sachs's life on the experience of *Stern* journalist Niklas Frank.[13] Second, and more important, is the emphatic circumstance that the novel's Konrad Sachs figure is a German and not an Austrian. Now, the figure's model, Niklas Frank, really is a German, of course, but that is beside the point. Schindel's story is fiction. He can make of the characters anything he wants, and we should assume that he wants Sachs to be German. It is important that Sachs be German because in Germany the possibility of coming clean about the Nazi past is a more likely occurrence than in Austria, a country that Schindel has aptly called "die Republik des Vergessens"[14] Not only does Sachs do his remembering in public, but it makes a success of him, a national celebrity. The novel presents this commercial marketing of family guilt and Jewish suffering in all its moral dubiousness. Sachs insists on something like absolution from the Jews, Katz and Demant, who are intelligent enough and skeptical enough to realize that an inherited moral superiority is as specious a category as the inherited guilt of Sachs: "Das Mindeste, was wir tun können," says the arch-liberal Sachs to Katz when they first meet, "ist, unsererseits deutlich zu sagen, was wir über Hitler denken, über die Judenvernichtung und all das, was heute damit zu tun hat. Es gibt keine Normalität. Bloß Schuld und Unschuld."[15] Katz, while gratified to hear a German gentile speak so forthrightly, sees into the deeper complexity of what Sachs has said: "Mitschuld and Mitunschuld auch," he responds.[16] Neither Katz nor Demant is comfortable with the mantle of innocence that they have inherited simply by being born Jewish, and which Sachs compels them to wear.

Sachs's slightly comic misery of self-imposed exile, its basically comic mode points to the happy denouement of his story, when misery is transformed into cash and celebrity. It is matched in the novel by the misery of genuine exile. The novel's central figure is actually the protagonist of a novel that Katz has written, and which is being read by Demant, his literary editor. Demant carries the manuscript around with him and picks it up at intervals throughout his own story, which consists mostly of a soap-opera romance (getting rid of one girlfriend, trying to get along with another, an Austrian Catholic with two children and a husband who is headed in the direction of mental collapse). Katz has invented a fascinating figure, one along the order of Jean Améry and Bernhard's Schuster. His name is Herrmann Gebirtig, and he is a survivor of Austria's KZ Ebensee, a satellite camp of Mauthausen. In 1945 he emigrated to America and there became a successful playwright. Yet he is never able fully to become an American. He remains what he is by birth, an Austrian, but one who refuses to set foot in his native land or even (and here again we sense the presence of Thomas Bernhard, who attempted in his will to prevent publication of his works in Austria) allows his works to be translated into German.

In Austria an aging communist named Ressel, who like Gebirtig was interned at Ebensee, is out for a hike on the Rax with his grown daughter. There he catches sight of Hans Egger, now an old man who once had been an especially brutal guard at Ebensee, known in those days as the *Schädelknacker*. The police apprehend and jail Egger, but old Ressel's heart gives out before he can see justice done. He dies of a coronary, which leaves the prosecutors with no reliable witnesses to identify Egger as the war criminal he certainly is. Ressel's daughter turns to Gebirtig, who can positively identify Egger, but still declines to return to Austria for any reason. The attractive Viennese woman does what she can to persuade the obstinate émigré to come back for the trial. She does not attempt a seduction. Still, the sexual politics of the situation are alive for them both subliminally and for the reader symbolically.

Like Schuster, Murau, and Améry, Gebirtig has tried to undo his Austrian identity but cannot or, perhaps, at some deep level simply refuses to. Finally Gebirtig succumbs to the temptation to return. His sexual attraction to the right thinking, attractive Gentile woman embodies the seductive appeal of Vienna that he seeks to resist, for he knows but cannot admit to himself that he still longs for his natal city. He succumbs to his attraction to Susanne Ressel and returns home to Vienna, where civic authorities, eager to capitalize on his international fame, insist on celebrating him as a long lost son of the city. All the signs are favorable for reconciliation between Gebirtig and the land of his birth. He is returning triumphantly to see justice done to a war criminal and has become amorously entangled with a Viennese. The city ostentatiously heaps honors on him. Gebirtig begins to make plans for moving from New York to Vienna.

What could go wrong? This can go wrong: the war criminal Egger is found not guilty, and on the streets of Vienna, its newfound native son is greeted with unmistakably hostile stares. Gebirtig returns to his apartment on the East River, and the past stays buried. The gloomy conclusion of Katz's manuscript is necessary. A happy ending would have been kitsch, an aesthetic falsehood. But here it is probably important to remember that Katz's book is a fiction embedded in a fiction. Its gloom is reflected hazily in Danny Demant's failed romance with the Gentile doctor Christiane Kalteisen. The sexual politics of this failure are not exactly hard-hitting social commentary, but certainly a happy union of the two would also have been the most degraded sort of kitsch. The inherited friction and distrust between Jewish Austrians and their German-Catholic countrymen cannot be wished away in the bedroom frolics of a popular novel. The position of Jews in Austria remains too precarious to allow Schindel the indulgence of a happy resolution. Yet the gloom need not be exaggerated. The very fact that Schindel's book could be written and, more importantly, could be so successful, is in itself a minor victory of the Austrian ethical imagination. Thomas Bernhard never admitted of even a minor freshening of the atmosphere. Yet Franz-Josef Murau of *Auslöschung* claimed that he returned to Wolfsegg to give the place a good airing. Bernhard's unforgiving animadversions have thrown open the windows of Austria's literary culture. The praise for Schindel's *Gebürtig* at the time of its appearance was the breath of fresh air rushing in the open window of Wolfsegg's library.

Should Bernhard's admirers celebrate him for his role in Austria's gradual, if still tentative opening to its past? The events of the 1990s have shown Austrians to be more open to dealing with the Nazi past and its meaning for contemporary Austria; but the late 1990s, and in particular the rise of the reactionary "Freedom Party," founded by a former SS man, suggest to observers on the outside that a strange dialectic is at work within the country: two steps forward together with two steps back. In the present context, the contemporary Austrian political climate is relevant only insofar as it may have a bearing on our understanding of Thomas Bernhard, now dead for a little over a decade. Bernhard's writing has always been a sort of rallying site for dissenters unhappy with the state of postwar life and culture in Austria, or indeed anywhere. During Bernhard's lifetime his work survived the open hostility of the state and the enmity of its semi-official literary establishment. Now that he is dead, will his work survive the embrace of the literary critics — both inside and outside Austria — who are in the process of making him a literary classic?

Bernhard is now made the object of respectably professorial attention expressed in the formation of a Thomas Bernhard Gesellschaft, a Thomas Bernhard Museum in his former residence Ohlsdorf, and even an overarching Thomas Bernhard Privatstiftung. Along with scholarly conferences and publications honoring his legacy, a certain domestication of the writer and his rage is taking place. In life Bernhard wrathfully rejected attempts to objectify him as one of Austria's cultural celebrities. His notoriously insulting prize acceptance speeches are ample evidence of his refusal to be domesticated by the cultural establishment:

> Preisverleihungen sind, wenn ich von dem Geld, das sie bringen, absehe, das Unerträglichste auf der Welt, diese Erfahrung hatte ich in Deutschland schon gemacht, sie erhöhen nicht, wie ich bevor ich meinen ersten Preis bekommen habe, glaubte, sondern sie erniedrigen, und zwar auf die beschämendste Weise. Nur weil ich immer an das Geld, das sie einbringen, dachte, habe ich sie ausgehalten, nur aus diesem Grund bin ich in die verschiedensten alten Rathäuser und in alle diese geschmacklosen Festsäle hineingegangen. Bis vierzig. Habe ich mich der Erniedrigung dieser Preisverleihungen unterzogen. Bis vierzig. Habe ich mir in diesen Rathäusern und Festsälen auf den Kopf machen lassen,

> denn eine Preisverleihung ist nichts anderes, als daß einem auf den Kopf gemacht wird. Einen Preis entgegennehmen, heißt nichts anderes, als sich auf den Kopf machen zu lassen, weil man dafür bezahlt wird. Ich habe Preisverleihungen immer als die größte Erniedrigung, die sich denken läßt, empfunden, nicht als Erhöhung. Denn ein Preis wird einem immer nur von inkompetenten Leuten verliehen, die einem auf den Kopf machen wollen und die einem ausgiebig auf den Kopf machen, wenn man ihren Preis entgegennimmt. Und sie machen einem ***mit vollem Recht*** auf den Kopf.[17]

It is entertaining to speculate what Bernhard might have said at an academic conference dedicated to the exploration and, as is customarily the case, celebration of his work. We will never know, for it was his custom to ignore such invitations.

While he was alive Bernhard was an outsider and intended to remain so. He positioned himself in the observer's post, as he puts it in *Holzfällen,* as a critical onlooker, not a willing participant. Now that he is dead, he has little say in what is done with his work. He went so far as to block the performance of his dramas in Austria for seventy years, the duration of his copyright. Yet the Thomas Bernhard-Privatstiftung, founded in 1998 by the executors of his estate and by his former publisher, has seen it fit to ignore or somehow override Bernhard's testamentary instructions. This betrayal of him and his legacy by precisely those who claim to be upholding it seems to me to be a sign of some significance. The foundation receives funding from the state the writer spent most of his life execrating. Bernhard, too, was at certain points in his career the beneficiary of state support. But he was always on hand then to bite the hand that fed him. It may be that his admirers and supporters, academic critics included, are currently in the process of transforming him into a national institution of sorts, a tastefully mounted exhibit in the museum of Austrian cultural history, a historical literary monument.

By now the process is familiar. The most virulent opponents of affirmative culture in this century have been absorbed into the mainstream of modern consumerism. Even Kafka, Brecht and Beckett, writers whose work surely stands in sharpest protest against the emptiness of the modern spiritual condition, cannot keep entirely clear of posthumous re-absorption into the status quo. The logic of cultural life has been inevitably shaped by the postmodern culture of consumption. Cultural images likely to appear in magazines such as *Time* and *Newsweek,* or *Der Spiegel* and *Der Stern* are ineluctably transmuted into consumer items, hardly different from the images of Elvis or Princess Di. People gradually become famous for being famous, and what remains of their true achievement is converted into cliché. Nor is the academy excluded from this process. Even within the context of the university, the laws of cultural consumerism prevail. Students are presented with Great Writers and Master Works from canons of various sorts (national, Western, feminist, and so forth). Since television, radio, movies, magazines and newspapers have trained them in the ways of consumption, students are mostly content to concede their literary experience to a caste of privileged experts and theorists. This familiar and typically modern arrangement, the layman surrendering his sovereignty to the culture's official experts, positions the layman as consumer. And so students are likely to treat art, and the university experience itself, as an exercise in consumption. In a sense Kafka, Brecht and Beckett have been kidnapped and replaced with impostors. Broadway has claimed Brecht; the movies have claimed both Kafka and Beckett. As canonical twentieth-century masters, they have become cultural signifiers, universally respected icons (brand names in the marketplace of Great Writers) and consequently rendered all but permanently harmless, free-ranging wild beasts captured and put on display in a zoo. Perhaps it is still possible to read them with something approaching unmediated engagement, shock, and the pleasure of discovery; but it must be difficult. They are so encrusted with the sanction of high culture and the official certifications of media culture, including Beckett's Nobel Prize, that any clear and unprejudiced view of their works has been all but completely obscured.

Kafka believed we need literature that affects us like a personal calamity. Institutionalization militates against a literary work striking with this kind of impact; in fact annuls it. The blow is turned into a ritual gesture emptied of its original meaning and refilled with highly mediated connotations of prestige, cultural authority, and education. Thomas Bernhard — rude, simple, and fearless — is one of the few writers who are actually still able to deliver a major jolt, at least until he becomes so prestigious that he ceases to be controversial. The recent spate of photographic books about Bernard's life and haunts does not bode well. Enshrining him in coffee table books is a way of abolishing him. He is being displaced and repressed even as he is being celebrated. The way you treat a thing can change its nature. Bernhard's art, which is at bottom morally driven satire, thrives on controversy. The most certain way to trivialize him, as Bernhard himself plainly understood from the first time anyone tried to give him a literary prize, is to heap public honors on him, to patronize him by declaring him the composer of philosophical allegories,[18] or to reduce his wrathful art to its technical virtuosity, customarily celebrated as "musical." Yet this virtuosity is surely the key, its role is specific and identifiable apart from its supposed musicality. Bernhard's marginal position in society, his authentic individualism (radical to the point of something approaching the condition of exile), and his continual conflict with authority are crucially linked to his unique stylistic accomplishment, which must be described, in my view, as Bernhard's own peculiar ethics of language.

His inflexible moralism, not the self-righteous didacticism of philistine convention but a deeply disturbed and disturbing vision of modern history, positions him permanently on the outside. This solitude, recalling the ironic detachment associated most often with modernism (making Bernhard something along the order of a post-apocalyptic mutation of Tonio Kröger) has the advantage of creating a sense of critical opposition to the world. As an ethically serious and solitary outsider, Bernhard can experience reality only as fallen, flawed, and unacceptable. And in order to express this individual vision, an individual idiom is called for. Bernhard answers not with theory but with art. Unable to transcend or even accept the catastrophe of twentieth-century Austrian life religiously or philosophically or politically or intellectually, Bernhard transforms it into style. His style imposes form on the spiritual experience of his time. His startlingly original prose art is in itself an act of civil disobedience at the same time that it is an expression of his estranged individuality as well as a frontal assault on the literary status quo. The underlying ethical situation is one that Joseph Brodsky has described with considerable force:

> The surest defense against Evil is extreme individualism, originality of thinking, whimsicality, even — if you will — eccentricity. That is, something that can't be feigned, faked, imitated; something even a seasoned impostor couldn't be happy with. Something, in other words, that can't be shared, like your own skin: not even by a minority. Evil is a sucker for solidarity.[19]

Like Brodsky, Bernhard was no joiner of schools, movements, or collectives. Autonomous individuals did not become Nazis or Stalinists, and they do not acquiesce in the media-propagated deceptions of the Western postwar culture of consumption, Austrian or otherwise. In literature, ethical autonomy naturally finds its most powerful ally in formal autonomy, as a style that both defines and isolates. Bernhard's idiosyncratic style fits him like a skin; it cannot be shared, borrowed, or imitated. By dint of its sheer creativity Bernhard's style militantly opposes and unmasks the canned language of television, magazines, law, ordinary fiction, and bureaucratic officialese, the discourses that define and constrain our daily lives. To this extent Bernhard's prose is a paradoxically liberating experience, suggesting that the possibilities of verbal representation (and of the novel as form) must still be endless. It is paradoxical because Bernhard's overt message is so often that art is useless and at an end. Yet I am perhaps justified in speculating that the reading experience of countless readers belies his professed view.

The achievement of his style may also have a function that is linked to but essentially separate from the vilification of Austria and all it stands for. Joseph Brodsky again: "The revulsion, irony, or indifference often expressed by literature toward the state is essentially the reaction of the permanent — better yet, the infinite — against the temporary, against the finite."[20] Literature outlasts the political system in which it arises. Bernhard's writing exists in the permanent present of the act of reading him. Long after the Austria he hated has disappeared, his prose will still stand as permanent cry of outrage against self-deceit, smallness of mind, and official repression in any context. But there is a metaphysics at work here, too. Bernhard's cry of outrage is also against history, time, and death itself. He was condemned by bad luck, historical circumstance, and ill health (exacerbated by the state health system's shabby treatment of him while he was still young) to an early death. Because he lived his entire adult life under a cloud of serious pulmonary disease, Bernhard experienced basic human vulnerability more immediately and acutely than most. That he may have felt an impulse to transcend death in artistic creativity, or at least seek to register his indignation permanently, can come as no surprise. It is this aspect of Bernhard's work that speaks directly, and with all the urgency his style can muster, even to those with little or no interest in Austria.

Notes

[1] Wolfram Bayer. "Das Gedruckte und das Tatsächliche: Realität und Fiktion in Bernhards Leserbriefen," *Thomas Bernhard: Beiträge zur Fiktion der Postmoderne. Londoner Symposion,* ed. Wendelin Schmidt-Dengler, Adrian Stevens, and Fred Wagner (Frankfurt: Peter Lang, 1997), 1–23.

[2] Robert Knight, "The Waldheim Context: Austrian and Nazism," *TLS* 13 (October 1986): 1083–84.

[3] Peter Jankowitsch, Peter. "Die verschämte Republik," *Profil* (12 January 1987): 33. See also Gordon A. Craig, "The Waldheim File," *The New York Review of Books* (9 Oct. 1986): 3–4; followed up in the issue of 26 February 1987: 44.

[4] Gerhard Botz was one of the historians to whom Jankowitsch wrote. I am citing Botz's quotation from the letter: Gerhard Botz, "Österreich und die NS-Vergangenheit: Verdrängung, Pflichterfüllung, Geschichtsklitterung," *Ist der Nationalsozialismus Geschichte? Zu Historisierung und Historikerstreit,* ed.

Dan Diner (Frankfurt: Fischer, 1987), 141–52, 276–79; here 142. Cf. also Charles S. Maier, *The Unmasterable Past: History, Holocaust, and German National Identity* (Cambridge, Massachusetts: Harvard UP, 1987), 162–63, 215; and "Überaus bedenklich," *Profil* (15 December 1986): 16, 19.

[5] See C. Vann Woodward, *The Burden of Southern History* (Baton Rouge: Louisiana State UP, 1960).

[6] Hilde Spiel (writing before German reunification seemed even remotely possible) rebukes the "pious lie" of an Austria "liberated" from German Nazism. Austrian amnesia, she suggests, goes back to the pious lie of an Austria supposedly liberated in 1945: "The Allies tolerated the proposition — nourished by Austrian émigrés — that Hitler's Ostmark was not much different from Czechoslovakia: a country that had been overrun, forcibly *gleichgeschaltet,* and incorporated into the Third Reich. . . . And once "denazified" [the same people who on March 13, 1938, had rejoiced over Austrian union with Germany], forgot those seven dark years like a bad dream. Their children, the generation of today's young writers, have disavowed all responsibility. Not so the Germans west and east of the border. The division of Germany served them as a permanent reminder of their fall from grace, a thorn in their flesh that could not be ignored." Spiel's comment condenses into a few words the general trend of Austrian theater and fiction up into the 1980s to tiptoe around the question of Austrian Nazism and the problems it raises for constructing a new Austrian identity. As she implies, the refusal to confront Austrian involvement in the Third Reich was fueled not least of all by the "Moscow Declaration" of 1943, in which the Allies declared Austria to be the first victim of external Nazi aggression. The official culture of postwar Austria has willingly accepted the role of first victim. So it is that the concept *Vergangenheitsbewältigung,* or "mastering the past" is associated with Germany instead of Austria. See Hilde Spiel, *Die Feder, Ein Schwert?* ed. Harald Seuter (Graz: Leykam, 1981), 171–72. For a defense of Austria against this and other examples of what she regards as overstatements, see Gabriele Holzer, *Verfreundete Nachbarn: Österreich/Deutschland, Ein Verhältnis* (Vienna: Kremayr und Scheriau, 1995), 115–36.

[7] Thomas Bernhard, *Auslöschung* (Frankfurt: Suhrkamp, 1986), 108.

[8] In 1993 Schindel was honored in Vienna with the Erich Fried Prize. In his acceptance speech he discusses his path from sanctimonious dogmatism to a more relaxed, clement way of sorting out human experience. See Robert Schindel, "Erich Friedpreisrede," *Gott schütz uns vor den guten Menschen* (Frankfurt: Suhrkamp, 1995), 136–48.

[9] Schindel's experience here is part of a larger European phenomenon. The gradual collapse of left-wing cultural and political commitment forced Europe's generation of "sixty-eighters" to search elsewhere for a new identity. Alain Finkielkraut documents this turn in his book *The Imaginary Jew,* trans. Kevin O'Neill and David Suchoff (Lincoln and London: Nebraska UP, 1994). Like the Austrian Schindel, the Parisian Finkielkraut rediscovered his

Jewish identity from the wreckage of his generation's political illusions. Whereas religious Jews could escape from the travails of postwar life by fleeing into their faith, Marxist Jews could escape their uneasiness with Jewish identity by immersing themselves in the universal solvent of Marxist ideology: there are no Jews, no Gentiles, just good comrades. European Jews discovered the emptiness of this claim at about the same time leftist women turned from politics to feminism, and for the same reason. Leftist culture was no less blind to gender and ethnicity than the culture it rejected.

[10] Günther Kaindlstorfer, "Auf Wiederschaun, Herr Schindel," *Falter*, No. 32 (7–13 August 1992): 18.

[11] Hans Haider, "Sieben Worte im voraus: Gespräch mit Schindel," *Die Presse*, Literaricum (22 February 1992).

[12] *Auslöschung*, 291.

[13] Niklas Frank, *Der Vater: Eine Abrechnung* (München: Bertelsmann, 1987).

[14] Erika Wantoch, "Von '68 zu '38: Ein Gespräch mit Robert Schindel," *Profil* (21 December 1987): 62.

[15] Robert Schindel, *Gebürtig* (Frankfurt: Suhrkamp, 1994), 115.

[16] *Gebürtig*, 115.

[17] Thomas Bernhard, *Wittgensteins Neffe* (Frankfurt: Suhrkamp, 1982), 107–8.

[18] It is patronizing to insist that Bernhard's novels are philosophical parables because it implies an apologetic subtext, that is to say that Bernhard's buffoonery needs some kind of legitimation. Mere art, it would seem, is not serious enough on its own. Bernhard is not to be aligned with the man-of-ideas novel (for instance, fiction by Thomas Mann or Hermann Broch), but is instead much closer to writers along the order of Witold Gombrowicz: "The artist doesn't think, if by 'thinking' we mean the elaboration of a chain of concepts. In him thought is born from contact with the matter which it forms, like something auxiliary, like the demands of matter itself, like the requirement of a form in the process of being born. Truth is less important to the artist than that his work should succeed, that it should come to life. My 'thoughts' were formed together with my work, they gnawed their way perversely and tenaciously into a world which gradually revealed itself." Witold Gombrowicz, *A Kind of Testament*, trans. Alistair Hamilton, ed. Dominique de Roux (London: Calder and Boyars, 1973), 59. So it is with Bernhard's prose; he does not borrow or allegorize the prefabricated systems of historical philosophers. His thought should be allowed to emerge from his fiction.

[19] Joseph Brodsky, *Less Than One: Selected Essays* (New York: Farrar Straus Giroux, 1986), 385.

[20] Joseph Brodsky, *On Grief and Reason: Essays* (New York: Farrar Straus Giroux, 1995), 46.

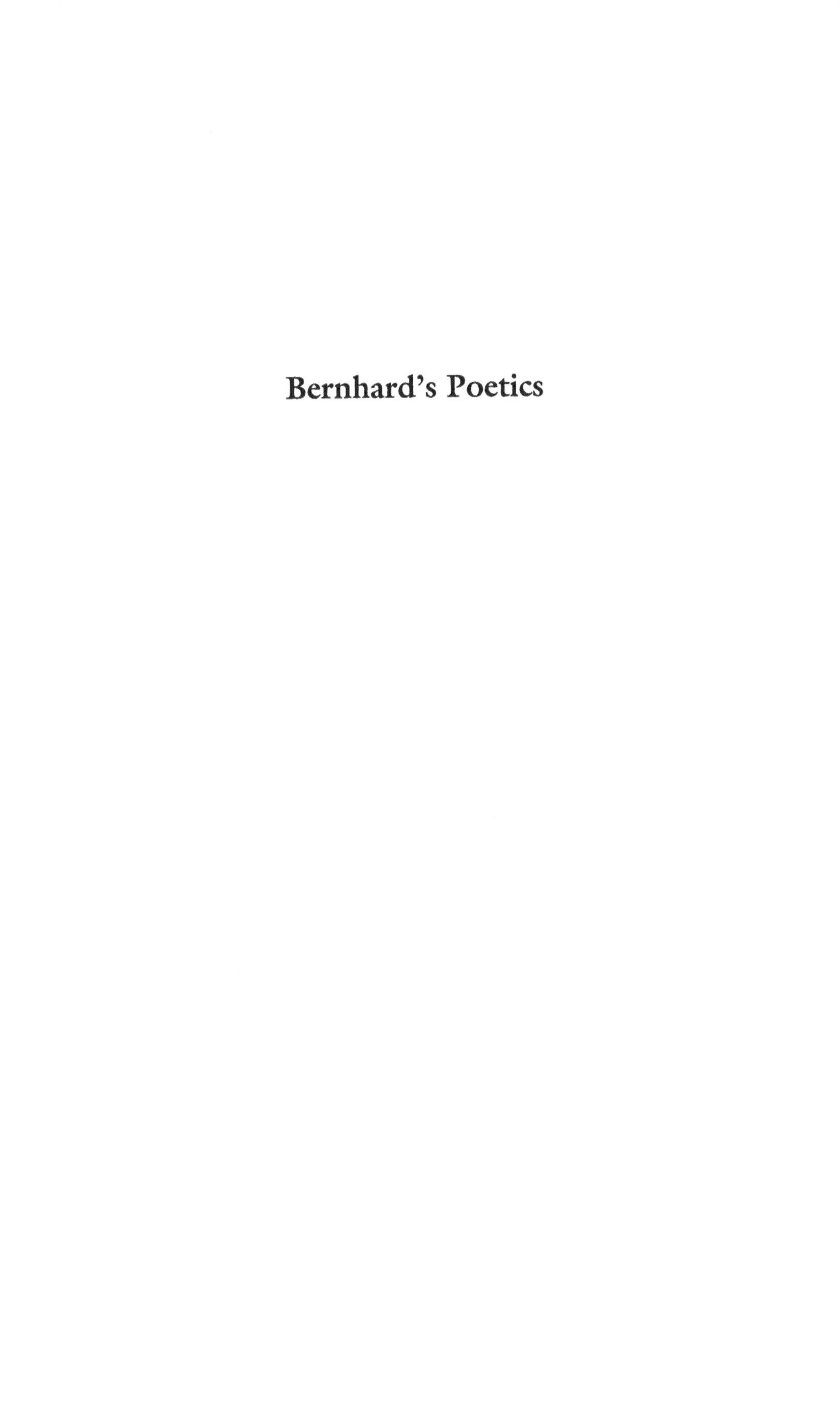

Bernhard's Poetics

Paola Bozzi

Homeland, Death, and Otherness in Thomas Bernhard's Early Lyrical Works

ALTHOUGH THOMAS BERNHARD IS widely acknowledged as a master of prose and drama, it is easily forgotten that his literary career began with some poems written at the age of sixteen and the publication of a short prose piece, "Vor eines Dichters Grab" in the *Salzburger Volksblatt* in 1950. It was not until the early 1960s that critics started to take an interest in Bernhard's writing. By then he had already published three volumes of poetry. Their biblical references, ecstatic mysticism, and intense yearning for salvation surprise today. Speaking about Bernhard's literary beginnings, it has become almost a commonplace of scholarship to cite the haunting shadow of his serious illness that in the end proved fatal. However, I would like to suggest that Bernhard's own rebellious streak is well rooted in the historical and cultural agony of postwar Austria. This background carries as much weight as the literary foreground — something that should be taken more into consideration. Bernhard's poems and prose works of the early 1950s are idylls of an untouched regional world (*Salzburger Land*) such as "Die Landschaft meiner Mutter."[1] This period was nevertheless decisive for his literary apprenticeship.[2] Indeed, there is a gulf between the sunny rhymes of "Mein Weltenstück"[3] and the poems Bernhard will write soon afterward. His poetic works will shortly afterwards speak of a world full of suffering and brutality, of a long biography of sorrow.[4] "Biographie des Schmerzes" is the programmatic title of a poem from Bernhard's first collection *Auf der Erde und in der Hölle*.[5]

In Salzburg, Thomas Bernhard survived various predicaments and dangers: the NS boarding-school; the air raids; the first bombings; his attempted suicide in the autumn of 1945; his short stint at the *Humanistisches Gymnasium* that he left to serve an apprenticeship with a grocer; pleurisy and tuberculosis; the death of his grandfather and mother which he learned from the newspapers; and the reality of everyday life in postwar Austria which he discovered directly as a reporter and columnist for the *Demokratisches Volksblatt* (1952–1954), the local organ of the Austrian social democratic party SPÖ. Occupied by American, British, French, and Soviet forces until 1955, postwar Austria had to struggle for survival, and the way to normalization was still very long. On May 15, 1955, representatives of the four powers finally signed the treaty that restored Austrian sovereignty. It formally re-established the Austrian republic in its pre-1938 frontiers as a sovereign, independent and democratic state. It prohibited *Anschluß* between Austria and Germany as well as the restoration of the Habsburgs. The United Kingdom, the United States and France relinquished to Austria all property, rights, and interests held or claimed as former German assets or war booty. The Soviet Union, however, obtained tangible payment for the restoration of Austrian freedom. The treaty came into force on July 27, 1955. A month later all occupation forces were withdrawn and a constitutional law of perpetual Austrian neutrality was proclaimed.

After liberation from the Nazi rule, the country faced complete economic chaos. Everyday life was gray, insecure, and lean, marked by the need for indispensable articles, clothes, fuel, and housing. At this time, Bernhard's large family of seven lived in a two-room flat in Salzburg (on Radetzkystraße). Barracks characterized the image of towns and suburbs, foodstuffs were rationed out. Only aid (food, vitamins, clothes, and medicines) provided by the United Nations Relief and Rehabilitation Administration (UNRRA) and, from 1948, support given by the United States under the Marshall Plan made survival possible. Heavy industry and banking were nationalized in 1946, and, through a series of wage-price agreements, the government tried to control inflation. Interference by military commanders in political and economic affairs in the Soviet zone of occupation caused a considerable migration of capital and industry from Vienna and Lower Austria to the formerly purely agricultural western provinces. This brought about a far-reaching transformation of the economic and social structure of the country.

In the immediate postwar era, Austria faced an awkward and chaotic situation. On the one hand, the exponents of the new political order held little sway. On the other hand, the occupying powers had limited knowledge of the local structures. Plundering was rife while people often settled their disputes by means of murder and conspiracy. The church regained its old position and the traditional parties — black (conservatives) and red (socialists) — reappeared. In the postwar years, the Austrian People's Party (corresponding to the Christian Socialists of the prewar period) and the Socialists (corresponding to the Social Democrats and Revolutionary Socialists) were the sole partners in a coalition government that was formed in proportion to the parties' strength in parliament. The influence of the Socialists in the coalition government, which had been relatively strong under Leopold Figl's chancellery, was reduced when the Austrian People's Party replaced Figl with Julius Raab in the spring of 1953 and had Reinhard Kamitz appointed minister of finance. The subsequent economic reconstruction and the advance toward a prosperity unknown to Austrians since the years before World War I is generally identified with the so-called Raab-Kamnitz course that was based on a modified free-market economy. The nationalized steel industry, electrical-power plants, and oil fields, together with privately owned lumber and textile industries as well as the increase in tourism were Austria's major economic assets. The Austrian economy came to be dominated to a disproportionate extent by a trend toward the tertiary sector because of the importance of *Fremdenverkehr*, which transformed the economic and social character of the rural Alpine areas.

Young Bernhard knew the human and social misery of these formative years of postwar Austria. He will later describe it as the basis for his "wilde und große Literatur"[6] derived from personal experience and in his capacity as a reporter. As a case in point, his first article in the *Demokratische Volksblatt* deals with the problems of the refugees in Salzburg. As a columnist, he had the chance to confront both contemporary culture and the Austrian cultural tradition. On the whole Bernhard wrote nearly 250 articles about diverse cultural topics such as American literature and Salzburg writers, Mozart's *Zauberflöte* in a marionette theater and Grabbe's *Don Juan und Faust.* He also reported on "Wirtshäuser, Wiesen und Felder," skiing in Austria, and iodine treatments against goiter. Bernhard's articles display a strain of traditionalism and attachment to his roots. Bernhard describes "die Geschichte eines grundnatürlichen Lebens, die Welt einfacher, arbeitsamer Menschen in einer schönen Landschaft," and the beautiful Salzburg scenery seems to be "berufen . . ., die frohe Armut in hohem Maße zu verkörpern."[7] By the same token, he claims that books should be as positive (that is good, affirmative and sound) as the Austrian landscape:[8] "Wir sollten uns hinwenden an das reine, nicht angekränkelte Buch, das problemlos gestaltet ist und doch fähig ist, uns ein klares Weltbild zu erweisen."[9]

It is necessary to keep in mind that Bernhard's literary beginnings followed in the tradition of a strong anti-modern vein shared by the Austrian mainstream. The author eventually had to free himself of this cheerful historical amnesia that he witnessed in the *Salzburger Land.* Bernhard held fast to poetry during all his free-lance journalistic activity and even during his attendance of the music conservatory Mozarteum. The collections of poems, published one after the other since 1957, demonstrate that from this point onwards writing played an important role in his life. Bernhard never left these poems behind, as some critics claim. A note in his own handwriting on the jacket of the collection *Unter dem Eisen des Mondes* proves the existential and aesthetic authenticity that these lyrics harbored for him during all his life: "mein einziges Exemplar, das mir heute — 7.12.1980 — s e h r g u t gefallen hat" (GG, 335). In the 1980s, Bernhard edited a personal choice of Christine Lavant's (1915–1973) poems.[10] In the 1950s, when Bernhard had to earn a living, he seemed inclined to write lyrics and short prose. Moreover, the period between the end of the Second World War and the so-called big monetary reform of 1947 (1945–1948) ravaged the Austrian book market and industry. Given these circumstances, good connections were vital in the postwar era as young writers were excluded from state subventions.[11] The old generation dominated every sector. It depended mostly on individual initiative to link cultural policies with literary interests.[12] Hans Weigel's *Stimmen der Gegenwart,* which published some of Bernhard's early texts, should be mentioned here.[13] The state supported mostly representative art, an indirect attempt to boost tourism and an expression of the Austrian great tradition, which wanted to pass the last seven NS years off as negligible and meaningless, or merely as an occupation.[14]

After the end of the Habsburg millenary Empire, Austria kept on with its millenary culture without any discussion about *Anschluß.* At this time, Austrian literature was divided into a literary vanguard experimenting with language and an officially supported group of antimodern writers who had dominated the cultural life since the 1930s and produced prizewinners even after 1945.[15] The Cold War gradually changed the political climate, leading to a political polarization between progressive and conservative powers in the official cultural sphere. Writers back from their emigration were either engaged in trench fights or played a negligible role.[16] The above-cited Brecht-boycott, supported by the conservative Jewish writers Hans Weigel and Friedrich Torberg, shows the blurred ideology of Austria in the 1950s.[17] The necessary and desirable open discussion about the NS-past and Austrofascism was replaced by a convenient Austrian ideology of national self-assertion. In 1955, the year of the *Staatsvertrag,* the Vienna Burgtheater opened its doors again as the foremost national theater, while the construction of the Salzburg festival house, Austria's premiere conservative cultural institution, was finished in 1960.

Peter Rubel, editor of the survey "Tribüne der Jungen" on the literary review *Plan,* commented on the postwar era from the perspective of a younger generation. He did so with more critical detachment and less reconstructive fervor:

> Die beiden großen politischen Parteien Österreichs bemühen sich, der Welt einzureden, daß das österreichische Volk an den Ereignissen der letzten acht Jahre völlig unschuldig sei . . . das österreichische Volk greift in seiner Mehrheit gierig nach der beglichenen Rechnung. . . . Und prompt — viel prompter als alles andere — stellte sich der Freispruch ein.[18]

Rubel put the question of morality bluntly: "Aber können wir eine neue Geschichtsepoche mit einem pharisäerhaften Taschenspieltrick beginnen?"[19] The young authors born around 1920 to 1925 had no "pre-past" (*Vorvergangenheit*) to which they could refer back. They belonged to a "geschlagene Generation," a lost generation.[20] As the NS-edifice collapsed in 1945, the past weighed in their stomach "wie ein Stein."[21] Since social life was pervaded with a tremendous sense of meaninglessness, art and literature worked as a sedative. The boom of poetry in the postwar years can be easily explained. The poem is a quick form of artistic production, which corresponds to the need to express feelings and have a personal, intimate, and secret refuge. The genre realizes the dual demands of super-personality or generality and individuality.

For Bernhard, *Vergangenheitsbewältigung*, the attempt to come to terms with the past, was not a political problem but a personal one. While psychoanalysis believes that the establishment of a chain of cause and effect will assist in understanding and overcoming trauma, Bernhard took the opposite road and sought freedom in a form of lyrical self-exorcism. Bernhard initially held onto the peasant world as a poetical subject, but his innocent pastoral poems soon changed into a landscape of sorrow. Many circumstances worked together to make him the writer we know today. He was motivated by hunger, unrestrained ambition, great intelligence and unappeasable restlessness, as frequent changes of residence show. Salzburg and Vienna, later Vienna and Maria Saal in Carinthia, are the most important places in his literary career. Bernhard traveled south, to Italy and Yugoslavia, formed new impressions after the gloominess of his war and postwar life, and at the end of the 1950s visited England and Sicily.

Bernhard's first collection of poems *Auf der Erde und in der Hölle* describes a journey discovering the urban world that has a domestic, religious, geographic, and spiritual dimension.[22] Travel experience not only opens up the limited horizons of the lyrical subject, but also involves a new self-knowledge and awareness of the world. Conforming to the legs of the journey, the collection consists of five sections. The lyrical narrator takes leave from his own peasant country ("Hinter den Bäumen ist eine andere Welt") and sets out for the towns. Yet the European cities are only a loud, destructive, and poor bustle ("Die ausgebrannten Städte"). The desire for a new era arises along with a contemplation of one's inner life in an effort to approach a transcendental dimension ("Die Nacht, die durch mein Herz stößt"). The lyrical subject reminds himself of the journey, evokes his own death, his dead parents and his homeland ("Tod und Thymian"), his old "love," to whom he finally returns ("Rückkehr in eine Liebe"). Loss of metaphysical certainties, mourning, torment, guilt, and senselessness are the scenery of this fictive journey.

The individual poems relate the experience of darkness, solitude, and the tension between yearning for death and longing for life. Indeed, the very titles convey the melancholy and spirituality of these early poems: "Novemberopfer" (GG, 18), "Fäulnis" (GG, 20), "Traurigkeit" (GG, 59), "Schwarze Hügel" (GG, 84), "Tod und Thymian" (GG, 99), "Der Tod" (GG, 113). Death and mourning provide the dominant vocabulary:

> Hinter den Bäumen ist eine andere Welt,
> ein Gras, das nach Trauer schmeckt, eine schwarze Sonne,
> ein Mond der Toten,
> eine Nachtigall, die nicht aufhört zu klagen
> von Brot und Wein
> und Milch in großen Krügen
> in der Nacht der Gefangenen. (GG, 31)

In fact, Bernhard's poetry presents a variation in the most central of concepts in modernist writing, the intrusion of *Schrecken,* of terror and horror, into everyday reality. In such a moment of shock one inevitably looks at one's own existence and relationship with the world in a new light.

The entire collection of poems describes the situation of a modern beleaguered subjectivity through the varied and reiterated representation of a cold world ("Der Schnee verfolgte mich mit seiner vernichtenden Poesie," GG, 106),[23] a rising darkness ("eine schwärzliche Stunde der Welt im Novemberwind meines Daseins," GG, 45) and a general decay ("Ich will die Stimme / der Vergängnis hören!" GG, 76).

The drama of the reflection on "Herkunftskomplex"[24] begins with the ingredients of the traditional *Bauernroman:* with earth, homeland, cattle, weather and black coffins. However, earth and homeland do not figure in Bernhard's lyrical world simply as nature but rather serve as biographical and historical background. With reference to his poems Peter Hamm points out rightly: "Land ist bei Bernhard nie identisch mit Natur, sondern mit den ihr Ausgelieferten und von ihr Zugrundegerichteten, den vielen Versoffenen, Verkrüppelten, Verrohten, Verrückten, die nicht nur Bernhards Prosa, sondern auch schon seine Lyrik bevölkern."[25] In *Auf der Erde und in der Hölle,* everything portrays a sorrowfulness emanating from the guilt of the Austrian postwar society:

> Morgen ist der Tag der Gesichter, die in
> die Kartoffelerde gefallen sind. Ich kann
> nicht leugnen, daß ich
> an diesem Sterben der Triebe schuldig bin. (GG, 11)

One of the first poems of this collection presents the image of the "schwarze Truhen der Bauernerde" — of a gloomy heritage, a menacing past which prevents the speaker from living:

> Auf den schwarzen Truhen der Bauernerde
> steht geschrieben, daß ich sterben muß im Winter,
> verlassen von meinen Sonnen und vom Geraune der Kübel, der
> vollgemolkenen. . . . Ich werde nicht nur Verlassenheit erdulden
> müssen, sondern
> das Vieh meiner Väter und Mütter durch die Jahrtausende treiben!
> (GG, 16)

The use of material with specifically Austrian overtones is particularly evident.[26] One could mention the oft-repeated clichés and commonplaces about Austrian literature — its continuing indebtedness to the Baroque tradition, its conservative and anti-realistic nature, its musicality, its melancholy mood, its emphasis on language and theater as central themes, the passivity and lack of action, and, last but not least, its fascination with decay and death.[27]

Certainly, one can find in Bernhard's poems identifiable features of the Austrian tradition or history. Bernhard's obsession with death suggests a close affinity to a type of Austrian anti-modern modernism which turns away from reality in favor of introspection and the cultivated pursuit of melancholy, ascribing to death a mythical quality as the ultimate source of truth. Bernhard puts his speaker into a spiritual landscape, a symbolically significant space, and provides a mythological framework. Thus, the office of the poet becomes a vocation for probing the legacy of a culpable world and bringing it into harmony:

> Ich weiß, daß in den Büschen die Seelen sind
> von meinen Vätern,
> im Korn
> ist der Schmerz meines Vaters
> und im großen schwarzen Wald.

Ich weiß, daß ihre Leben, die ausgelöscht sind
vor unseren Augen,
in den Ähren eine Zuflucht haben,
in der blauen Stirn des Junihimmels.
Ich weiß, daß die Toten
die Bäume sind und die Winde,
und das Moos und die Nacht,
die ihre Schatten
auf meinen Grabhügel legt. (GG, 121)

Timelessness gets to the heart of poetry, creating a place for myth, leaving history behind. The result of this lyrical adventure is a form of metaphysical certainty. *Auf der Erde und in der Hölle* refers to a poetic understanding of the world, which is a kind of theodicy.[28] In contrast to the prevalent litany of resignation, many passages display a will to resurrect God in writing:

Ich werde an den Rand gehn,
an den Rand der Erde
und die Ewigkeit schmecken.
Ich werde die Hände anfüllen mit Erde
und meine Wörter sprechen,
die Wörter, die zu Stein werden auf meiner Zunge,
um Gott wieder aufzubauen,
den großen Gott,
den alleinigen Gott,
den Vater meiner Kinder,
am Rand der Erde,
den uralten Vater,
am Rand der Erde,
im Namen meiner Kinder. (GG, 75)

Poetry and its language guarantee sense and meaning. Bernhard's first lyrical collection can be viewed as "Kunst als Enklave des zeitlos Absoluten."[29] "Metaphysische Seinsdichtung"[30] grants the poem magical rather than expressive or communicative functions. An obviously undervalued socio-historical reality is compensated by means of an overestimation of the anthropological and social power of art. Art and artist join in an anti-historical mystification of "being" in order to breed an auto-referential literature tied solely to the literary world and private life. Gottfried Benn's normative influence on the 1950s characterizes the aesthetic and ideological direction of these years.[31] Like other authors of his generation, young Thomas Bernhard had an Alexandrian spirit of metamorphosis, study and repetition. The journey of the speaker in his first lyrical collection of poems is thus to be understood as an initiation into "unerschöpfliche Poesien" (GG, 46). Bernhard was soon to become a "Stimmenimitator im Museum der modernen Poesie."[32]

In the postwar period, literary reviews, especially the *Plan*, promoted, through essays and translations, English, Russian, and French literature. Expressionism, French modern literature (symbolism and surrealism), Baudelaire's *Fleurs du mal*, and the revival of Trakl[33] helped Bernhard in his need to find an adequate expression for his psychic wounds. In July 1946, the *Plan* published an anonymous, but programmatic "Bekenntnis zu Georg Trakl":

> Inmitten von Verfall und sinnlosem Tun eines entheiligten Geschlechts begegneten wir Georg Trakl. Es war die Trauer einer sterbenden Zeit in seinen Versen, die Melancholie der Einsamkeit und die unsagbare Schönheit der menschlichen Landschaft.

It seems as if the experience of wartime destruction could only be overcome in dreams. The sweet decadence, melancholy, controlled pathos, somnambulism of Trakl corresponded exactly to the mood of the younger generation who found here the possibility to express their derangement poetically without falling into dilettantish consolatory verses: "Wir glauben, daß die verschwiegenen Verse Trakls uns vor allen anderen gelten. Den ungeborenen Enkeln, die den gewaltigen Schmerz, der sie nährte, noch nicht zu nennen gewagt haben."[34] The acknowledgment of Georg Trakl had of course formal consequences, and by imitating this model, the strongest talents worked out their own sounds and their own poetical form. However, it is also a matter of convenient selective reception of modern literature, for Trakl's (and Benn's) irrational poetry reveals itself in the longing for myth, for stopping history. After the *Staatsvertrag* (1955) such a conception of poetry relied on the acceptance of a cleared and innocent Austria, not because it was poetically understood, but rather useful for a peculiar restorative modernity.

In his subsequent volume of poetry, *In hora mortis,*[35] written several years after his brush with death, Bernhard shows but a fleeting glimpse of the rebellious self-assertion that was to become the trademark of his later writing. Nine psalms had formed the center of Bernhard's first collection. Due to its rhythmically reiterated set of phrases, prayer came even closer to Bernhard's ideal of musical writing. He therefore chose this form for his second collection. The topic of the collection, if indeed it can be said to have one, is the death of meaning. The poems' speaker attempts to overcome his fear of death through religious faith, but without success, for he receives no answer from his God. An ambivalence of affirmation and pessimism is peculiar to the volume: on the one hand trust in language, on the other the recognition of the "illness" of his own words ("die Krankheit / meiner Lieder / dieser Verse Krankheit," GG, 137). *In hora mortis* describes the mystical desire to raise the spirit through suffering. However, it is no longer possible to escape doubts and ambivalence. The speaker acknowledges skeptically a betrayal by suffering, "Leid/ das .. betrogen hat" (GG, 145). The cycle ends in a cry of mental anguish that is clearly expressionistic in both idiom and pathos:

> tot ist längst
> mein Rot
> mein Grün
> mein Stachel sticht
> zerschnitten
> ach
> zerschnitten
> ach
> zerschnitten
> ach
> ach
> ach
> mein
> Ach (GG, 150)

It remains questionable whether Bernhard's apocalyptic visions suggest a possible redemption through an exorcism of anxiety. Bernhard's skeptical attitude has its roots in the linguistic and philosophical dilemmas of the turn of the century. Hugo von Hofmannsthal, despite the despair of the *Chandos Letter,* still believed in a new form of poetic language and in the possibility of salvation through art. For Bernhard this avenue is no longer open. He shows a much greater control over his personal pain and seems to follow Ilse Aichinger's "Aufruf zum Mißtrauen" which ends with the following words: "Werden wir mißtrauisch gegen uns selbst, um vertrauenswürdiger zu sein!"[36]

In fact, it is as archivist of the negative that Bernhard gives up every form of sense in his third lyrical work *Unter dem Eisen des Mondes.*[37] The collection does not refer to transcendence or prophesy a religious-metaphysical utopia, and is fixed on the sadness of the real world. The metaphysical desire typical of his early writings (*Auf der Erde und in der Hölle, In hora mortis*) changes here to a topography of unvarnished corporeality and alienation (GG, 156, 160, 191). These aggressive and explicit poems all seem intent on destroying every myth and exposing the artificiality and lies through which the unrealistic, fairytale-like image of Austria is maintained. Death is here the liquidation of the old order and the ultimate realization of the chaos in life. Heterogeneous elements are combined without true connection. The result is a radicalized form of destruction, that is a fragmentary character of the form. The crisis of the language ("Weiß der Sprache," GG, 209), which is closely linked to a loss of individuality, exerts such a purificatory effect on poetry that tradition is now denied and a new phase is ushered in. In the subsequent collections this will beg some questions. For this disappointed metaphysician is now fixed on one goal, namely to demonstrate in an unmistakable and relentless way that everything is ridiculous in the face of death:

> Das blanke Eisen des Mondes
> wird dich töten und der starre
> Fuß eines Riesenvogels
> dem du
> Deine Trauer anvertraut hast
> im Winter. . . .
>
> Die Sonne wird ihr Wundenmal
> vergraben
> hinter den sterbenden Stämmen
> und deiner Lippen Feuer
> Flammen
> zu lachenden Blüten
> des Todes. (GG, 171)

One can see here the most prominent gesture of his works: repulsion by and destruction of aesthetic forms, philosophical assumptions, and social practices of the consciousness that ignore the finality of death and despair.

The treatment of homeland (*Heimat*) and death unexpectedly shifts the reader's attention away from the bleakness and the self toward otherness, challenging the myth of a cultural center and exploring various avenues of critique. Modernity is now understood as a break with harmony and perfection and a turn towards open forms. In *Ave Vergil*,[38] Bernhard turns the artificial and hermetic language of modern poetry into prosaic forms of life experience. The sublime and the commonplace, pathos and everyday life are now side by side. Poetry concentrates on the finite, unsuccessful, and disparate, and draws the truth from the miseries of life:

Ich bin . . .
Verkünder der Mißgestalten,
oben
und unten . . .

ich, der Metzgersohn,
sitze mit meinem PASCAL im Schlachthaus . . .
(GG, 266)

The legs of the journey — once theme of the first collection — become in *Ave Vergil* a palimpsest in which one can read a millenary history of death. However, the sadness over the loss of God, nature and people that provide sense, happiness, and security, is present in this lyrical work only as "legend" (GG, 251). Returning to the world, Bernhard's poetry becomes a "Selchfleischapostolat" (GG, 245) so that one can see the second basic pre-condition for Bernhard's writing: the experience of the inward collapse of illusionistic art and art-forms. He now follows in Eliot and Pound's footsteps. Through locations (such as "*Im Kornfeld*," "GASTHOF FREUMBICHLER"), direction ("*Durch das Fenster*," "*und dann*," "*Viermal, fünfmal, immer eindringlicher*"), roles ("*Braut*," "*Bräutigam*"), and through layout Bernhard's collection foreshadows his dramatic work. This procedure transforms Bernhard's aesthetic of sorrow into a performance. The dialogue of the voices within the same text or expression gives rise now to a plurality of discourses. The poem is no longer a badly sung choral (the first collection spoke of "schlecht gesungener Choral," GG, 93). Bernhard's lyrical work becomes polyphony: a multiplicity of songs (GG, 252–54, 265–67). This is a poetical program too. It is the intertextual plan of an author, who — moving between exhaustion and replenishment — arranges, combines, and deconstructs through a continual pla(y)giarism the Babylonian library of writing and the imaginary museum of all images.

In *Die Irren. Die Häftlinge*, the sober and lapidary style of *Ave Vergil* becomes biting and coarse.[39] Bernhard's poetical evolution shows that the road to the inner mind, the descent into the abyss of Bernhard's own personal existence is also a road to this world beyond hope, to the extremities of society. In fact, only collective types (the madmen and the prisoners) arranged according to a particular schema (the poem of *Die Irren* on the right page and the one of *Die Häftlinge* on the left, interrupted by eight aphorisms) keep up the lyrical play in Bernhard's last collection. The lyrical texts serve only as allegorical illustrations ("Der Bucklige mit dem Wassereimer, / die mit den Zöpfen, ganz wild, / die Nonnenschwänze weiß, die Vögel / schwarz auf dem grünen Bild," GG, 214), while the aphorisms reflect about insanity and limitation in terms of freedom and determinism: "*Das Gehirn ist so unfrei und das System, in das mein Gehirn hineingeboren worden ist, so frei, das System so frei und mein Gehirn so unfrei, daß System und Gehirn untergehen*" (GG, 213). With a skeptical attitude Bernhard definitively replaces the fading image of a horizon by a lyrical universe of dissonance:

> In Lumpen geht der Mensch, in faulen Fetzen.
> Das sagt der Schinderwind. Ich bin nicht dumm!
> Die Hosenröhren und den Hund zu hetzen,
> kommt der in meinen Kopf und haut mich um. (GG, 215)
>
> Vom Mörtel blind, in meinen Holzschuhkufen,
> schreien mir die Schädelfetzen die Befehle
> aus ihrem Wachmannstumpfsinn . . . auf den Stufen
> vertrotteln mir die Kutteln meiner Seele. (GG, 223)
>
> Was bist du für ein Wein, mein Herr Urin?
> Besoffen geh ich durch die kahlen Köpfe
> der Unterunterwelt, durch den Ruin
> und flecht aus meinem Hunger ihm die Zöpfe. (GG, 227)

The question of the copula between language and reality raised in Bernhard's last collections gives to author, language, and to the reader/interpreter new liberty of action. They censure the fiction of that mythological being that Barthes defined as God-Author (*Auteur-Dieu*).[40] The shadow of an author's "I" as central subject (GG, 134) is here deconstructed and replaced by a multiple fringe subjectivity as product of a discursive play and complement to the writing of an empirical individual. At the same time, the play of signifiers freed of meaning and reference replaces the semantic depth.

As the texts present themselves primarily as signs rather than message, they lead the readers/interpreters to their capability to produce signs. *Ave Vergil* and *Die Irren Die Häftlinge* illustrate a newfound capacity to invest an individual dilemma with universal significance and to create a new norm, that of a life lived in the aftermath of the experience of *Schrecken*. There are no standards that might help the reader to assess the distortions portrayed. Poetry cannot interpret the world or put it into perspective but it is able only to present it in a detached manner with moments of grotesque and ironic lightening. Though Bernhard maintains the humanistic tradition of searching for the meaning, he remains an interpreter of the world always keenly aware that the artist can create nothing but lies and deceit. Like Beckett, his work retains a link with traditional western rational humanism by virtue of its heartfelt pathos of the demise of this tradition. Such literature may be said to affirm an objective order of values, not by permitting the assumption that such an objective order actually exists, but by assuming that the loss of such an order is deprivation.

Notes

[1] See "Die Landschaft der Mutter," *Handschreiben der Stifterbibliothek,* 13 (1954), here cited from *Thomas Bernhard Werkgeschichte,* ed. Jens Dittmar (Frankfurt: Suhrkamp, 1990): "Noch lachen die Kinder aus dem Stubenfenster, noch werfen die Bäume Schatten auf die Landstraße, riecht der Most uns herb an den Abenden. Dieses Dorf ist mir mehr als nur Heimstatt und Rastplatz. Seine Bewohner sind richtige Menschen. Sie schaffen, beten und handeln" (10).

[2] This essay participates in a critical tradition that calls into question the thesis of a break (*Bruch*) in Bernhard's literary career. I fully concur with Grazia Pulvirenti, "'Con la morte negli occhi.' La produzione poetica di Thomas Bernhard: un apprendistato giovanile," *AION. Annali. Sezione Germanica,* N.S. 1 (1991), 1/2 (1992): 213–65; and Hans Höller, *Thomas Bernhard* (Reinbek: Rowohlt, 1993), 49–67. Josef Donnenberg and Burghard Damerau do not share this opinion. See Donnenberg, "War Thomas Bernhards Lyrik eine Sackgasse?" *In Sachen Thomas Bernhard,* ed. Kurt Bartsch et al. (Königstein: Athäneum, 1983), 9–34; and Damerau, *Selbstbehauptungen und Grenzen. Zu Thomas Bernhard* (Würzburg: Könighausen und Neumann, 1996), 74–85.

[3] Thomas Bernhard, "Mein Weltenstück," *Münchner Merkur,* 22 April 1952; *Demokratisches Volksblatt,* 20 September 1952.

[4] See on the topic of suffering Alfred Barthofer, "Berge schwarzer Qual: Zur thematischen Schwerpunktstruktur der Lyrik Thomas Bernhards," *Acta Germanica* 9 (1976): 187–211; and Paola Bozzi, *Ästhetik des Leidens. Zur Lyrik Thomas Bernhards* (Frankfurt/Berlin/Bern: Lange, 1997).

[5] Thomas Bernhard, *Auf der Erde und in der Hölle* (Salzburg: Müller, 1957); also in *Gesammelte Gedichte,* ed. Volker Bohn (Frankfurt: Suhrkamp, 1991), 7–121; here 62f. All subsequent references to Bernhard's lyrical works will be drawn from this edition and will be provided parenthetically in the text (GG).

[6] *Die Kälte. Eine Isolation* (Salzburg: Residenz, 1981), 141.

[7] Quoted from Michael Töteberg, "Höhenflüge im Flachgau. Drei Anläufe, dreimal abgestürzt: die Vorgeschichte des Autors Thomas Bernhard," *Text und Kritik* 43 (1991), 5.

[8] See Georg Schmid, "Die 'Falschen' Fuffziger. Kulturpolitische Tendenzen der fünfziger Jahre," in *Literatur der Nachkriegszeit und der fünfziger Jahre*

in Österreich, eds. Friedbert Aspetsberger et al. (Vienna: Österreichischer Bundesverlag, 1984), 7–23; here 22.

[9] *Demokratisches Volksblatt,* 21 November 1953.

[10] Christine Lavant, *Gedichte,* ed. Thomas Bernhard (Frankfurt: Suhrkamp 1987).

[11] On Bernhard's literary connections in the 1950s, see Höller, 54–61.

[12] Heinz Lunzer offers an incisive analysis of the stifling effect of the conservative cultural policies in the 1950s on younger and less traditional writers; see his "Der literarische Markt 1945 bis 1955," *Literatur der Nachkriegszeit und der fünfziger Jahre in Österreich,* eds. Friedbert Aspetsberger et al. (Vienna: Österreichischer Bundesverlag, 1984), 24–55.

[13] Thomas Bernhard, "Großer, unbegreiflicher Hunger," *Stimmen der Gegenwart 1954,* ed. Hans Weigel (Vienna: Albrecht Dürer, 1954), 138–43; "Der Schweinehüter," *Stimmen der Gegenwart 1956,* ed. Hans Weigel (Vienna/Munich: Herold, 1956), 158–79.

[14] See Schmid, 9.

[15] On this subject see Karl Müller, *Zäsuren ohne Folgen. Das lange Leben der literarischen Antimoderne Österreichs seit den 30er Jahren* (Salzburg: Müller, 1990), 267ff.; see also Klaus Amann "Vorgeschichten. Kontinuitäten in der österreichischen Literatur von den dreißiger zu den fünfziger Jahren," *Literatur der Nachkriegszeit und der fünfziger Jahre in Österreich,* eds. Friedbert Aspetsberger et al. (Vienna: Österreichischer Bundesverlag, 1984), 46–58; esp. 47.

[16] Amann, 57.

[17] On Brecht's reception in Austria see Kurt Palmer, *Vom Boykott zur Anerkennung. Brecht und Österreich* (Vienna/Munich: Löcker, 1983).

[18] Peter Rubel, "Wir sind schuldig!" *Plan* I/9 (1946), 781; Volume I of the *Plan* appeared from October 1945 to January 1947, volume II from February 1947 to the beginning of 1948. All references to this review are quoted from Albert Berger, "Schwieriges Erwachen. Zur Lyrik der jungen Generation in den ersten Nachkriegsjahren (1945–1948)," in *Literatur der Nachkriegszeit und der fünfziger Jahre in Österreich,* eds. Friedbert Aspetsberger et al. (Vienna: Österreichischer Bundesverlag, 1984), 190–206.

[19] *Plan* I/9 (1946), 781.

[20] Rüdiger Wischenbart, "Zur Auseinandersetzung um die Moderne. Literarischer 'Nachholbedarf' — Auflösung der Literatur," *Literatur der Nachkriegszeit und der fünfziger Jahre in Österreich,* eds. Friedbert Aspetsberger et al. (Vienna: Österreichischer Bundesverlag, 1984), 351–66; here 352.

[21] Berger, 193.

[22] See on this topic Kurt Klinger, "Flucht durch Europa: Thomas Bernhard," *Kindlers Literaturgeschichte der Gegenwart,* vol. 6/II, ed. Hilde Spiel (Frankfurt: Fischer, 1980), 137–39.

[23] See on this subject Paola Bozzi, "Nel freddo dei pensieri. La tragica 'Aufklärung' lirica di Thomas Bernhard," *Studia austriaca,* Vol. I, ed. Fausto Cercignani (Milano: Edizioni dell'Arco, 1992), 47–60.

[24] *Auslöschung. Ein Zerfall* (Frankfurt: Suhrkamp, 1986), 201. See also *Korrektur* (Frankfurt: Suhrkamp, 1975): "worunter wir immer gelitten haben, die Herkunft und alles, was mit unserer Herkunft zusammenhägt . . ., alles, das ist vor allem und in erster Linie unsere Herkunftsgeschichte für uns auch nichts als Marter" (272).

[25] Peter Hamm, "Auf der Erde und in der Hölle. Thomas Bernhard als Lyriker," *Die Zeit* (26 April 1991).

[26] I examined in detail these Austrian nuances in *Ästhetik des Leidens,* esp. 71–75.

[27] See Otto Basil et al., *Das große Erbe* (Graz/Vienna: Stiasny, 1962). Scholarship by critics such as Weiss, Màdl, Bodi, and Jarka, which has illuminated a significant tradition of realistic and engaged literature in Austria, has made such a thesis totally untenable. See Antal Mádl, "Entwicklung der österreichischen Literatur," in *helikon.* Sondernummer, ed. Ilona T. Erdély (1979), 17–42; Walter Weiss, "Österreichisches in der österreichischen Literatur seit 1945," *Literatur aus Österreich — Österreichische Literatur. Ein Bonner Symposion,* ed. K. Pohlheim (Bonn: Bouvier, 1981), 73–92; Leslie Bodi, *Tauwetter in Vienna. Zur Prosa der österreichischen Aufklärung 1781–1795* (Frankfurt: Fischer, 1977); Jura Soyfer, *Das Gesamtwerk,* ed. Horst Jarka (Vienna: Europa Verlag, 1980).

[28] I have emphasized elsewhere the religious side of Bernhard's lyrical works. See "'Das Wort des Todes.' Thomas Bernhard und Charles Péguy," *Thomas Bernhard. Traditionen und Trabanten,* eds. Joachim Hoell, Kai Luehrs-Kaiser (Würzburg: Könighausen und Neumann, 1999), 151–58.

[29] Peter Rühmkorf, *Die Jahre, die ihr kennt. Abfälle und Erinnerungen* (Reinbek: Rowohlt, 1972), 94.

[30] Otto Knörrich, *Die deutsche Lyrik seit 1945* (Stuttgart: Kroener, 1978), 250–68.

[31] See Arnold Gehlen, *Die Seele im technischen Zeitalter. Sozialpsychologische Probleme in der industriellen Gesellschaft* (Reinbek: Rowohlt, 1957), 118.

[32] On this issue see *Ästhetik des Leidens,* 75–78, 226.

[33] See Gerald A. Fetz, "Thomas Bernhard und die österreichische Literatur," *Österreichische Gegenwart. Die moderne Literatur und ihr Verhältnis zur Tradition,* ed. Wolfgang Paulsen (Bern/Munich: Francke, 1980), 189–205; esp. 194ff.

[34] *Plan* I/7, 556.

[35] Thomas Bernhard, *In hora mortis* (Salzburg: Müller, 1958); also GG, 123–50.

[36] *Plan* I/7, 588.

[37] *Unter dem Eisen des Mondes* (Köln: Kiepenheuer & Witsch, 1958); also GG, 151–209.

[38] *Ave Vergil* (Frankfurt: Suhrkamp, 1981); also GG, 229–77.

[39] Thomas Bernhard, *Die Irren. Die Häftlinge* (Klagenfurt: Kleinmayr, 1962). Manfred Mixner has referred to this collection as an "Objektivierung der subjektiven Bewußtseinserfahrung." See Mixner, "Vom Leben zum Tode. Die Einleitung des Nagations-Prozesses im Frühwerk von Thomas Bernhard," *Bernhard. Annäherungen,* ed. Manfred Jurgensen (Bern: Francke, 1981), 65–97.

[40] Roland Barthes, "La mort de l'auteur," *Manteia,* 5 (1968), 12–17; here 15.

Rüdiger Görner

The Broken Window Handle: Thomas Bernhard's Notion of *Weltbezug*

SOME ABSURDITIES CAN MAKE SENSE; some dusky corners may provide the right setting for illuminating thoughts; and some smoky *Kaffeehaus* in Vienna's first district can be the venue for strikingly clear insights. These are the sentiments that I continue to associate with the memory of my one and only encounter with Thomas Bernhard, just a few months before he died. Such memories are, of course, in line with one striking aspect of the aftermath of Bernhard's death. Few postwar writers have been subjected to a similarly busy personal-memoir industry like Thomas Bernhard. At times it looked as if the interest in his well-guarded private life became more intrinsic than the discussion of his literary works. But what was, and is, the reason behind this interest?

Much of it seems to originate in the enigma of this writer, who, on the one hand, needed privacy to the point of seclusion, yet on the other hand, was a controversial public figure. One could see him sitting on a bench on Vienna's most traditional grounds for *flaneurs,* the Graben, the city's commercial center, receiving both devotional greetings from his admirers and at the same time, verbal abuse from outspoken critics. This was a writer who indulged in verbal onslaughts against Austria and the rest of the world. Yet, he clearly enjoyed his public appearances taking his bows on stage with a wry smile in spite of a booing audience. But at the end he even made those whom he despised applaud him. There was an undoubtedly masochistic dimension to Bernhard's love-hate relationship with his fellow Austrians — and vice versa.

Any anecdotal approach to Bernhard hopes to generate a sense of authenticity in what is otherwise an artificial discourse on the distinctly artificial world of his prose and plays. Part of this approach is the ongoing fascination with Bernhard's bewildering generalizations, which were as prominent in his conversations and interviews as in his fiction. Many of these sweeping judgments provided the stuff headlines are made of. "Alles ist grauslich," this was the very essence of Bernhard's generalizing views.[1] It summed up his notion of a world in which he came to regard contemplating the various ways of committing suicide as the most meaningful way of living.

Is then this following episode, or anecdote, just another reminiscence to the Bernhard-saga? I mention my encounter with him, because of one particular object that featured in it rather prominently and since I cannot help but to regard it as a peculiar symbol of Bernhard's awkward *Weltbezug*, his relation to the world. It is by no means improper to read this brief episode and what I try to make of it as a parody of Bernhardian anecdotalism that still dominates our writing on this advocate of the absurd, whose literary forms of despair and black humor have divided the reading community into admirers and critics, as has been remarked by most critics long ago.[2] But to put it paradoxically, the poignancy of Bernhard's deliberately appalling generalizations has continued to concern us in various ways. These generalizations, together with his use of exaggeration and repetition, belong to the same rhetorical register. More than anything else, they were meant to parody the generalizations, exaggerations and repetitive way of speaking, that are commonplace in public debate. This approach is strongly reminiscent of the rhetorical features in Nietzsche's eighth book of *Jenseits von Gut und Böse* that plays with the various degrees of prejudice.

But let me come back to my actual anecdote. During my conversation with Thomas Bernhard, he suddenly took a broken window handle out of his pocket and placed it quite carefully in front of him on a table with some newspapers. As it happened, the window handle was lying on a copy of the Viennese newspaper *Die Presse*. Bernhard was visibly displeased by this fact and decided to re-arrange the papers so that his window handle came to lie on the *Neue Zürcher Zeitung*. All of this happened without him commenting on what he was doing. But once his broken window handle had found its proper place between the two of us, I could not help noticing a sly smile on his face.

Bernhard now embarked on telling me about the history of this broken window handle and that he had been searching all over Vienna to find a duplicate. He stressed several times that he was only interested in an exact replica, identical replacement or absolutely the same thing. Without it he felt that he could never open his favorite window in his Viennese domicile again. The point was that only an *identical* object could help him in this matter. Being able to open this very window seemed to have been of vital importance to him. Perhaps it symbolized to him the ability to open up to the outside world, which would have explained why he was so particular about placing his broken window handle onto the *Neue Zürcher Zeitung* with its decidedly international flair and not on any Austrian paper that represented to him deplorable provincialism. I was reminded of the symbolic significance of the *Neue Zürcher Zeitung* in his novel *Wittgensteins Neffe* where its two major protagonists travel many miles across Austria to locate a review in this journal.

But the real point was still to come. After some moments of silence Bernhard said that if he was really looking for the absolutely identical duplicate of this *broken* window handle, then he could only hope for yet *another broken* window handle. Consequently, he would never be able to open his favorite window again. What I had the honor of observing was the creation of an obsession with all the verbal patterns of repetition and exaggeration that characterize his literary style. Eventually though, Bernhard wrapped his broken window handle in one or two sheets of the *Neue Zürcher Zeitung* and put it back into his pocket saying that he should better bury this parcel now. With these words he rose, left his favorite *Kaffeehaus* and disappeared into the labyrinth of Vienna's first district.

Am I overstating the significance of this episode? Am I already overinterpreting the symbolic meaning of this small object, especially in view of the fact that things, or objects, play a relatively small part in Bernhard's *œuvre*? It looks though as if this broken window handle, and even more so Bernhard's almost melancholic affection for it, epitomized the fragility of his *Weltbezug*. What is meant by this concept? It refers to the attempt to attain some strong connection with what is beyond one's own limited sphere of life. It emphasizes the willingness to define one's own identity in terms of the larger context in which one operates. Finally, it suggests putting our own concerns into perspective. In *Alte Meister,* for example, the main protagonist Reger stresses the fact that he was once married to an intelligent and wealthy "cosmopolitan."[3] This reference, together with his being a music critic for *The Times* and his experience of the various lavatories in many a metropolis, are his credentials that make him a man of the world, at least in the eyes of the narrator and the museum attendant Irrsigler who is of decidedly provincial origin.

This feature was one prominent pattern of Bernhard's narrative strategy. The "world" is present in the form of sweeping generalizations and comparisons. By referring to a particular newspaper or a certain city, Bernhard's narrator creates a sense of cosmopolitanism. But this kind of *Weltbezug* strikes the reader as utterly pretentious and much, indeed, of the comic effects in Bernhard's prose and plays derive from this exaggerated pretentiousness of his characters. At the same time, such pretentiousness signals that Bernhard's protagonists are ill at ease with the "world" since their *Weltbezug* is fundamentally flawed. These protagonists are all in need of covering up their inability to communicate with each other, which is at the heart of their disturbed relationship with the outside world. The notion of otherness does not really occur, at least not as a potential area of recreation for the battered self. On the contrary, in a Sartre-like fashion, the other person, as a messenger of the world beyond one's own self, only seems to represent one thing — hell. Or as in Bernhard's play *Am Ziel*, the mother tells her daughter in no uncertain terms: "Ich unterhalte mich mit mir allein am besten / Ich bin nur gestört von den Andern / [. . .] Ich habe mich tödlich an dich gewöhnt tödlich ja."[4]

The "world" is explicitly referred to only in a few titles of Bernhard's texts. Most prominently of course, in *Der Weltverbesserer*, but also in two of his early poems "Mein Weltenstück" and "Hinter den Bäumen ist eine andere Welt." The central point in the play *Der Weltverbesserer* is the protagonist's "Traktat zur Verbesserung der Welt" with its claim that the world could only be improved if man abolished it. In Bernhard's first publication, the poem "Mein Weltenstück" (1952), the "world" is defined by the view from a window (!) onto repetitive daily occurrences: "Und jeder neue Glockenschlag / Bringt tausendmal denselben Blick / Durchs Fenster in mein Weltenstück."[5] The difference between these two approaches to the "world" is obvious. While the poem does not draw any consequences from its limited view of life, the "Weltverbesserer" enters into a lengthy lament on the boredom of repetition that conditions human existence and the necessity to extinguish these conditions.

In the second of Bernhard's poems on "Welt," the reader is made to enter another world behind the trees that cannot provide any consolation. On the contrary, it refers to the realm of mourning, black suns and the moon of the dead.[6] It is a world after the abolishment of the world. With his early poetry (all published prior to his first works in prose) Bernhard appears to have prepared the ground for his narrative explorations of a world that he saw in a state of dissolution. It is a world of broken identities and fragments of abandoned cultures. At the same time, Bernhard the lyrical poet was acutely aware of the need to recall the grand epic tradition and hence his implicit references to Vergil, Dante, Hölderlin and T. S. Eliot.[7] Through his poetry Bernhard conjured up an epic spirit of which he hoped that it could be sustained for the sake of developing a provocative interplay between self-creation and self-annihilation.[8] It is this provocative element and verbal anarchism in Bernhard's writings that must be recognized and should not be neutralized by secondary comments on them. These are texts full of outrage even though these outbreaks of emotion and challenges to conventional thinking were carefully crafted and skillfully orchestrated by the author's linguistic virtuosity.[9]

Recently, Alfred Pfabigan attempted to evaluate the analytical dimension particular to Bernhard's prose. In the center of his study stood the writer's supreme ability to analyze the pathological dimension of people's outlook on life and their image of the "world."[10] Pfabigan called his study, somewhat ambiguously "ein österreichisches Weltexperiment," suggesting that Bernhard had experimented with the world from an Austrian perspective. He also appears to suggest that Bernhard himself was, and up to a point still is, at the heart of an Austrian experiment summarized in the following question: How can one find access to larger contexts and a way of thinking that can transcend parochial preoccupations. The laboratory where this twofold experiment was/is taking place is, according to Pfabigan, in most of all Bernhard's prose. Epic narration of, say, the scale of *Auslöschung* requires a significant amount of breath in a literal and non-literal meaning of the word. In addition to Pfabigan's understanding of experiment, I would like to add that Bernhard's life and work represent a continuous experiment with the notion of breath, or "Atem" as one of his key-novellas is called.[11] In many respects Bernhard's experimental writing was first of all a case of experimenting with himself. The German word "Selbstversuch," an experiment performed upon oneself, highlights the fact that such experiments are also the result of being tempted by one's self to explore it. The self-referentiality of Bernhard's works is obvious, but often it does not seem to be clear what this entails. To begin with, such self-referentiality should not automatically be associated with self-indulgence or self-obsession. In Bernhard's case it means an existential interest in what enabled him to create his own space, as he put it in his last interview.[12] Furthermore, it implies the experience of one's own limitations and the attempt to overcome them. Within this space and its boundaries Bernhard created his own world. The question remains how unique and distinctly different was this world from other worlds? More importantly, how credible was Bernhard's criticism of Austria and the Austrians, if his measures were taken from a world that he had constructed with literary means?

Pfabigan points out that Bernhard was in fact very close to the *Zeitgeist* and unusually well informed about what was going on in Austria and elsewhere. However, the intriguing point is that Bernhard transformed his knowledge in a way that suggested a rather superficial understanding of world matters. Through obsessive reproduction of social prejudice and generalizations of political issues, often presented in deliberately monotonous monologues, Bernhard seems to have subjected himself to an overwhelming sense of futility. Yet to put it paradoxically, this futility mattered, for he could demonstrate in his art of repetition that the frequent recurrence of the same sentiment or thought can assume a meaning of its own.[13] In *Der Atem,* the reader learns of two kinds of breaths: The angelic breath of art, especially music, and the ever endangered breath of life. Whereas the former informs a sense of optimism, the latter undermines it: "Meine Atemzüge waren die einer, wie mir vorgekommen war, vollkommen zerstörten Lunge gewesen, ein fürchterlicher Zerstörungsprozess war jedesmal, wenn ich ein- oder ausatmete."[14] This remark is not only the reflection of a writer who was suffering from a lung disease but also of an intellectual who was intimately familiar with spiritual connotations of breath, or *pneuma,* in the tradition of the *Book of Revelations.* In his novel *Verstörung,* for example, the narrator speaks of "metaphysische Luft" which is in line with the biblical interpretation of *pneuma.* The main revelation, however, is that there is also a negative dimension to breath, namely the supposedly self-destructive effect of breathing.

One can regard Bernhard's self-classification as a "Geschichtenzerstörer"[15] as a consequence of this fundamentally disturbing experience. But the real point is that Bernhard may well have destroyed stories, whether in a postmodern sense or not, though he did not destroy narration as such. On the contrary, his artistically structured syntax and various forms of repetition suggest an unbroken confidence in the effect of narrating. The art of narration was Bernhard's connection with the world in a decidedly existential meaning of the word. His life-long illness required him to restore some of the breath he was lacking through incessant writing. The words and never-ending sentences became his breath, as Elfriede Jelinek rightly remarked in her brief but splendid homage to Bernhard, written shortly after the news of his death had reached her.[16] Jelinek argued that in his works, Bernhard's "breath" had turned into a permanent rage, which paradoxically granted him life, but also suffocated him at the end.

"Welt" served Bernhard as a point of reference with both vague and negative connotations. The potential grandeur of the "world" was, in his view, most seriously undermined by the either laughable or sinister aspirations of the *petit bourgeois:* "Die sogenannte Harmlosigkeit des Kleinbürgers ist in Wirklichkeit ein grober und fahrlässiger und sehr oft direkt in die Weltstörung und Weltzerstörung führender Trugschluß, wie wir wissen müssen," the narrator says in *Die Ursache.*[17] In *Die Ursache,* like in all other autobiographical novels, the "world" is represented by the names of the great artists of the past, but also by the menacing obscurity of ideologies, by fear and repression. Yet the very instrument that should provide meaningful access to the world mediating between the small world of the province and *tout le monde,* as well as enabling the petit bourgeois to become a genuine cosmopolitan, is education. However, according to Bernhard's narrators, this instrument called education fails completely to accomplish this aim. *Die Ursache,* for instance, refers to schools and other educational institutions as "Verrottungszentren" where talents are repressed and the notion of *Bildung* is perverted. *Die Ursache* portrays an uncompromisingly bleak outlook onto the world from the perspective of a Catholic boarding school in Salzburg. Here, Bernhard's *Weltbezug* only occurs in the form of unprecedented destruction. The outside world comes to visit these anguished boys as a menace. In front of their eyes the icons of the past have become exchangeable: Christ replaces the portrait of Hitler. Discussions on what had actually happened in the world outside the Salzburg boarding school are not allowed; news only exists as rumors.

The great names of the artistic world can no longer provide any sense of orientation. On the contrary, they seem to cripple Bernhard's protagonists and diminish their productivity while turning them into shadowy existences. In *Beton,* the unheroic hero fails to succeed in completing a study on Mendelssohn-Bartholdy. The protagonist of *Der Untergeher* has worked for years on a study on the legendary pianist Glenn Gould only to find out in the end that he needed to destroy his own writings. Bernhard's characters inhabit secondary worlds and yet their only aspiration in life is to become authentic. What does make them authentic at times is their relentless (self-) hatred and sense of destruction, or, extinction. The only originality left consists of images of annihilation. Bernhard's novel *Verstörung,* for example, confronts the reader with such strikingly original images of destruction. An aristocrat imagines that he had asked for all the trees on his estate to be cut down and turned into sawdust or tree-powder. He imagines the tree-powder to have suffocated everything and everybody. It is possible to read such images as extrapolations of the fundamental experience of destruction as depicted in *Die Ursache.* Eye-witnessing the air raids on Salzburg was, in a sense, one of Bernhard's *Urerlebnisse,* perhaps only matched by the fact that his mother, time and again, had accused him of being in this world at all. It was these experiences that inspired Bernhard's haunting autobiographical account *Ein Kind.*

In Bernhard's works we learn that any attempt to assert oneself can have self-destructive consequences. Moreover, in plays like *Der Ignorant und der Wahnsinnige* and in novels like *Verstörung* we are made to believe that the only possible connection with the outside world is to share its insanity. Bernhard's protagonists cannot help but live against their own existence.[18] They seem to exist in spite of nature and history. They act, if at all, against any traces of the *élan vital* that might still be in them. They can only entertain some interaction with the "world" if any such activity is defined in negative terms. Thus, the only possible definition of objectivity that Bernhard's characters can accept is negativity. By the same token, reality of any sort is determined by a continuously diminishing sense of what reality essentially is. Given this overwhelming sense of *Realitätsverlust,* it is somewhat surprising to find but a few of Bernhard's protagonists who are running out of words. For it seems that what applies to the issue of breath and language, is also true for the complex interrelationship between *Realitätsverlust* and words: The less reality is left, the more essential it becomes in constituting a surrogate world by means of incessant talking and writing. If reality does no longer exist, at least some form of verbally generated reality must be in its place. Pointlessness must have a point and the meaninglessness of communication must be communicated if not in plain words then in multi-layered sentences, full of repetitions, variations, and subordinate clauses which signify the relativity of any statement.

In Bernhard's works pointlessness as such is treated like *the* fact of life. It is a fact that is part of the very totality of facts that, according to Wittgenstein, constitute the world. The influence of Ludwig Wittgenstein on Bernhard is undeniable.[19] One of the most striking aspects of this influence is the notion of *Weltbezug*. When Wittgenstein stated in his *Tractatus* that the "Die Grenzen meiner Sprache bedeuten die Grenzen meiner Welt," then this statement, surely, comes close to Bernhard's view that the act of producing words conditioned his world.[20] With Walter Schulz we can argue that Wittgenstein had portrayed language increasingly as a *Lebensform,* a form of life, which precisely coincides with Bernhard's concern to preserve, if anything at all, language as his means of life.[21] To an unusual extent, however, Bernhard was prepared to widen the limits of language. In his works there is a Wittgensteinian desire to be precise about facts and, at the same time, this precision is counteracted by vague generalizations. The latter seem necessary to keep the various monologues afloat and to cause the impression that incessant talking could prolong the license to live. Bernhard was not easily prepared to accept Wittgenstein's famous last statement in the *Tractatus* that what cannot be spoken about must be passed over in silence. On the contrary, his protagonists speak about silence and preferably about such things that normally are passed over in silence, perhaps most notably in the play *Ein Fest für Boris.*

Quite different from Wittgenstein however, Bernhard viewed "life" as synonymous with experiencing, and trying to cope with the absurd. While at least part of Wittgenstein's philosophy represented an attempt to suppress, or contain the threat of meaninglessness and the intrusion of the absurd into the world of logic, Bernhard was quite prepared to embrace pointlessness and to accept it as the main *condition de vivre.* One could argue that Wittgenstein employed logic as an instrument to gain control over the ever-stronger sense of absurdity that began to penetrate modernism. Yet Bernhard, in his plays and prose, allowed the absurd to adopt pseudo-logic and thus allowed absurdity to unfold its own momentum. Language was not only to reflect the paradoxes of life but also to assist the absurd in voicing a sense of pointlessness. Wittgenstein's phrase "was der Fall ist" might have been taken literally by Bernhard; for in German "Fall" can mean "case" or "fall." In this instance it would not be a fall from grace, but a fall from sense. Bernhard's work suggests a re-interpretation of Wittengenstein's essential first statements in the "Tractatus": The world is falling into disrepute, because the logic it relies on is a mere construction and as such equally absurd as the conditions of life. Furthermore, Wittgenstein's claim that the world divides into facts reads slightly more dramatically in the original: "Die Welt zerfällt in Tatsachen."[22] Again, Bernhard is likely to have interpreted this sentence literally with the emphasis on "zerfällt," meaning "disintegrates" or "dilapidates." To him Wittgenstein's differentiation between facts and things — "Die Welt ist die Gesamtheit der Tatsachen, nicht der Dinge"[23] — would not have made sense; for Bernhard tends to regard things as facts. Bernhard's broken window handle was to him, quite evidently, a thing and a fact, an object and an emblem of a world in a state of disintegration.

The fall from an assumed height of intellectualism and banality into the abyss of nonsense is the subject matter of *In der Höhe/Rettungsversuch, Unsinn,* one of Bernhard's earliest prose pieces (1959), but published posthumously as his last book in 1989. Needless to say, the rescue operation (*Rettungsversuch*) in this prose is doomed to fail. The fundamental fact on which this prose rests is spelled out at the beginning of *Rettungsversuch:*

> Tatsache, daß das, was wir aussprechen, niederschreiben, zehnmal dümmer ist, als das, was wir denken, trotzdem lassen wir uns, wie die großen Schriftsteller, darauf ein, als viel dümmer zu gelten, als wir sind, und begehen den Unsinn etwas zu sagen, niederzuschreiben, eine Meinung zu äußern, eine Richtung zu vertreten, uns für einen Gedanken einzusetzen.[24]

Communication is viewed as a mere caricature of thought. Or to be more precise, our desire to communicate and share our thoughts with others makes us susceptible to ridicule, for the very means of communication are insufficient. Already at the outset of our attempt to create

Weltbezug through an act of communication we fail in our ambition. The narrator mocks the obsession with *Weltbezug* and its various, and inevitably ludicrous, forms:

> *was haben Sie denn für eine Weltanschauung?*, ich habe keine Weltanschauung, wenn man davon absieht, daß ich die Weltanschauung habe, die ich haben *muß* die jeder hat, die ganzen Schriften und die ganzen Gespräche der Leute sind angefüllt mit ihrer *Weltanschauung* und: *Weltbild, Weltbund, Welthysterie, Weltkrise, Weltbankrott, Weltpakt, Weltgesundheit*, das ist alles unerträglich.[25]

The other, and probably most crucial form of *Weltbezug* in Bernhard's works is the reference to *Weltliteratur*. This is most evident in the mottoes to his prose and plays.[26]

One of Bernhard's few works without a motto is, in fact, *In der Höhe/Rettungsversuch, Unsinn;* though the text supplies us with one possible reason for this omission:

> Vorlesen von Shakespearebrocken, Dantebrocken, Köpfe, die nicht NEIN sagen, Köpfe, die in der Luft hin- und hergeworfen werden, Hauptstraßen, die alle Städte untereinander verbinden: ein Schiff fährt aus meinem Gehirn heraus und schneidet die Welt auseinander.[27]

This suggests that both, mere allusions to world literature (". . . -brocken") and actual connections with parts of the world (the main streets) are of no use. In the end it is the vehicle of imagination, the ship, that destroys any notion of unity. There is a striking similarity between the ship in this context and Rimbaud's famous poem "Le Bateau ivre,"[28] which gained some popularity in the German-speaking world through Paul Zech's translation and his play "Das trunkene Schiff" (1986).[29] Although it cannot be argued that Bernhard was familiar with both texts, then (1959) or at a later stage, the analogy is nonetheless worth pointing out. In a sense, Rimbaud's ship was cutting his world in half: One part still belonged to his origins, while the other was the unknown territory of his uncertain future. It was the *bateau* of a *poète maudit* that was supposed to divide up Rimbaud's world. In this case though, the ship itself hoped to break up ("Oh! que ma quille éclate! Oh! que j'aille à la mer!"[30]). But while Rimbaud felt ready for the sea, that is to say, a new life without further guidance, Bernhard sought answers in vain: "du stehst vor dem Grab der Mutter: keine Antwort, du stehst im Schnee: keine Antwort."[31]

Bernhard's mottoes, or *Brocken* of the great and the famous, often taken from Pascal, Voltaire, Kierkegaard, but also Diderot, Novalis and Alexander Block, read like islands of mental tranquility and firmness, that bode both ill and good for what is to come. Yet, in all cases these mottoes prove to be a short prelude to the destruction of any such tranquility. One gains the impression that Bernhard's protagonists only refer to the great artists to have a worthwhile target. The dismantling of idols is, for example, the main occupation of the characters in his play *Die Berühmten*. The truly famous artists, such as Lotte Lehmann, Toscanini and the pianist Elly Ney, are only present in the shape of puppets, while their present-day equivalents indulge in talking about the necessity to kill talent in artists and to liberate oneself from the oppressive presence of the great names of the past. Finally, one singer tries to destroy the puppet of Lotte Lehmann by beating it with a champagne bottle.[32] The deconstruction of once revered old masters is, of course, one of the central subject matters in *Alte Meister* and in *Auslöschung*. What only seems to matter in this, as in other works by Bernhard, is the originality of deconstructing this connection to world literature; and this originality is often limited to the degree of verbal attacks on the names of names:

> Bruckner ist ein genauso schlampiger Komponist wie Stifter ein schlampiger Schriftsteller, diese oberösterreichische Schlampigkeit haben beide gemein. Beide machten sie eine sogenannte gottergebene und gemeingefährliche Kunst, sagte Reger . . . Prosaverwischer, sagte er, der Eine, Musikverwischer der Andere, . . . zwei maßlos überschätzte Blindgänger.[33]

In the novel *Auslöschung* it is Murau who instructs his disciple Gambetti to read world literature, with deconstruction and devaluation in mind: "das Goethesche Werk ist ein philiströser philosophischer Schrebergarten."[34] An essential tool in this deconstructive strategy is, as mentioned earlier, the means of repetition. Through repeating an argument, often several times, Bernhard empties the content of the repeated subject matter, or exposes it to ridicule.

The art of exaggeration and repetition are, after all, closely related.[35] As is often the case with musical compositions, Bernhard tends to avoid identical repetitions; he insists on slight variations when repeating a phrase. This is often connected with constructing absurdly logical arguments as given in this grotesque conversation in *Die Berühmten:*

> VERLEGER
>
> Im übrigen ist unsere verehrte Abwesende
> auch eine Verwandte von Thomas Mann
> und dieser ist
> wie ich gerade herausgefunden habe
> mit James Joyce verwandt

PIANISTIN *ausrufend*

Mit Joyce
mit Joyce
was Sie nicht sagen

SCHAUSPIELERIN *fast hysterisch*

Tatsächlich mit Joyce

VERLEGER

Tatsächlich mit Joyce
Joyce und Mann
Sind Verwandte
Und Joyce habe ich entdeckt
ist mit Rilke verwandt

PIANISTIN

Dann ist ja auch Mann
mit Rilke verwandt
wenn Joyce mit Mann verwandt ist
Und Rilke mit Joyce

VERLEGER

Das ist eine Sensation

REGISSEUR

Sensationell

KAPELLMEISTER

Unglaublich

VERLEGER

Und mit Rilke sind so viele verwandt
daß gar nicht gesagt werden kann
mit wie vielen Rilke verwandt ist[36]

The structure of this verbal exchange and parody of name dropping is unmistakably operatic in character. Moreover, it aims to discredit a certain understanding of (high) culture that believes in combining everything with everything. Indirectly, it argues in favor of retaining differences in culture: Rilke is Rilke, and Joyce is Joyce. The concept of culture and the actual historical context where a given culture unfolds must be differentiated. Bernhard's *Weltbezug* is historically concrete rather than culturally universal.

Finally, some brief reflections on what appears to have been one of Bernhard's favorite words may be helpful in examining the last aspect of his *Weltbezug;* it is the word *sogenannt* (so-called) with its evidently depreciatory undertone. The restrictive meaning of this word is obvious. It signals to the reader that a word associated with "so-called," can merely be a construction or approximation of what is really meant. But by "calling" something just "so," the speaker has either made a highly individualistic selection from numerous other possible words or adopted a certain linguistic convention according to which one calls a particular something in a particular way. The use of "so-called" in Bernhard's case implies a considerable ironic distance to his language community. Something "so-called" allows for alternatives if one can bring oneself to depart from linguistic conventions. Such conventions were, according to Bernhard, merely awkward conveniences. Sheer indolence often prevents us from calling things other than they have been called for all too long. In Bernhard's way of thinking, as far as one can tell, alternatives, even (or shall we say especially) absurd ones, mattered a great deal. In his rhetorical registers the phrase "either/or" played a significant part. His notion of either/or was to challenge one-dimensional thinking and to undermine conventionalism. What the word "so-called" alludes to, namely the instability of assumptions and conventional modes of language, becomes in Bernhard's vocabulary, aggravated by either/or constructions. One could therefore argue, that to Bernhard, the "world" was rather a question of the means with which we try to access it; to him the actual *Bezug,* whether in the shape of a participle, conjunction or [broken] window handle, seemed to have mattered more than "the world as such."

In lieu of a conclusion, I should like to tell the rest of my Bernhard-anecdote. When he had left the *Kaffeehaus,* the waiter came and opened the window close to the table where I had had my encounter with Bernhard. He responded to my questioning look by saying: "It is rather stuffy, isn't it? But, you see, Herr Bernhard does not like open windows; for he is afraid of draughts."

Notes

[1] Cf. *Zeit-Magazin* 46 (1988): 40–50. See also Kurt Hofmann, *Aus Gesprächen mit Thomas Bernhard* (Munich: dtv, 1991).

[2] See, for example, Peter Demetz in his review of *Der Untergeher,* "Der Anti-Jedermann": *Frankfurter Allgemeine Zeitung* (17 September 1983); or Reinhard Baumgart's review of *Alte Meister,* "Die vergrauste Komödie": *Frankfurter Allgemeine Zeitung* (14 September 1985).

[3] Thomas Bernhard, *Alte Meister. Komödie* (Frankfurt: Suhrkamp, 1988), 198.

[4] Thomas Bernhard, *Die Stücke 1969–1981* (Frankfurt: Suhrkamp, 1983), 102.

[5] Thomas Bernhard, *Gesammelte Gedichte,* ed. Volker Bohn (Frankfurt: Surhkamp, 1991), 294.

[6] *Gesammelte Gedichte,* 31.

[7] This point was first made by Peter von Matt in his review of Bernhard's collected poems that became quite influential for the wider reception of his poetry. Peter von Matt, "Unbekannte Dichter. Thomas Bernhards poetische Paradiese," *Frankfurter Allgemeine Zeitung* (10 August 1991).

[8] This partly ironic, partly melancholic interplay between "Selbstschöpfung und Selbstvernichtung" was identified by Gerhard Gamm as a hallmark of Bernhard's approach to literary composition that can be traced back to Friedrich Schlegel. Gerhard Gamm, "Korrektur. Über Thomas Bernhard und die Melancholie der Moderne," *Lettre international* 56 (1999): 56–61.

[9] Cf. Robert Vellusig, "Thomas Bernhards Gesprächs-Kunst," *Thomas Bernhard. Beiträge zur Fiktion der Postmoderne. Londoner Symposion,* eds. Wendelin Schmidt-Dengler, Adrian Stevens, Fred Wagner (Frankfurt: Suhrkamp, 1997), 25–46.

[10] Alfred Pfabigan, *Thomas Bernhard. Ein österreichisches Weltexperiment* (Vienna: Zsolnay, 1999).

[11] Thomas Bernhard, *Der Atem* (Salzburg: Residenz, 1978).

[12] "'Ich bin nur mehr kurz da.' Thomas Bernhard in seinem letzten Gespräch [mit Kurt Hofmann]," *Der Spiegel* 5 (1990): 168.

[13] Cf. Rüdiger Görner, "Gespiegelte Wiederholungen. Zu einem Kunstgriff von Thomas Bernhard," *Thomas Bernhard. Beiträge zur Fiktion der Postmoderne. Londoner Symposion,* 111–25.

[14] Thomas Bernhard, *Der Atem. Eine Entscheidung* (Munich: dtv, 1981), 72.

[15] Thomas Bernhard, *Der Italiener* (Salzburg: Residenz, 1971), 152.

[16] Elfriede Jelinek, "Atemlos," *Die Zeit* (24 February 1989): 57.

[17] Thomas Bernhard, *Die Ursache. Eine Andeutung* (Munich: dtv, 1977), 102.

[18] Cf. Herbert Gamper, "Thomas Bernhards philosophisches Theater," *Neue Zürcher Zeitung* (29 January 1988): 40.

[19] Cf. Albrecht Weber, "Wittgensteins Gestalt und Theorie und ihre Wirkung im Werk Thomas Bernhards," *Österreich in Geschichte und Literatur* 25 (1981): 86–104. Recently, Manfred Mittermayer argued against overrating this influence; he does not however discuss his point in sufficient detail. See Manfred Mittermayer, *Thomas Bernhard* (Stuttgart: Metzler, 1995), 73.

[20] Ludwig Wittgenstein, *Schriften: Tractatus logico-philosophicus, Tagebücher 1914–1916, Philosophische Untersuchungen* (Frankfurt: Suhrkamp, 1960), 5.6; 64.

[21] Walter Schulz, *Wittgenstein. Die Negation der Philosophie* (Pfullingen: Neske, 1979), 51.

[22] *Tractatus,* 1.2; 11.

[23] *Tractatus,* 1.1; 11.

[24] Thomas Bernhard, *In der Höhe Rettungsversuch, Unsinn* (Frankfurt: Suhrkamp, 1990), 8; first published 1989 (Salzburg: Residenz Verlag).

[25] *In der Höhe,* 56. Italics in the original.

[26] For further discussion of the theory of mottoes see Jan Erik Antonsen, *Text-Inseln. Studien zum Motto in der deutschen Literatur vom 17. bis 20. Jahrhundert* (Würzburg: Königshausen & Neumann, 1998).

[27] *In der Höhe,* 142.

[28] Arthur Rimbaud, *Sämtliche Dichtungen. Französisch und Deutsch,* ed. Walter Küchler (Heidelberg: Laubert Schneider, 1982), 132–39.

[29] Paul Zech, *Rimbaud. Ein biographischer Essay und die szenische Ballade "Das trunkene Schiff,"* ed. Hermann Haarmann et al. (Rudolstadt: Greifenverlag zu Rudolstadt, 1986).

[30] "Rimbaud," 136.

[31] *In der Höhe,* 142.

[32] Thomas Bernhard, *Die Stücke 1960–1981* (Frankfurt: Suhrkamp, 1983), 504.

[33] *Alte Meister,* 76, 78.

[34] Thomas Bernhard, *Auslöschung* (Frankfurt: Suhrkamp, 1986), 576.

[35] Cf. Wendelin Schmidt-Dengler, *Der Übertreibungskünstler. Studien zu Thomas Bernhard* (Vienna: Sonderzahl, 1989); and Rüdiger Görner, "Gespiegelte Wiederholungen," 113–25.

[36] Thomas Bernhard, *Die Berühmten* (Frankfurt: Suhrkamp, 1976), 476.

Wendelin Schmidt-Dengler

Thomas Bernhard's Poetics of Comedy

Liver Dumpling Soup or Fried Crêpe Soup

ALL OF BERNHARD'S CHARACTERS have to make decisions. The more they ponder the possible alternatives, which are mutually exclusive, the more insecure they become. The more the alternatives are being weighed, the more the opposite choices begin to resemble one another. A decision made is tantamount to a decision made in favor of misfortune. We, as outsiders, are not privy to this moment of decision. Because the alternatives cannot be reconciled, they risk becoming irrelevant. Bernhard once remarked in an interview that he talks about death in the same manner he talks about a roll of bread. In the play *Der Theatermacher* the hero is continuously faced with the choice between Liver Dumpling Soup (*Leberknödelsuppe*) and Fried Crêpe Soup (*Fritatensuppe*).[1] We are not too far off the mark when we assume that in this cosmos with its pervasive sense of Bernhard's poetics of comedy, the choice between Liver Dumpling Soup and Fried Crêpe Soup could assume the same validity as that between life and death.

The similarity of opposites turns into a line of argument used in a manner worthy of scholastics and at the same time facilitates a form of writing that no longer emphatically insists on truth. By circumventing the truth through a lie, one even claims to recognize the truth:

> Die Wahrheit, die wir kennen, ist logisch die Lüge, die, indem wir um sie nicht herumkommen, die Wahrheit ist. Was hier beschrieben ist, ist die Wahrheit und doch nicht die Wahrheit, weil es nicht die Wahrheit sein kann.[2]

"Wahrscheinliches, Unwahrscheinliches" (The Likely and the Unlikely) was the original title given to the collection of short prose published under the title *Der Stimmenimitator*. Here we read that Stanislaw Jerzy Lec always told the truth and of his absurd claim that the most dangerous enemies of the Polish regime had been buried under the *Nowy Swiat* in Warsaw.[3] By taking a lie close to the border of truth — and I phrase this in a cautious manner — Bernhard opens up a new dimension within truth. The choice between truth and untruth, he suggests, may well be decided in the same egalitarian manner as other alternatives, such as the choice between two soup dishes. At the end of the novel *Der Keller* (*The Cellar*) the German word "egal," which can roughly be rendered as "all the same," is spoken of almost in terms of a hymnic eulogy: "Ein schönes, ein klares, ein kurzes, ein einprägsames Wort: *egal*!" (DK, 165). Because equality is impossible, one could infer from this phrase, it is all the same. The man behind the jackhammer or the man behind the typewriter — both despair.

It would be easy to let Bernhard off the hook and present him as some kind of prophet of indifference who takes the easy way out by not addressing issues pertaining to social and ethical responsibility. Abandoning all commitments he is said to play the game of the laughing philosopher with the gesture of a Baroque theater director. In doing so, literary scholars are able to see him how they always wanted to see him and pin him down precisely where they want to have him, namely in the tradition of a secret continuation of the Austrian Baroque. The repetition of analogous antitheses typical of Bernhard's works makes scholars inclined to look at his oeuvre in terms of such opposites. Bernhard's principle of reconciling differences or opposites is also taken over by critics in order to suspend the unsettling sense of instability that ensues from his antithetical manner of writing.

The Comedy-Tragedy (*Komödientragödie*)

At any rate, this play on antitheses has become more or less binding for Bernhard's work. And critics have willingly adopted this notion and claim to come up with a label for the difficult characterization of Bernhard's writings. However, it is worth the effort to take a closer look at these antitheses. In my view, the antithesis of comedy and tragedy seems to be especially relevant for the constitution of his oeuvre. Perhaps it will thus be possible to discover a narrative dynamics within Bernhard's oeuvre. I use the word "oeuvre" to avoid the questionable term "development." "Is it a tragedy? Is it a comedy?" This title of a short story has become a standard quote in Bernhard criticism. In his oeuvre, the characters reflect at length about comedy and tragedy. Here I would like to offer some relevant examples, beginning with a statement by the painter Strauch in the novel *Frost:*

> Ich habe Mitleid mit dieser Tragödie, Komödie, ich habe ***kein*** Mitleid mit dieser Tragödie, Komödie, mit dieser von mir allein erfundenen Komödientragödie, mit diesen von mir allein erfundenen Schatten.[4]

There is an interesting parallel passage in *Der Keller* published thirteen years later which similarly suggests the blurring of boundaries between comedy and tragedy:

> Zuerst habe ich hundertprozentig eine Tragödie aufgeführt und dann eine Komödie und dann wieder eine Tragödie, und dann vermischte sich das Theater, es ist nicht mehr erkennbar, ob es eine Tragödie oder eine Komödie ist. (DK, 152)

I am not overstating matters by suggesting that Bernhard claims to have a patent on his own original form of drama. It is not merely a matter of viewing his dramas as a *genus mixtum,* as is the case, for example, with the tragi-comedy with its easily understood structure. Willi Huntemann recently made this entire complex genre the subject of a thorough study. He is correct in saying that Bernhard has gone farther than "die moderne Tragikomödie, die sich als Genre wenigstens noch ernst nimmt, wenn auch Komik und Tragik in ihr bis zur Untrennbarkeit miteinander verschmelzen."[5] One has to read Bernhard's texts for both their comic and tragic elements. These elements work on the basis of shifting images (*Umspringbilder*) and the spectator (in other words the reader) has the opportunity to perceive, in a flash, first one side and then the other side of the subject matter. The text called "Empfindung" ("Sensation") from the *Stimmenimitator* projects this insight from the sphere of reception back onto that of production. A stage writer scores a success by virtue of the fact that he advertizes his comedies as tragedies, and vice versa: "Im Gegensatz zu seinen erfolglosen Kollegen [sei er] ehrlich genug, seine Komödien immer als Tragödien, seine Tragödien aber immer als Komödien auszugeben" (DS, 117). And Bernhard Minetti, the famous actor, directly confirms the thesis of the shifting image in his memoirs:

> Bernhard ist für mich der absolute Souverän auf dem Gebiet der Tragikomödie. Wie oft treffe ich Zuschauer aus meinen Bernhard-Aufführungen, die mir jeweils dieselbe Stelle zitieren: Die einen finden sie komisch, die anderen tragisch, aber ich denke weder an Komik noch an Erschütterung, während ich spiele.[6]

Minetti, just like Bernhard himself, has unconsciously placed the emphasis in his acting style on "Empfindung," on feeling. The opposites of comedy and tragedy exist alongside rather than in mutually exclusive terms. Bernhard's virtuosity reveals itself in that he gives the reader the opportunity to re-enact this constant crossing of borders between the two genres. He appears to be a tap-dancer who, with the speed of lightning, dances on the border between the comic and the tragic. Claude Porcell, for his part, introduces Bernhard's dramaturgy as follows: "Bernhard brouille les cartes, on le sait, des genres litéraires. La 'tragedie' se donne sans cesse pour une comedie, 'et inversement.'"[7] Bernhard, claims Porcell, clouds the issue of literary genres. Tragedy is constantly being presented as comedy, and inversely. Jean-Louis de Rambures speaks of an "énorme farce 'shakespearienne.'"[8] Chantal Thomas opens her monograph on Bernhard with a chapter about "Le rire tragique de Thomas Bernhard."[9] This consensus of opinion reached in France in the 1980s cannot be encountered in the early scholarly literature on Bernhard in German. The first reference to a possible, indeed serious reception of the writings of Thomas Bernhard dealing with the aspect of the comic is from Eckhard Henscheid, published under the title "Der Krypto-Komiker: Wie der österreichische Schriftsteller Thomas Bernhard seine Bewunderer, seine Kritiker und wahrscheinlich sich selber an der Nase herumführt."[10] Henscheid, referring to Bernhard as a crypto-comic, claims that Bernhard leads his admirers, critics and even himself around by the nose. Henscheid advises people for the time being not to trust the man.

From Appearances to Revelations

The ambivalence of the tragic and the comic eventually did not go unnoticed by German language critics. In a recent analysis of the play *Theatermacher*, Herbert Gamper writes:

> Ab etwa der Mitte der siebziger Jahre hat Bernhard die in den ersten Stücken und vor allem in den großen Prosawerken entfalteten Themen und Motive mehr und mehr als formelhafte Versatzstücke zu immer neuen Variationen eines mehr oder weniger konstanten Musters montiert, wobei sie häufig zur routinemäßig wiederkehrenden, ohne Kenntnis der Werkgeschichte kaum mehr verständlichen Abbreviatur verkürzt, oder verzerrt und ins Lächerliche gezogen sind.[11]

Roughly from the mid-1970s onward, claims Gamper, Bernhard took themes and motifs from his works and used them increasingly as stereotypical clichés to create new variations of a more or less constant pattern. While one does not necessarily have to agree with the judgment implied in this statement, the observation is nonetheless applicable to Bernhard's complete works. Bernhard's fundamental statement "Es ist alles lächerlich, wenn man an den *Tod* denkt"[12] ("Everything becomes ridiculous when one thinks of *death*") is valid for the period that begins with the caesura of the mid-1970s.

However, it must be said that in the preceding epoch the tragic and the deplorable, the element of horror/fright/agony and misery, and obsessive thought about death are at the forefront. This emphasis changes only gradually as death takes on less prominence and becomes a foil to more comical events. This change, which by no means indicates a sharp line of separation, is marked by the collection of short prose *Der Stimmenimitator*. The prose text "Ernst" ("Seriousness"), contained in this collection, persistently invokes this ambivalence. An incredibly successful comedian, wearing a traditional Tyrolean hat on his head, stands on the edge of a mountain in Salzburg in front of a group of vacationers who break into loud laughter when he announces that he is going to jump off the edge. Serious about his threats, the comedian throws himself off the mountain: "Der Komiker soll aber gesagt haben, daß es ihm ernst sei und habe sich tatsächlich und augenblicklich in die Tiefe gestürzt" (DS, 48). It does not matter whether it is a tragedy or a comedy. Because we have lost the utopia of a better or different condition, we have committed ourselves to the farce, the ridiculous. In the mere process of writing we serve the interests of the ridiculous, which helps us to cope with time and thus life itself. The joke is, like the tragic, affirmative. That brings to mind an early criticism voiced years ago by Michael Scharang, which came from the other side, namely that of death: "Diejenigen die bei Bernhard in Tod und Metaphysik flüchten, flüchten in der Realität in den Faschismus."[13] Those who seek refuge in death and metaphysics in Bernhard's works, seek in real life refuge in fascism. These criticisms, which have very different points of departure — in one case the fascination with death, in the other the play of the "crypto-comic" — merge at the precise moment when critics assume that Bernhard's texts, sometimes in virtuoso manner, sometimes less so, really signify nothing at all and thus prevent any critical and dialectical confrontation with reality. Herbert Gamper writes: "Bernhards Denken spielt sich in Aporien ab, in Gegensätzen, die keine wirklichen Alternativen sind: *einerseits — andererseits*, weitgehend mechanisch, vereinzelt sogar sinnwidrig gebraucht, ist davon die erstarrte Formel."[14] Bernhard's mode of thinking, claims Gamper, is aporetic and offers no real alternatives. Consequently, the alternatives are only spurious alternatives, and even if that were the case, one would nevertheless like to ask, whether they reveal something after all.

Total Comedy

Gamper's criticism is obliged to ethical goals and wants to uphold the sanctity of that which Bernhard's technique of irritation destroys. This means to uphold the moral mission of literature, to offer resistance to indifference and passivity and to all distortions of the human. Faced with a tribunal that takes Bernhard to task in such a manner, he would seem to have no adequate attorney or defense. I think that Bernhard's poetics offer at least a legitimate basis for argument which does not examine his texts in order to determine the quality of the moral fiber in these texts, but instead considers their organization and attempts to illuminate more closely the function of their so called spurious alternatives.

The fact that Bernhard obviously did have something specific in mind when he used the term comedy and did not use it in an arbitrary manner is evident in his early works and becomes even clearer in his later works. I would even go so far as to say that his chief concern, to exaggerate somewhat, is a poetics of comedy and that it is possible to provide evidence to back up this assertion. The ideally conceived comedy would appear to be the telos of the work's development. In the story *Ungenach*, the lawyer Moro makes the following remark in a rather dark monologue: "Wem es gelingt, auf dem Totenbett eine Komödie oder ein reines Lustspiel zu schreiben, dem ist alles gelungen."[15] A person who can manage to write a comedy on his deathbed has succeeded totally. And Bruscon, man of the theater, has come up with a plan for a universal comedy containing all comedies ever written: "Die Idee war ja / eine Komödie zu schreiben, in der alle Komödien enthalten sind / die jemals geschrieben worden sind."[16]

It has been noted, and rightly so, that in the moment of the worst horror there is even a place for laughter, as, for example, at the close of *Ein Fest für Boris* (*A Party for Boris*). The character "Goodness" breaks into "fürchterliches Gelächter" (frightful laughter) after everyone has left the stage and she is left alone with the dead Boris.[17] The comic element in Bernhard's works always arises through ridiculous triviality. The poetics of ludicrousness also determine the concepts in the novel *Frost:*

> Keine Tragödie regt die Welt auf. *Nichts ist tragisch.* Das Lächerliche sei "allgewaltiger als alles andere." Innerhalb des Lächerlichen gebe es "Tragödien, in die man vorstößt, ohne mit einem Licht ausgerüstet zu sein, in ein finsteres Bergwerk." Verzweiflung sei in der Lächerlichkeit.[18]

Nothing is tragic. The ridiculous is more powerful than anything else. Comedy arises, according to a remark made by Count Saurau in *Verstörung*, due to the fact that the ridiculous nature of people lies in their complete inability to be ridiculous, "*ihre totale Unfähigkeit, lächerlich zu sein.*"[19] And in *Kalkwerk* this poetics of comedy is consistently continued. Ever since the comic exists, ridiculousness becomes bearable:

> Aber nichts sei komischer als alles und dadurch, soll er [Konrad] gesagt haben, ist ja alles erträglich, weil es komisch ist. Wir haben nichts anderes als den Innbegriff der Komödie auf der Welt und wir können tun, was wir wollen, wir kommen aus der Komödie nicht heraus, der Ver-

such der Jahrtausende, die Komödie zu einer Tragödie zu machen, hat naturgemäß scheitern müssen.[20]

We can do whatever we want, but we cannot escape comedy. The attempt throughout the centuries to turn comedy into tragedy was doomed to failure. Viewed in this light, and Alfred Barthofer has already demonstrated it in his study, a coherent theory of comedy is in the making in the context of Bernhard's works, a theory whose task is of a compensatory nature.[21] Comedy alone is in a position to guide the ridiculous, to which in turn it owes its own existence. Because everything is ridiculous in the face of death, tragedy is a method that offers no consolation for the ridiculous, not even temporary relief. Bernhard's characters all experience themselves in their own ridiculousness. As a consequence, Bernhard's protagonists (and along with them their author) devote themselves to the program of comedy. It is as if the tragic had become ridiculous: This process can always be measured by the height of the person's fall, but falls in the case of Bernhard, as moving as they may be, amount to only stumblings.

As far as Bernhard is concerned the term comedy appears not to be an arbitrary one. It is remarkable, however, that in the complete edition of his plays from the years 1969 to 1981, published in 1983, this genre of drama, namely comedy, is missing, although the term would be more than appropriate in the case of *Die Macht der Gewohnheit, Immanuel Kant* or *Über allen Gipfeln, ist Ruh,* and all the more appropriate in the case of *Vor dem Ruhestand.* It is important here to refer back to the initial publications, since in Bernhard's later oeuvre the generic terms of comedy and tragedy enter into a more complex and revelatory relationship.

Among Old Men and Fools

We should make a minor adjustment in the chronology of Bernhard's oeuvre in terms of when a work was actually written as opposed to when it was first published. *Auslöschung* (*Extinction*) published in 1986 was definitely written before *Alte Meister* (*Old Masters*) that appeared in 1985. For our purposes it appears necessary to discuss these texts in their chronological order. In *Auslöschung* we encounter the hero and the first-person narrator Murau in a situation bordering on the ridiculous. Murau has come to his father's estate at Wolfsegg to attend the funeral of his parents and his brother. He is standing naked in the hallway, his sister Amalia sees him and he sticks his tongue out at her, a pleasure that he has not had for a good thirty years or more. While standing in front of the mirror, the joker consoles himself over his poor state of health and the metaphor of the theater is invoked. His parents and his brother died in a traffic accident — that was the tragedy, but the drama is not yet over: "Der Vorhang ist zugegangen, dachte ich. Noch nicht ganz, dachte ich, sozusagen das Satyrspiel hat begonnen. Das Schwierigste des Ganzen."[22]

Murau is committed to *Übertreibungskunst*, the art of exaggeration, since it alone makes events visible (A, 128). It functions as *Existenzüberbrückung* (A, 611), a relief for existence, even at the risk that one may be called an old fool: "Wenn wir die Möglichkeit dazu haben, sollten wir uns spätestens mit vierzig zum Altersnarren ausrufen und versuchen, unser Narrentum auf die Spitze zu treiben" (A, 129). If we have the chance to do so, the narrator advises, we ought to proclaim ourselves old fools at the age of forty at the latest and take our foolery to ultimate levels. In front of the mirror, Murau exposes himself unsparingly, naked and fascinated by his own distortion. His face takes on grotesque features. The mirror turns into the misanthrope's most dangerous tool. While Raimund's hero Rappelkopf shatters the mirror, Bernhard's Murau needs a mirror to entertain himself. Through clownish disfigurement the misanthrope comes to recognize himself and becomes thereby a Narcissus. Fundamental condemnation turns against the hero himself. The unsparing self-parody, the act of self-disfigurement relativizes the malicious criticism of others.

Explicit tragoedia, incipit comoedia would be one way of describing the finale of *Auslöschung*. It is appropriate that comedy is the subtitle of Bernhard's final novel *Alte Meister*. Yet the question remains unsolved why this work, which we would normally call a narration or novel, is indeed a comedy? In this comedy, the eighty-two-year-old art critic Reger launches a counterattack on art. Whereas art and writing figured earlier as a means or trick to survive, these efforts of survival are now annihilated. It is an extremely dangerous game in which Bernhard indulges. The old art critic Reger regularly sits in the museum every other day in front of the same painting. He searches for its lethal flaw, a procedure that, according to Reger, is bound to succeed every time when one observes a piece of art. In other words, it is a procedure serving the falsification and negation of art. In the novel's surprising conclusion, Reger offers his friend Atzbacher a ticket to attend Kleist's comedy *Der zerbrochene Krug* (*The Broken Jug*). Both attend the performance at the National Theater, the Burgtheater, and reach the final hostile verdict: "Die Vorstellung war entsetzlich."[23]

Reger attends the theater in the hope of seeing a consummate work of art. Instead the play delivers the same result he has elaborated in his criticism of art, namely it presents the art of the destruction of art and its distortion to the point of caricature. The play, while in actuality a comedy, can only be described as a tragedy by the manner in which it was performed. Reger's sublime strategy of subverting art is rendered superfluous by the heavy-handed strategy of the existing practices of performance in the theater. What Reger had painstakingly developed as a form of resistance against total perfection can be found almost anywhere in Austria's theaters. Art can be disqualified with much less effort and Reger with his diatribes against the old masters, and the Austrian canon of art in particular, turns into a pitiful and ridiculous old fool, becoming the central focus of this comedy.

The use of the term "Keine Komödie" ("No Comedy") for Bernhard's penultimate drama *Elisabeth II* is entirely consistent. The term "No Comedy" does not necessarily imply tragedy. Furthermore, it appears as if the author is trying to write a drama beyond the common alternative comedy-tragedy. An old fool who is eighty-seven and thus five years older than Reger guides the play. The play's final surprising twist shows the social gathering waiting to see the English Queen during her Vienna visit fall to its death as the balcony on which they assemble collapses. The only survivor is the stubborn old man who had no desire to be a part of this spectacle. His "no" protects his life.[24] The development that has taken us in the early discussion back and forth between comedy and tragedy finally to a play that claims to be "no comedy" is in itself consistent. This attempt to deal with the ridiculous is not merely an attempt to conform to a contemporary spirit in which alternatives are dismissed as unimportant and irrelevant. This constant crossing between comedy and tragedy irritates the spectator and the critic who cannot come to dwell in either genre. This rapid shift between the two genres places Bernhard's work beyond the reach of literary criticism, at least as far as the terms tragedy, comedy, jest and merriment are concerned. Comedies and tragedies are posited as identical. However, this equation is immediately subjected to doubt and discontinuity. While it is not really a matter of deciding between tragedy and comedy, it definitely is important whether something functions like a tragedy or a comedy.

Attempts to compare Bernhard's texts with those of Shakespeare, Chekhov or Dürrenmatt are just as admissible as is the intention to link his theory of comedy to that of Schopenhauer. However, one would also want to demonstrate that Bernhard through his playful use of comedy and tragedy gradually begins to set himself apart from these examples. His brand of poetics is determined by the dynamic change between tragedy and comedy. Both occupy the same territory and the difference between them only becomes glaringly evident at the moment when it is negated. Gerhart Hauptmann jotted down a revealing insight in his travel diary *Griechischer Frühling* (Greek Spring) that seems very appropriate in the case of Bernhard:

> Als höchste menschliche Lebensform erscheint mir die Heiterkeit: die Heiterkeit eines Kindes, die im gealterten Mann oder Volk entweder erlischt oder sich zur Kraft der Komödie steigert. Tragödie und Komödie haben das gleiche Stoffgebiet: eine Behauptung, deren verwegenste Folgerung zu ziehen der Dichter noch kommen muß.[25]

Cheerfulness, claims Hauptmann, is the highest form of human existence, particularly the cheerfulness of a child that in an aging man or people either wanes or takes on the power of the comedy. Tragedy and comedy therefore have the same basic substance. This assertion, he states, has yet to be brought to its most audacious conclusion by a poet. To be sure, Hauptmann saw mostly himself in the role of this poet. In any case, with Thomas Bernhard we have come a lot further in proving that comedy and tragedy do not only converge in a person but also on the terrain of literature.

Notes

[1] Thomas Bernhard, *Der Theatermacher* (Vienna: Burgtheater, Programmheft 1986), 11. The two soups are local Viennese specialties.

[2] Thomas Bernhard, *Der Keller. Eine Entziehung* (Salzburg: Residenz, 1976), 44; hereafter quoted in text as DK.

[3] Thomas Bernhard, *Der Stimmenimitator* (Frankfurt: Suhrkamp, 1978), 135; hereafter quoted in text as DS.

[4] Thomas Bernhard, *Frost* (Frankfurt: Suhrkamp, 1972), 184.

[5] Willi Huntemann, *Artistik und Rollenspiel. Das System Thomas Bernhard* (Würzburg: Königshausen & Neumann, 1990), 219.

[6] Bernhard Minetti, "Ein Autor namens Bernhard. Erinnerungen eines Schauspielers," *Thomas Bernhard. Portraits. Bilder & Texte,* ed. Sepp Dreissinger (Weitra: Bibliothek der Provinz, 1991), 219.

[7] Claude Porcell, "Théâtre: La scène obscure," *Thomas Bernhard: Ténèbres,* ed. Claude Porcell (Paris: Nadeau, 1986), 137.

[8] Jean-Louis de Rambures, "Dans le labyrinthe," *Arcane* 17 (Nantes, 1987): 175.

[9] Chantal Thomas, *Thomas Bernhard* (Paris: Seuil, 1990), 11–39.

[10] Eckhard Henscheid, "Der Krypto-Komiker: Wie der österreichische Schriftsteller Thomas Bernhard seine Bewunderer, seine Kritiker und wahrscheinlich sich selber an der Nase herumführt," *pardon* Heft 7 (1973): 21–23.

[11] Herbert Gamper, "Theater machen oder Schluß machen," *Schauspiel. Staatstheater Stuttgart: Thomas Bernhard: Der Theatermacher* (1990), n.p.

[12] Quoted in Anneliese Botond, ed. *Über Thomas Bernhard* (Frankfurt: Suhrkamp, 1970), 7.

[13] Quoted in Franz Schuh, "Thomas Bernhard in Anekdote und Selbstzeugnis," *salz* 1, Heft 2 (1975/76): 8.

[14] Gamper, n.p.

[15] Thomas Bernhard, *Ungenach* (Frankfurt: Suhrkamp, 1968), 44.

[16] *Der Theatermacher,* 178.

[17] Thomas Bernhard, *Stücke 1* (Frankfurt: Suhrkamp, 1998), 77.

[18] *Frost,* 258.

[19] Thomas Bernhard, *Verstörung* (Frankfurt: Insel, 1967), 211.

[20] Thomas Bernhard, *Das Kalkwerk* (Frankfurt: Suhrkamp, 1970), 69.

[21] Alfred Barthofer, "Vorliebe für die Komödie: Todesangst," *Vierteljahresschrift des Adalbert-Stifter-Instuitut des Landes Oberösterreich* 31 (1982): 77–100.

[22] Thomas Bernhard, *Auslöschung* (Frankfurt: Suhrkamp, 1986), 432; hereafter quoted in text as A.

[23] Thomas Bernhard, *Alte Meister. Komödie* (Frankfurt: Suhrkamp, 1985), 311.

[24] Thomas Bernhard, *Elisabeth II. Keine Komödie* (Frankfurt: Suhrkamp, 1987), 126.

[25] Gerhart Hauptmann, *Sämtliche Werke. Band 7,* ed. Hans-Egon Hass (Berlin: Ullstein, 1962), 47.

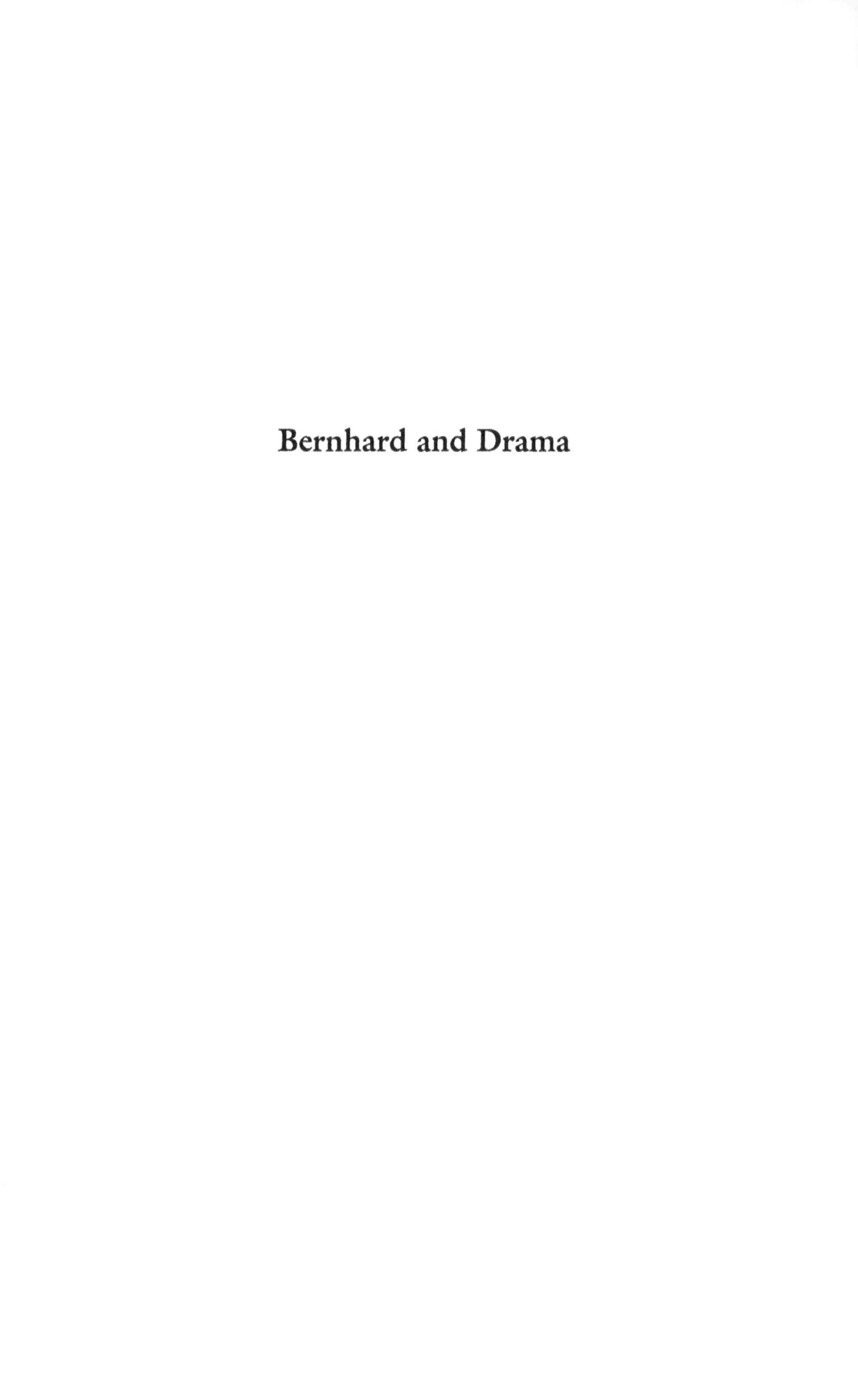

Bernhard and Drama

Mark M. Anderson

Fragments of a Deluge: The Theater of Thomas Bernhard's Prose

> Ein Buch hat er veröffentlichen wollen, aber dazu ist es nicht gekommen, weil er sein Manuskript immer wieder geändert hat, so oft und solange geändert, bis von dem Manuskript nichts mehr dagewesen ist, die Veränderung seines Manuskripts war nichts anderes, als das völlige Zusammenstreichen des Manuskripts, von dem schließlich nichts als der Titel *Der Untergeher* übriggeblieben ist. (*Der Untergeher*, 78–79)

DURING HIS LIFETIME Thomas Bernhard's texts provoked more than the usual share of scandals. But perhaps the most enduring scandal will turn out to be his very last text, his will, which ordered that everything he had written, whether published during his lifetime or as part of his *Nachlaß* (literary estate), could not be performed, printed or even recited for the duration of legal copyright within the borders of Austria, "wie immer dieser Staat sich kennzeichnet." Bernhard had taken care not to reveal the contents of this will before he died; in fact, he even stipulated that news of his death not be announced until he was buried. This parting slap in the face of his native country thus came not only as a surprise, it came from the hand of a dead man, whose laughter rang out from the grave.[1]

To be sure, it was absurd laughter that had elements of a bad and willfully unpatriotic joke. But then so did most of Bernhard's literary works. In his last play *Heldenplatz,* one of the members of a Jewish family that was driven into exile in 1938 and has returned to Vienna fifty years later characterizes the country as a pigsty with only "black" (fascist) and "red" (socialist) pigs living there:

> In diesem fürchterlichsten aller Staaten
> haben Sie ja nur die Wahl
> zwischen schwarzen und roten Schweinen
> ein unerträglicher Gestank breitet sich aus
> von der Hofburg und vom Ballhausplatz
> und vom Parlament
> über dieses ganze verluderte und verkommene Land

ruft aus
Dieser kleine Staat ist ein großer Misthaufen.[2]

Contemplating his decision to return to Austria, one of the characters, Schuster, concludes that it had been an absurd idea after all: "Das Ganze war ja eine absurde Idee."[3]

This laughter at an "absurd" world, fueled by suffering, moral outrage and philosophical stoicism, is the motor behind what Bernhard called his "Kunstmaschine," the formidable writing apparatus that generated an uninterrupted deluge of texts from the late 1960s until his untimely death in 1989. Born in Holland in 1931, a citizen and (reluctant) resident of Austria, Bernhard studied music and theater at the Mozarteum in Salzburg, working as a reporter and drama critic for a local paper. His first literary publications were collections of lyric poetry, followed by a novel, *Frost* (1963), and several short stories. But only in 1967, with the appearance of *Verstörung*, did the deluge begin: twelve novels, three collections of stories, two full-length film scripts based on earlier stories, more than a dozen plays and short plays (*Dramoletten*), and five volumes of an autobiography that, had death not intervened, would surely have continued with similar intensity.[4] His last novel, *Auslöschung.Ein Zerfall* (1986), written on the heels of this immense literary output and while his health was rapidly disintegrating, is over six hundred pages long.

Just as astonishing as the volume of this deluge was its form: a stream of prose, unbroken by any paragraph or chapter markings, that circles around the themes of illness, death, madness, and artistic or intellectual ambition in a developmental spiral somewhere between Bach's *Art of the Fugue* and the twelve-tone repetitions of Schönberg and Webern. One book after another, the prose flowed forth unbroken, startlingly urgent, always identifiably Bernhard, so that even the breaks between publications came to seem largely arbitrary. Working the line between fiction and autobiography, these prose works arose from the immediate conditions of Bernhard's surroundings, with recognizable empirical scraps of his biography still clinging to them, while, at the same time, they engaged in manifestly invented plot scenarios. Whether "autobiographical" or "fictional," however, these texts are deeply personal and deeply performative. For they all spring, or appear to spring, from the obsessive monologue going on inside Bernhard's head, a continuous text uttered by a single droning voice that is endlessly reformulated, corrected, and filtered through a hundred different registers.

Bernhard himself attributed the conspicuous lack of breaks in his work to the modern impossibility of closing a text off into a legitimate totality. "Es darf nichts Ganzes geben," he insisted in an interview of 1970, "man muß es zerhauen. Etwas Gelungenes, Schönes wird immer mehr verdächtig." Comparing his writing to that of Virginia Woolf and E. M. Forster, he demands that no chapter or book should have a proper ending or conclusion, since this is also the case with human relationships:

> So ist es auch falsch, ein *sogenanntes Kapitel* in einem Buch wirklich zu Ende zu schreiben. Und so ist es falsch, überhaupt ein Buch zu Ende zu schreiben. Und *der größte Fehler* ist, wenn ein Autor ein Buch zu Ende schreibt. Und im Umgang mit Menschen ist es auch sehr gut, wenn man die Beziehung *plötzlich abreißt.*[5]

Reinforced by Bernhard's peculiarly emphatic and ironic voice, the concept of what one might call his "deluge fragments" emerges. Because it cannot be brought to a conclusive end, this monstrously long, unbroken stream of prose is still a fragment. One might compare the language of Bernhard's obsessively prolix narrators to a phonograph needle stuck in a groove, producing a language spinning on itself in a perpetually arrested inconclusiveness. The lack of breaks in and between his texts meant, for Bernhard, that everything was broken.

But if he ruled out a traditional ending for his texts, one that would reconcile their various intentions into an aesthetic and logical totality, Bernhard mastered the staging of abrupt *coups de théâtre* as the provisional, self-consciously unsatisfying means of closing off a particular fragment. These theatrical breaks in his narratives invariably involve the death of close friends, internationally known artists or simply unknown suicides, at once strange and tragic. Never a form of reconciliation or unity, death in his writing comes as a random, unjustifiable, but unavoidable cut in existence that cancels all previous hope and striving. The thought of death makes life absurd, ridiculous; it turns all his protagonists into versions of Lear's Fool. Incidentally, this figure strongly preoccupied the author Bernhard and his acting "double," Bernhard Minetti. As Bernhard claimed in his scandal-provoking, anti-Austrian acceptance speech for the Austrian State Literary Prize: "Es ist nichts zu loben, nichts zu verdammen, nichts anzuklagen, aber es ist vieles lächerlich; es ist alles lächerlich, wenn man an den Tod denkt."[6]

Those who see only bleakness in his work, especially in the United States, have usually overlooked that Bernhard's preoccupation with death was also the driving force behind his writing. In his texts, death always comes to a character who is close to but is not the first-person narrator himself, shocking him out of a previous writing block and starting up a kind of automatic, denotative prose machine that seems to function without the narrator's active or even conscious intervention.

With an immediacy that lies somewhere between a newspaper report and a murderer's dazed confession (one cannot help thinking here of his early employment as a local crime reporter in Salzburg), Bernhard's texts narrate *someone else's suicide,* one which simulates the narrator's own death and triggers an immediate attempt to recount it, obsessively, in interminable fragments. These proximate deaths thus provide the provisional closure for, but also, one realizes in retrospect, the detonating force behind Bernhard's stories, which take the unsettling form of exultant mourning. The death narrative is always also the record of survival, a survival through a grotesquely jubilant, at times comic writing. As the French critic Chantal Thomas has noted, Bernhard's morbid stories invariably give rise to a *rire tragique* akin to the cathartic effect produced by dramatic spectacles of catastrophe.[7]

Bernhard's brilliant semi-autobiographical memoir, *Wittgensteins Neffe,* is a case in point. It begins with an unattributed quotation as its epigraph: "Zweihundert Freunde werden bei meinem Begräbnis sein und du mußt an meinem Grab eine Rede halten."[8] Bernhard then proceeds to relate in the first person the story of his friendship with Paul Wittgenstein, the philosopher's brilliant but insane nephew. Both are confined to adjoining pavilions of the same hospital in Vienna, Bernhard for a nearly fatal tumor in his lungs, Wittgenstein for his most recent bout of insanity. Written as if spoken by an actor on an empty stage, the text masterfully and almost mathematically establishes so many parallels between Bernhard's illness and Paul Wittgenstein's madness, between Paul Wittgenstein's inspired philosophical performances and his famous uncle's genial, but also, in Bernhard's account, insane writings, that the three figures become interchangeable apexes of the same triangle. At the end of the book Paul Wittgenstein has a fatal attack of madness, at which point the now identifiable epigraph-quotation is repeated in italicized form. Bernhard's voice has the last word:

> An seinem Begräbnis hatten aber nur acht oder neun Leute teilgenommen, wie ich weiß und ich selbst war zu diesem Zeitpunkt auf Kreta gewesen, ein Theaterstück schreibend, das ich, als es fertig gewesen war, gleich wieder vernichtet habe. . . . Er liegt, wie gesagt wird, auf dem Wiener Zentralfriedhof. Sein Grab habe ich bis heute nicht aufgesucht.[9]

Despite this unsentimental gesture of rejection, Bernhard's text accomplishes what he fails to do in real life. *Wittgensteins Neffe* is the funeral oration he never delivered, the ritual catharsis of his spiritual relative, the textual visiting of his grave. Writing becomes the performance of "exultant mourning," a jubilant act of semi-public *Trauerarbeit* that memorializes an insanely idiosyncratic human existence. Reading Bernhard's book is akin to participating in a funeral.

"An der Baumgrenze," an early, little known story of fifteen pages, offers a powerfully condensed version of all Bernhard's later "deluge fragments" that can help us trace both the thematic constancy and formal development in his writing. Its subject is the incestuous love between a brother and a sister who both eventually commit suicide. But the point of view is that of a police officer who happens to be sitting in the isolated mountain inn where their tragedy unfolds. The conversation, which he overhears in bits and pieces, distracts him from the letter he is writing to his pregnant fiancée. Without knowing they are brother and sister, he becomes obsessed with the two lovers for no discernible reason, even asking himself whether he is sick or insane to be so curious. The next day the woman is found unconscious from an overdose of sleeping tablets. A doctor is called but comes too late to save her. Her parents arrive, at which point the village residents learn to their horror that the lovers were siblings. Several weeks later two woodcutters find the man's frozen corpse just below the timberline, covered by two chamois-bucks he has killed, presumably in a last attempt to keep warm.

This sparse narrative, as chilling as any in postwar German literature and directly akin to certain dream narratives in Kafka's diaries, offers what might be called an *Urtext* or prototype of Bernhard's mythic narrative structures: two siblings in a love-hate conflict are observed by an unnamed, apparently disinterested witness-narrator; their suicide impels his immediate attempt to recount it in writing. Marked stylistically by fairly conventional paragraph breaks and a sequential plot structure, the story is disturbing for its extreme stylistic impersonality, which is primarily a function of the officer's brutally descriptive and cold manner of narration. What does he think of the couple's death? Why is he so absorbed by their behavior? Is there some parallel between the incestuous couple and the narrator's own engagement? None of these questions is answered. More than just a disinterested, objective witness, the narrator seems to be shallow. For instance, when the doctor arrives too late and the woman dies, his only expressed reaction concerns the administrative arrangements for her corpse: "Das vereinfacht jetzt alles, dachte ich, das Mädchen bleibt in Mühlbach."[10] As a result, the text sounds like a kind of police report, a bureaucratic *Protokoll,* not unlike the newspaper chronicles of court proceedings that Bernhard wrote for a local Austrian newspaper as a young man.[11]

This impression is contradicted, however, by the story's final sentence: "Gestern, den achtundzwanzigsten, fanden ihn überraschend zwei Holzzieher knapp unterhalb der Baumgrenze über Mühlbach erfroren und mit zwei von ihm erschlagenen schweren Gemsen zugedeckt" (AB, 74). The word "gestern" introduces immediacy into the writing of the report that belies the narrator's apparent reserve. It acts like a temporal shock, transporting the reader not so much to the moment and place of the corpse's discovery as to the scene of its bureaucratic transcription, to the officer's desk and paper. Before, the narrator was an indecisive writer of love letters: "In letzter Zeit schreibe ich alle Briefe drei- bis vier- bis fünfmal, immer gegen die Erregung während des Briefschreibens, meine Schrift selbst sowie meine Gedanken betreffend" (AB, 63). Afterwards, he writes the story of the couple's suicide automatically, without "Erregung," but as if unburdening himself of an awful confession. Death is the catalyst in this transformation; it imposes itself on the narrator as something that must be written down, put down, gotten rid of as names, information and the brute facticity of life and death, however pointless this search may be: "Namen, Daten, dachte ich, Daten, und ich durchsuchte die Handtasche des Mädchens, erfolglos" (AB, 73).

This sudden reversal of the narrator's attitude forces the reader to re-evaluate the story. Similarities between the incestuous couple and the officer's relationship with his pregnant fiancée, whom he is less and less willing to bring to Mühlbach and to marry, suddenly seem more important. One realizes that the narrator is not a neutral, disinterested observer but that in fact he identifies with the man. Through a careful series of undeveloped allusions, juxtapositions, and slightly non-grammatical sentence constructions, the text establishes an identity between three couples: the narrator and his fiancée, the brother and sister, the inspector and his fatally ill wife. The following passage, which presents the contents of the narrator's letter and his external observations in an undifferentiated flux, is typical in its syntactic irregularity:

> Die Gendarmerie sei eine gute Grundlage für uns beide, von der Gehaltserhöhung, von einer im Spätherbst in Wels zu absolvierenden Waffenübung schrieb ich gerade, *als die beiden, seltsamerweise das Mädchen zuerst, hinter ihr der junge Mann, in das Gastzimmer eintraten,* von der Frau des Inspektors, die in den Lungen krank und verloren sei. (AB, 63)

Here the "outside" entrance of the couple into the inn (marked in italics above) is slipped inside the folds of the narrator's sentences to his fiancée. By merging distinct frames of reference, letter text and visual field of observation, the story interweaves all protagonists in a hopelessly fatal relationship, breaking down the borders not only between individual protagonists but also between external landscape and psychic interiority.[12] Prisoners of Mühlbach, the protagonists represent different forms and different stages of one undifferentiated tragedy "at the timberline," evoking isolation, cold, death, and hence intimately the narrator's own emotional, psychic register, which remains "officially" undisclosed. The closing image of a frozen corpse covered by two heavy, dead animals, though visually striking, is not mimetic, but is rather a figure for an inner, metaphysical landscape. Everything in the text is turned in on itself, becomes an artificial "theater of darkness." As Bernhard once noted in an interview, "In meinen Büchern ist alles künstlich, das heißt, alle Figuren, Ereignisse, Vorkommnisse spielen sich auf einer Bühne ab, und der Bühnenraum ist total finser. . . . In der Finsternis wird alles deutlich."[13]

The peculiar narrative logic of Bernhard's "An der Baumgrenze" consists in the collapse of the differences between distinct characters until they form interchangeable parts of the same geometric construction. But this identity is metonymic rather than metaphoric; it is not based on any essential similarity between the three couples but on their contingent proximity to one another. The narrator *happens* to be in the inn when the couple arrives, *happens* to witness the fatal dénouement of their conflictual relationship. From this accident of shared location derives the metaphysically justified but mimetically irrational effacement of the substantial differences separating the three couples, who come to resemble each other through a negative relation to their surroundings. In this sense the narrator is insane to identify with the brother, a fact he himself notes and attributes to his secluded existence: "Eine solche Abgeschiedenheit wie die in Mühlbach, dachte ich, ruiniert die Nerven. Bin ich krank? Bin ich verrückt?" (AB, 67). However, as he answers these questions, the narrator can no longer simply be thought of as a bureaucratically neutral, objective, reliable source of notation. Beneath its frigid surface the text harbors a latent but extreme subjectivity that constantly veers toward insanity, undermining its apparent facticity and infusing it with the kind of philosophical irony Friedrich Schlegel described in his *Kritische Fragmente*.

The textual insanity brought on by the merging of narrator and suicide-subject of narration exists in "An der Baumgrenze" only in a latent form. In later writings Bernhard's narrators are more conspicuously delirious. But this madness also manifests itself as the will for an exhaustive, total denotation of the world, a form of "scribe madness" not unlike that of Flaubert's *Bouvard et Pécuchet,* which, in dissolving the distance between phenomenal reality and the narrator, gradually eclipses the latter's subjective identity. The subject is absorbed, swallowed up by the object of its obsessive attention. Typically, this narrator is a scholar writing the "definitive" study of some famous writer or composer, a doctor or scientist attempting a rigorous description of empirical reality, or a mathematical philosopher working on a formally pure, geometric or logical construction. In all cases, however, the narrator's dedication is so extreme that it empties him of his own subjectivity, turning him into an insane, mechanical double of some external identity or idea. He becomes a quotation machine not unlike the parrot in Bernhard's play *Immanuel Kant* that recites the philosopher's lectures word for word in an exact but meaningless performance.

This grotesque amalgamation of scholarly rigor and insanity (or the potential insanity of all scholarly rigor) results in the complex irony of Bernhard's novel *Korrektur* (1975), which is loosely based on Ludwig Wittgenstein's construction of a house for his sister in Vienna. An unnamed narrator and friend of the main character, Roithamer, recounts the events leading to the latter's suicide. An expatriate Austrian who once taught natural sciences at Cambridge, Roithamer renounced his family fortune and dedicated himself to constructing a geometrically pure, cone-shaped house for his sister in the isolated forest where they spent their childhood. Roithamer's obsessive love for his sister is displaced into an obsessive architectural formalism, and the resulting house makes her intensely happy but also causes her suicide, which in turn triggers his own. The narrator visits Roithamer's study, the attic of a house built over a rushing stream recalling Frank Lloyd Wright's "Falling Water," with the intention of ordering and publishing the mass of Roithamer's notes and sketches for the house in a "definitive edition," as a posthumous homage to his friend. In a decisive moment, however, his hand slips, and the manuscripts fall into an irrevocably disordered pile on the floor.

In a letter to the Austrian novelist and critic Hilde Spiel, Bernhard once explained: "Die Frage ist nicht: schreibe ich über Wittgenstein. Die Frage ist: *bin* ich Wittgenstein *einen* Augenblick, ohne ihn (W.) oder mich (B.) zu zerstören?"[14] This question evidently motivates the narrator's obsession with Roithamer. To break down the barrier between self and other, between narrating inside and narrated world, between ultimately life and death, is always the impossible, insane project behind Bernhard's texts. In *Korrektur* the narrator is already a partial double of Roithamer: a childhood friend, he too is an expatriate Austrian teaching at Cambridge. Roithamer's suicide brings him back to the room where his friend worked on the sketches for the cone-shaped house, a room still animated, as it were, by the dead man's voice. Rehearsing in his mind his past life with Roithamer, burying himself deeper and deeper in Roithamer's papers, books, and quotidian objects, the narrator is gradually absorbed into Roithamer's voice. What starts out as the narrator's own recollections of his deceased friend, merges, especially in the novel's second part, into the cited voice of Roithamer from the papers the narrator intends to publish. The dead man is brought to life, but only at the expense of the narrator's own subjectivity. He is Roithamer, but he destroys himself.

Or does he? The last words of the novel are Roithamer's. In effect they are his dated suicide note: "Wir können solange in der höchsten Intensität existieren, als wir sind, so Roithamer (7. Juni). Das Ende ist kein Vorgang. Lichtung."[15] The final image of a *Lichtung* or clearing (the same term that Heidegger uses in his writing on art) designates the space in the forest where the cone house is built, but at the same time refers to Roithamer's endlessly corrected manuscript, to the blank space of his and his sister's death. The question posed by this open conclusion is whether the narrator, having doubled Roithamer's life and thought, will also follow him into the "final correction." Or will he pull back in time, break off his obsessive mimesis, and re-establish his previous identity as the mere friend and publisher of Roithamer's writings?

These are the two fictional alternatives proposed by the fiction of *Korrektur*. The text itself provides a third possibility, namely the successfully written Wittgensteinian meditation on Roithamer formulated in a series of *Sprachspiele* (language games) by the narrator. The existence of the text stands in contradiction to suicide, insanity, or endless correction and reordering of notes, which are fictionally described as the narrator's only possible alternatives. In the end the narrator is not Roithamer; their relationship is not transparent but conflictual and jealous. Instead of committing suicide or publishing Roithamer's notes, the narrator speaks *Korrektur*, a "grave" speech that is mathematically objective and irrationally subjective, precise and hysterical, ordered and irremediably fragmented. Hence the profound irony of an existing text, both eloquent and long, that insists on the impossibility of either starting or finishing a text, an irony that harks back to the *Sprachkrise* (language crisis) of Hofmannsthal's eloquently written *Lord Chandos Letter* (*Ein Brief*) from the turn-of-the-century. Formulated as one protracted quotation that eventually obliterates the unnamed narrator's identity, *Korrektur* is also the written record of the narrator's survival. Death engenders writing, not another death.

Bernhard's masterful novel *Der Untergeher* (*The Loser*, 1983) recounts the attempt of an unnamed narrator to come to terms with the suicide of two friends. Organized in terms of musical repetition and variation rather than architectural form, the narration presents itself as the uninterrupted soliloquy of someone who, much like the messenger in a Greek play, steps onto an empty stage to describe to the audience the violence and death he has just witnessed. Having just returned from the funeral of his friend Wertheimer (the "Untergeher" in the story's title), he recalls the events that led up to Wertheimer's suicide. Twenty-eight years beforehand, Wertheimer, the narrator, and Glenn Gould studied piano together in Salzburg in a master class taught by Vladimir Horowitz. Wertheimer and the narrator had been students at the Mozarteum and were planning careers as concert pianists. But the young Gould, whom Bernhard describes as a genius already greater than Horowitz, indeed as the "größte Pianist des Jahrhunderts" convinces them of their own relative pianistic mediocrity. Since they cannot be the best in their field, they give up music and embark on academic careers, the narrator in philosophy, Wertheimer in the human sciences.

The details of their careers are deliberately kept vague. Neither of them has ever published anything, yet both are working on manuscripts that betray their ongoing obsession with Gould, who has since become world famous. The narrator's text "Über Glenn Gould" consists of a large number of provisional sketches that he endlessly destroys and rewrites. Wertheimer, who has had an unfulfilled incestuous relationship with his sister — her marriage is one of the motivating factors in his suicide — is working on a manuscript entitled "Der Untergeher," which is the ironic moniker Gould gave him in Salzburg at their first meeting. It consists of ideas jotted down on scraps of paper but is eventually destroyed by an endless process of correction. Gould's death provokes Wertheimer's decision to hang himself in front of his sister's new house. After the funeral the narrator returns to Wertheimer's country house, where he learns that his friend burned all his manuscripts shortly before his death. The last sentence in the novel reads as follows: "Ich bat den Franz, mich für einige Zeit in Wertheimers Zimmer allein zu lassen und legte mir Glenns *Goldbergvariationen* auf, die ich auf Wertheimers Plattenspieler liegen gesehen hatte, der noch offen war."[16]

The choice of a musical rather than an architectural theme is appropriate not only because of the temporal affinity between literature and music but also because Bernhard's obsessively spiraling prose inevitably recalls the logic of the Bachian fugue and baroque music generally. Gould's eccentric career began in 1955 with his recording of the *Goldberg Variations,* a beginning that foreshadowed nearly everything he did thereafter, including his re-recording of the piece not long before his death.[17] Bernhard's choice of Glenn Gould as a main character is a stroke of genius, at once unexpected and eminently logical. In a teasing mixture of novel and biographical memoir, fantasy and recent history, unnamed fictional characters and famous personalities like Gould and Horowitz, *Der Untergeher* transforms the real Canadian pianist into a prototypically Bernhardian protagonist. Genial, idiosyncratic, obsessed, fatally uncompromising, Bernhard's Gould is the musical cousin of Roithamer and Paul Wittgenstein. Interestingly enough, the same process of identification that animates *Korrektur* seems to have generated Bernhard's tribute to Gould. Gould died in October 1982 at the age of fifty. Bernhard, fifty-one at the time, must have written *Der Untergeher* immediately afterwards, almost in a single operation of his *Kunstmaschine* (artistic machine) since he published it with Suhrkamp early in 1983. Gould's death evidently struck Bernhard with all the force of the vicarious suicide he so often details in his novels. Comparison of the novel with Bernhard's five-volume autobiography, published in English in 1986 as a single volume entitled *Gathering Evidence,* suggests that the portrayal of Gould, like his other artist and writer protagonists, is a veiled self-portrait, a foil for his own ideal artistic self, with which he find himself in constant struggle.[18]

In Gould we recognize the paradox of all Bernhard's writing, a will toward artistic and intellectual perfection so intense that the results are pathological, deformed, perverse, ultimately resulting in the eclipse of the art itself. Bernhard's Gould wants to become the perfectly transparent vehicle for Bach's music, to merge with the piano itself: "Eines Tages aufwachen *und Steinway und Glenn in einem sein,* sagte er, dachte ich, *Glenn Steinway, Steinway Glenn nur für Bach*" (U, 119). The perfect interpretation is no interpretation at all. As a "reproduzierender Künstler," Gould's task is merely to repeat or quote Bach's music. However, both the real Gould and Bernhard's version of him give readings of Bach that are intensely personal. Gould's habit of humming while playing is only one obtrusive sign of the interpreter's presence rather than his self-effacement, a merging with the instrument that makes the interpreter opaque, an interventionist rather than transparent vehicle of transmission. In Bernhard's novel, Gould's humming ("seine Singstimme") becomes both the sign of his literally inspired musicianship and a deadly lung disease. Voice, music, sickness and art are woven together into a single life form. Like Kafka, who once interpreted his own tuberculosis as a kind of drawn-out, "singing" death, Bernhard's Gould plays and hums himself out to the point of physical exhaustion and extinction: "Glenn [hat] sich erst gegen vier Uhr früh *hingelegt, nicht um zu schlafen, so Glenn,* sondern um *die Erschöpfung ausklingen zu lassen*" (U, 62).

The irony of this absolutist desire to merge with one's writing, also present in Kafka's "In der Strafkolonie," is that it coincides with the artist's death. "*Die Natur ist gegen mich,*" Bernhard has Gould claim: "Die Natur [ist] stärker als wir, die wir uns zu einem *Kunstprodukt* gemacht haben aus Übermut. Wir sind ja keine Menschen, ***wir sind Kunstprodukte, das Klavier ist ein Kunstprodukt, ein widerwärtiges***" (U, 117–18). Hence Bernhard's reading interprets Gould's death as a suicide necessitated by the impossibility of carrying his art any farther, of "being the Steinway" and himself in the same instant. Even Gould cannot totally dismantle the self, cannot achieve the definitive rendition of the *Goldberg Variations* that he spent his life attempting. His recordings remain the inspired but ultimately failed attempt to efface the difference between artwork and artist, composer and interpreter, text and self, a difference effaced, theoretically, only when Bernhard's Gould suffers his fatal stroke at the piano: "vom Schlag getroffen, ***tot umgefallen am Klavier***" (U, 169).

The characterization of Gould has a palpable, immediate quality that is lacking in Bernhard's portrait of Roithamer, who remains an almost abstract, invisible figure. In *Der Untergeher* we see Gould hunched over the piano, hear his humming, his demonic laughter, and of course the music associated with his name. Gould, however, is not the subject of the novel but a resonant subtext or metonymy for the story of Wertheimer and the anonymous narrator. Gould as a romantic figure, a kind of Zarathustrian hero of inhuman will and talent, is ironized through two figures who fail in the attempt to "quote" him, to represent his genius in their writings. Both are prisoners of his example. Gould's obsessive but genial repetitions of Bach's original music (itself based on the principle of repetition and variation, and composed to cure Goldberg's insomnia by repeated replayings) are multiplied into the infinite regress of the two friends who repeat his life at the expense of their own identities. The subject of the novel is thus not Gould's music but the empty space of two unfinished, endlessly corrected manuscripts, Wertheimer's "Der Untergeher" and the narrator's "Über Glenn Gould." Like the recording of the *Goldberg Variations* in Wittgenstein's house at the open-ended conclusion of *Der Untergeher*, Bernhard's text turns endlessly upon itself, a moving funeral oration capable of an infinite number of replays.

These remarks should have made sufficiently clear the extent to which Bernhard's prose fragments are theatrical. They offer themselves as a spoken performance, punctuated more by the breath of an actor or a singer than the rules of a written grammar. As Elfriede Jelinek noted in her obituary of Bernhard, "Es ist ja kein Zufall, daß dieser Dichter ein Dichter des Sprechens (nicht des Schreibens) war. Die Erfahrung des in früher Jugend schon Lungenkranken hat ihm die großen Tiraden seines Werkes abgerungen: Ich spreche, also bin ich. Und solange ich spreche, bin ich nicht tot."[19] Moreover, these performances are always a re-citation of someone else's words and hence are implicated in the theatrical logic that requires the effacement of one identity in the acting out of another. But this logic is so extreme that it eventually calls into question the notion of any primary, authentic voice prior to citation. In Bernhard's short text "Der Stimmenimitator," a mimic amuses his audience by imitating a number of famous voices. He fails, however, to honor the audience's request to imitate his own voice: "Als wir ihm jedoch den Vorschlag gemacht hatten, er solle am Ende seine eigene Stimme imitieren, sagte er, das könne er nicht."[20] Imitation and citation become a kind of straitjacket, fettering and finally destroying the "original." It is no accident that Bernhard repeatedly turned to the theater, writing plays which both complemented and exceeded the prose texts in a monumental, grotesque absurdity recalling Jarry's Ubu Roi, Ionesco's *La Cantatrice chauve,* and Beckett's work for the stage. Common to both sets of writing is the will to distort, exaggerate, or just plain lie about the world rather than represent it realistically, an *Übertreibungskunst* (art of exaggeration), in the apt phrase of the Austrian critic Schmidt-Dengler, that uses theater as a framing device.[21]

During his lifetime Bernhard's exaggerations and distortions famously provoked their share of controversy and scandal in an Austria where, long before the Waldheim affair, he polemically insisted on airing his country's dirty linen from the Nazi period. In *Der Theatermacher,* for example, the director of a touring theatrical company is lodged in a country inn that has kept a portrait of Hitler on the wall years after the end of the war, causing him to fulminate that contemporary Austria consists of nothing but church spires, pigsties, and portraits of Hitler. To this kind of unfair characterization, Bernhard's critics responded in a variety of ways: physical attack, during the *Heldenplatz* furor an elderly lady assaulted him with an umbrella; smear campaigns in the Austrian media and even street graffiti; semi-official censure by Austria's political establishment; as well as more nuanced, though equally blinded critical reaction from feminist and politically progressive quarters. This is not surprising. In the context of political radicalism in which Bernhard's work first emerged in the 1960s and 1970s, readers objected to the presentation of a world so artificial that it seemed totally removed from a common, true realm of quotidian experience. Bernhard's narratives, their objection ran, take place in a rarefied, unrealistically bleak landscape "an der Baumgrenze"; they concern madmen, brilliant but self-destructive and unstable artists, diseased and morbid figures who lead each other into death, thereby undermining the mechanism for a positive reader reception. The distortions in his prose are always negative, "automatically black" (in George Steiner's phrase), decadent, and misogynist, in a word, inhuman.

Although the scope of this essay will not allow for a detailed examination of these charges, two points need to be made. The first is the polemically political implications of Bernhard's theatricality. No matter how distant his protagonists may seem from the common realm of experience, the performative nature of his texts aims their story directly at the reader, thus tending to deny the traditional distance between the production of narrative and its reception. The reader is spoken to, addressed, as if in the audience, and hence drawn into Bernhard's prose constructions with unusual force. The reader becomes a participant, an actor in the same staged funeral motivating all his texts. Evident in Bernhard's use of proper names like Wittgenstein and Gould in fictional works, this breakdown of the distinction between art and life disrupts the reader's conventional sense of a fictional interior space framed by an external historical context. We see it as well in the five volumes of Bernhard's autobiography that offers a highly selective, factually unreliable account in which Bernhard appears as a recognizable Bernhardian protagonist. Another fictional variation of Roithamer, Gould, the mad count in *Verstörung*, or the painter Strauch in *Frost*, but not as the mimetic double of the author Thomas Bernhard, Bernhard becomes a fully developed and fictive character.

The self-conscious theatricality of Bernhard's actual plays reinforces this breakdown with even greater political insistence. When Claus Peymann was forced to resign from his position as head of the Stuttgart State Theater by Hans Filbinger, a Nazi judge and then Minister präsident (governor) of Baden-Würtemberg, Bernhard responded by writing *Vor dem Ruhestand*, a viciously satiric comedy of the "German soul" which denounces Filbinger and the repressed Nazi past of major postwar German politicians. The best example of this tendency however is *Heldenplatz*, written in 1988 for the fiftieth commemoration of the *Anschluss* for a performance in the Burgtheater, located right next to the Heroes Square where jubilant crowds greeted Hitler in March 1938. The actual audience assembled for the performance, which no doubt included Austrians who had been part of the crowd welcoming Hitler, was thus forced to confront its own "voice" when recorded chants of "Sieg Heil" were piped onstage from the wings, as if this voice were coming from Heroes Square outside. The aesthetic sphere constituted by the theater gives way to history and politics; audience members become actors in a play that takes them fifty years back in the past to confront what might be called the *Urszene* (scene of instruction) of Austrian politics: the body politic's embrace of Hitler.

The second point, closely related to this theatricality, has to do with the sheer iconoclastic will of Bernhard's narrative project. The very instability of his voice, its hysterical excessiveness, tendentiousness, even fragility, when harnessed to the formidable energy of Bernhard's writing machine, has resulted in one of the most singular and recognizable styles in postwar German writing. For all its postmodern strategies of quotation and parodied imitation, there is nothing quite like Bernhard's narrative voice. He broke the rules, flouted the established literary and political authorities, and somehow managed to impose his idiosyncratic, "insane" idiom onto an initially reluctant or hostile audience. Now, more than a decade after his death, one can see how the mode of Bernhard's utterance, rather than this or that particular content, has had an empowering effect on a younger generation of emerging writers. To take only one recent example, Lilian Faschinger's hilariously audacious *Magdalene Sünderin,* a novel that consists of a female narrator's life confessions to a priest she has abducted from church and tied to a tree, is unthinkable without Bernhard's example of relentless *Redefluss* (speech flow), taking the same glee in polemical anti-Austrianisms, macabre humor, and the giddy performance of self. Similar traces of this political and aesthetic iconoclasm can be detected in the writing of Elfriede Jelinek, Robert Menasse and Josef Haslinger.

By insisting on the violation of traditional boundaries, Bernhard's theatrical prose texts achieve urgency, a direct and compelling passion that force the reader to confront an admittedly bleak narrative landscape. But Bernhard's depiction of human ugliness, stupidity, cruelty and death in the quite real world around him should not be confused with a resigned acceptance of their inevitability. For his scandalous attacks on this world were always carried out in the service of something he revered: the uncompromising philosophical rigor of Wittgenstein; the dedicated musicianship of Glenn Gould, Shakespeare's *Lear;* and even, in some instances, friendship and nonsexual love. To identify this level of feeling in Bernhard's work is admittedly no easy task, for it wears the satyr's mask of terrible beauty, a mask which laughs at all that is imperfect and all-too-human. But however one judges his writings, there is something grand in Bernhard's will to produce fragments of a discourse that he knew he would never be able to close off, finish, or perfect. They are corrections to a work that never existed and, if we read him closely, could never be written. That particular kind of failure still stands as a legacy for writers today.

Notes

[1] For a survey of the controversies Bernhard provoked throughout his life (starting with his early, factually unreliable criminal court reporting for the *Demokratisches Volksblatt*), see Jens Dittmar, *Sehr gescherte Reaktion: Leserbrief Schlachten um Thomas Bernhard* (Vienna: Österreichische Staatsdruckerei, 1993).

[2] Thomas Bernhard, *Heldenplatz* (Frankfurt: Suhrkamp, 1988), 164.

[3] *Heldenplatz*, 165.

[4] An exact count and classification are difficult given the protean nature of Bernhard's work, where *Erzählungen* (stories) can extend to hundreds of pages, and where the distinction between autobiography and fiction is constantly undermined.

[5] From an interview with the film director Ferry Radax entitled "Drei Tage," published in *Der Italiener* (Salzburg: Residenz, 1971), 158. Consistent with this logic of fragmentation and suspension of meaning, Bernhard wrote a disclaimer to this interview when it was published, noting that what he said now appears to him "mehr oder weniger zufällig und zusammenhanglos" and could have been said "vollkommen anders" (162).

[6] Quoted in Anneliese Botond (ed.), *Über Thomas Bernhard* (Frankfurt: Suhrkamp, 1970), 7.

[7] Chantal Thomas, *Le Rire Tragique: Thomas Bernhard* (Paris: Seuil, 1990).

[8] Thomas Bernhard, *Wittgensteins Neffe* (Frankfurt: Suhrkamp, 1982), 1.

[9] *Wittgensteins Neffe*, 164.

[10] Thomas Bernhard, "An der Baumgrenze," *An der Baumgrenze* (Salzburg: Residenz, 1969); edition cited here (Reinbek bei Hamburg: Rowohlt Taschenbuch, 1980), 74; hereafter quoted in text as AB.

[11] On Bernhard's early journalistic work, see the extremely helpful biographical and bibliographical volume compiled by Herbert Moritz entitled *Lehrjahre* (Weitra: Bibliothek der Provinz, 1992). A colleague of Bernhard's at the *Demokratisches Volksblatt* in the early 1950s, Moritz notes however the "humorvollen, immer menschlichen" (9) descriptive style of that paper's court reports.

[12] This merging of different frames of narration is at the root of one of Bernhard's most idiosyncratic and distinguishing prose techniques, namely the doubling or repetition of one person's thoughts and observations through another by means of discursive subjunctive ("so habe er, Roithamer," in die höllersche Kammer gehen müssen") or, more simply, by the shorthand, hammer-like use of "thus" ("so Roithamer").

[13] "Drei Tage," 150, Bernhard's emphasis. In subsequent quotes, the emphasis is always by Bernhard.

[14] Letter of March 2, 1971, reprinted in Hilde Spiel, *Briefwechsel,* ed. Hans A. Neunzig (Munich, Leipzig: List, 1995).

[15] Thomas Bernhard, *Korrektur* (Frankfurt: Suhrkamp, 1975), 363.

[16] Thomas Bernhard, *Der Untergeher* (Frankfurt: Suhrkamp, 1983), 243; hereafter quoted in text as U.

[17] The anthology of Gould's writings edited by Tim Page in 1985 presents astonishing parallels with Bernhard's fictional and semi-fictional narrators, particularly as regards the doubling, or multiplying of the narrative voice. Gould's spoof of the celebrity interview ("Glenn Gould Interviews Glenn Gould About Glenn Gould") demonstrates a *mise en abîme* of the authorial persona that constantly recurs in Bernhard's writings, and programmatically formulated in *Der Stimmenimitator.* See *The Glenn Gould Reader,* ed. Tim Page (New York: Knopf, 1984). See also Otto Friedrich's biography, *Glenn Gould: A Life and Variations* (New York: Random House, 1989).

[18] "Das Furchbarste ist für mich Prosa schreiben . . . Gerade die Autoren, die für mich die wichtigsten sind, [sind] meine größten Gegner oder Feinde. Es ist ein ununterbrochenes zur-Wehr-setzen, gerade gegen die, denen man einfach *restlos* verfallen ist" ("Drei Tage," 154, 157).

[19] Jelinek also notes Bernhard's conversational "performances" for friends, sometimes lasting up to ten hours, in which the "ausgebildete Musiker eine eigene Technik der Wiederholung entwickelt, aber in rhythmischer Gliederung . . . deren musikalischer Gesetzmäßigkeit sich niemand entziehen konnte." "Atemlos," reprinted in *Thomas Bernhard. Portraits,* ed. Sepp Dreissinger (Weitra: Bibliothek der Provinz, 1992), 311.

[20] Thomas Bernhard, "Der Stimmenimitator," in *Der Stimmenimitator* (Frankfurt: Suhrkamp, 1978), 10.

[21] Wendelin Schmidt-Dengler, *Der Übertreibungskünstler. Zu Thomas Bernhard* (Vienna: Sonderzahl, 1986).

Gitta Honegger

The Stranger Inside the Word: From Thomas Bernhard's Plays to the Anatomical Theater of Elfriede Jelinek

IT ALL LOOKS SO FAMILIAR, said Bernhard Minetti, one of the great German actors of the twentieth century, after the 1976 premiere of *Vor dem Ruhestand,* Bernhard's stinging "Comedy of the German Soul," as he subtitled his play.[1] It features a contemporary German judge and former concentration camp commander on the eve of his retirement celebrating Himmler's birthday together with his two sisters as they had done every year. Minetti was known at that time as the quintessential Bernhard actor through his definitive performances in *Die Macht der Gewohnheit* (The Force of Habit), *Die Jagdgesellschaft* (The Hunting Party) and *Minetti,* Bernhard's homage to his favorite actor. Bernhard Minetti, however, rejected the role of the camp commander when it was offered to him. Perhaps it was too familiar to the actor who first established himself during the Nazi years in Berlin's Staatliches Schauspielhaus under the patronage of Hermann Göring. Some of Germany's most influential critics hailed the play both as a first exposure after the Second World War of the persistent Nazi mentality among Germans and as a triumph of Bernhard's comedic vision. When the play was performed in Minneapolis in 1981 at the renowned Guthrie Theatre, only two people were laughing according to the production staff who listened backstage through the intercom: the Rumanian director, Liviu Ciulei and the play's Austrian born translator and production dramaturge (myself). Politically correct audiences were reluctant to laugh at a scenario that depicts an unrepentant Nazi, his devoted sister with whom he sleeps once a year in honor of his idol's birthday and a younger, wheelchair bound sister, an anarchist and quadriplegic who was struck as a child by an American bomb that hit a kindergarten in World War II. Not that Germans or Austrians reacted with unanimous mirth. None of Bernhard's plays had ever been crowd pleasers or unqualified critical successes. The bizarre, yet strangely familiar settings with characters who obsessively hold forth in monologues to defiantly monosyllabic partners elicited as much bored ennui even among admirers of Bernhard's prose as they irritated post-Brechtian activists who expected theater to take an active part in the changing of society.

Concerning the latter, *Vor dem Ruhestand,* for example, did not yield a critique of contemporary German society but rather a cynical variation of Bernhard's archetypal character modeled after his maternal grandfather: a tyrannical old man abusing those closest to him in his single-minded pursuit of one idea. That the retiring judge, after a distinguished career in postwar Germany still clung to the values of honorable citizenship as exploited and perverted by Hitler, was coincidental. His fixation on Nazi ideals could be exchanged with any obsessions of Bernhard's previous (as well as subsequent) characters. Die Gute, the Good One, of *Ein Fest für Boris* (A Party for Boris), a philanthropist without legs, has devoted her energies to a home for legless men, one of them her husband, for whom she prepares and hosts a birthday party with his fellow inmates. The celebrated soprano of his second play, *Der Ignorant und der Wahnsinnige* (The Ignoramus and the Madman), is driven by the conflicting demands of her art and her audiences. For years, Caribaldi of *Die Macht der Gewohnheit,* the director of a traveling circus, has been drilling members of his company to play Schubert's *Trout Quintet* with him without ever making it through the first bars. The writer of *Die Jagdgesellschaft* is obsessed with staging life as a text for his next play, while the one-armed General, who has fought in Hitler's army at Stalingrad hosts hunting parties in his decaying forests. The President and his wife of *Der Präsident,* are driven by their (well-grounded) fear of assassins, possibly led by their own son, while diverting themselves with affairs, the former with a young actress, the latter with a butcher and a priest. *Die Berühmten* (The Famous), the leading artists at the Salzburg Festival are haunted by the legendary names of those, now dead who preceded them in their respective fields. *Minetti* features an actor by that name who spent thirty years reciting Lear alternately in English and German in front of a mirror in his sister's attic, after he was dismissed as the theater's director for rejecting the classics. *Der Weltverbesserer* (World Improver) of the play with the same title, also written for Minetti (1905–1998), has spent his life working on a treatise about improving the world, which calls for its total destruction. In *Der Theatermacher,* one of Bernhard's most produced plays, a director, actor, playwright and head of a traveling theater company that consists of his wife and their son and daughter, undauntedly performs his play "The Wheel of History" featuring the great dictators and geniuses from world history in run-down rural taverns.

Finally, *Heldenplatz* echoes the rhetoric of *Vor dem Ruhestand* in a bizarre reversal: the speaker is Jewish. An eminent professor and refugee from Hitler returns to his native Vienna to find himself surrounded by the sort of values espoused by the retiring judge and his family. Venting his outrage in characteristically hyperbolic Bernhard-speak, he becomes indistinguishable from other Bernhard characters. The mechanism of Bernhard's dramaturgy is its disturbing message. Language speaks. It constitutes culture. The victim merges with the perpetrator in the stranglehold of language that keeps restaging their shared history. The stranger inside the word is the feared other who sounds so terrifyingly familiar that he must be silenced. One speaks; the other is always silent in Bernhard's dramaturgy. The real drama is located within the language. The minimal physical action on stage is its melodramatic perversion. The speakers are exchangeable. Their actions are no longer motivated by choices and are instead animated by grammar. Heidegger meets Wittgenstein in a deadly lock of history and syntax.

High Art, so dear to the German (and even dearer to the Austrian) heart, is the opiate for an elite of survivors. The former camp commander and later honorable judge (*Vor dem Ruhestand*) listens to his sister playing Mozart on the piano for him and puts on a record of Beethoven's *Fifth* during Himmler's posthumous birthday party that would end abruptly with his heart attack. The General (*Die Jagdgesellschaft*), who survived Stalingrad listens to Mozart's *Haffner Symphony* before shooting himself at the end of a long night of philosophical musings with his guests. Professor Schuster (*Heldenplatz*) and his suicidal brother had returned to Vienna for the love of music. While the former could enjoy a concert even though the hall was filled with Nazis — "in den Konzerten lauter Nazis" — and listen to Beethoven without thinking of the Reichsparteitag in Munich, it was always a nightmare — "es war ihm immer entsetzlich" — for the latter: "Denn er hat die Musik nur hören können / indem er zuerst die nationalsozialistische Gesinnung / der Musikvereinsbesucher überhört hat."[2] In *Ritter, Dene, Voss,* the philosopher's sister puts on Beethoven's string quartet after a disastrous welcoming meal for her brother who had just returned home from the mental institution. The *Eroica* (conducted by Knappertsbusch) underscores her fall to the ground with a tray of the beautiful Bohemian *Großmuttergeschirr.*

Art is amoral. It does not improve human nature as recent history had shown and it fails as a redemptive force. The cornerstone of Austrian culture, the transcendental center of the Austrians' (re-) construction of identity after the Second World War, gets smashed to pieces with grandmother's china. The last survivor on Bernhard's stage is only the actor lending his name to the stranger in the broken word. Bernhard's stage characters are the last representatives of a humanist patriarchy that extinguished itself in two world wars. Their roles are recast over and over. In the native tradition of great performances they come back to life, a ghostly theater of the dead, on stage and off, animated by the strings of language. The bizarre scenarios have the familiarity of an ancestral cult in decline. The language — distilled from local idioms stretched to their limits by repetitions, variations and inversions — has the familiar ring of the commonplace distorted in the echo chamber of its past. Bernhard's endlessly exchangeable cast of characters and the repetitiousness of his mise-en-scènes are intrinsic to his world-view.

Bernhard's theater of the dead is his most problematic legacy to Austrian, if not German theater. What life could there be found beyond it? Fellow-Austrian playwright and novelist Elfriede Jelinek draws the most extreme conclusion: "Den Wunsch Leben zu erzeugen auf dem Theater, der fast alle Schriftsteller angezogen hat, lehne ich ab. Ich will genau das Entgegengesetzte: Unbelebtes erzeugen. Ich will dem Theater das Leben austreiben. Ich will kein Theater."[3] In her later texts for the theater, she accomplishes her project by replacing conventional dialogue with what she calls "Sprachflächen," planes of speech. Appropriated from existing material — fragments from literary, philosophical and political texts as well as from commercials, tabloid columns and other popular sources — they are randomly assigned to individual or choral speakers. In the spirit of Barthes' deconstruction of myths, the resulting textual collages obfuscate meaning in the interplay of ideologies, past and present, hidden and overt, that determine contemporary German language culture. Roland Barthes speaks of myth as depoliticized speech, in which memory of actual historic processes has been replaced by belief in an eternal, natural order of things.[4] It is a speech all the more susceptible to the past which keeps infecting the present, as Jelinek demonstrates over and over again in her anatomical theater.

Although her early plays feature conventional characters of sorts, they are based on existing models, both historic and contemporary, often introduced by their actual names. In her first play *Was geschah, nachdem Nora ihren Mann verlassen hatte oder Die Stützen der Gesellschaft* (What happened after Nora left her husband or Pillars of Society), the icon of early feminism has become a factory worker. Inspired by Barthes' *Mythologies* and Brecht's Communist *Lehrstücke,* Jelinek deconstructs Ibsen's bourgeois myths of emancipation and their problematic persistence in feminist ideas of the seventies. Nora's liberation is the romantic illusion of a privileged woman. What is freedom to her is drudgery for working-class women. Bound by her bourgeois conditioning she remains a willing tool in the (male) capitalist power games both as whip-wielding dominatrix and sex-kittenish informer on her husband in a corrupt business deal. While the characters are still speaking to each other in recognizable dialogue, their language is discursive rather than dramatic, for the purpose of critical provocation rather than psychological information. The text, appropriating "dead matter" from earlier texts exposes an historic mechanism rather than human interactions. Its overall effect in performance is that of an animation, rather than any sort of quasi-Aristotelian imitation of "real life."

Like Bernhard, Jelinek thrives on hyperbole. Unlike Bernhard she extends it beyond the speech act into over-the-top physical actions that exploit pornography with as much gusto as rage. In her next play, *Clara S.,* subtitled "A musical tragedy," the young piano-playing daughter of Clara Schumann (the pianist and wife of composer Robert Schumann), is fondled in full view of his obliging mistresses. These acts of obscenity are also extended to her mother by the famous Italian writer and Mussolini protégé Gabrielle D'Annunzio. Later, at dinner with the women, the child is discovered under the table with her head in his crotch. The Romantic myth of phallic genius, absurdly propped up by women and Fascist fantasies, is graphically deflated by images of sexual indulgence and impotence. Their bourgeois notions of femininity cripple the women, all gifted artists in their own right. Female genius is accepted only in the little girl prodigy, soon devoured by her mentor. What's left is the stunted child-woman, her sexuality exploited, her gifts ingested by her teachers.

Unspoken residues of Jelinek's own *wundergirl* biography bind the anachronistic fragments of her play. Born after the Second World War and raised by an ambitious mother to become a concert pianist, she experienced both the drills of patriarchic genius cult and its persistent exclusion of women. Clara S's daughter, strapped at the piano in "einer Art Trainingsgestell," a kind of training frame, mirrors the granddaughter of the musician-circus director Caribaldi in Bernhard's *Macht der Gewohnheit,* who doesn't think much of her talent but drills her nonetheless in marionette like movements to become a tightrope artist and viola player.[5] Bernhard himself was no stranger to grandfatherly ambitions for his descendant's artistic development.

Jelinek contracts different time periods to establish the linguistic links between genius cult and fascism that still haunt contemporary culture by drawing from the novels and correspondence of D'Annunzio, the diaries and letters of the two women involved with him, and from journals and letters of Clara and Robert Schuhmann, who actually lived much earlier in the nineteenth century. The problematic role women play in further mythologizing the patriarchic myths even in the act of destroying them is highlighted by insertions of quotes from the first feminist critique of Thomas Bernhard, namely Ria Endres's book *Am Ende angekommen.*[6] A highly personalized meditation on Bernhard as the final apotheosis of a dying patriarchy, it gained considerable attention at the height of the feminist movement. Jelinek's appropriations for her female characters do not simply validate them as courageous forerunners of a common struggle; they also underscore the fallacies of a feminist idealism that fails to analyze historic processes and remains trapped in its narcissistic individualism — a predicament Jelinek herself has not escaped in the course of her controversial career as *Nestbeschmutzer* in the tracks of Thomas Bernhard and, like him, an accomplished self-performer. Her transformations as Austria's *femme fatale* of feminism, from leather-clad Marxist dominatrix in Austria's "second city" Graz, an early haven of the postwar avant-garde, to blond-braided, fortyish pseudo-Alpine maiden holding forth in Vienna's literary cafés to high fashion grand dame of letters parallel Bernhard's self-dramatizations from peasant outsider to country squire to cosmopolitan iconoclast. Her private life, not unlike Bernhard's, is kept a public mystery. (We do know that she divides her time between a husband in Munich and a mother at the outskirts of Vienna.) If Bernhard denounces (marital) sex as a dreary self-perpetuating mechanism that finally self-destructs in incestuous scenarios for the childless heirs of a doomed culture, Jelinek revels in the excessive tastelessness of equally sterile porno-parodies.

Her play *Burgtheater,* written in 1982 (published in 1984) invites comparison with Bernhard's 1976 play *Die Berühmten*. Both take on Austria's most treasured cultural institutions. (Neither was produced by either of them.) Jelinek zeroes in on Vienna's Imperial Theater and its first family of actors, active supporters of Hitler, stars of Nazi propaganda movies, who continued their distinguished careers on stage and as beloved idols of postwar Austrian *Heimatfilme. Die Berühmten* is a crass satire of culture as epitomized by the Salzburg Festival. Life-size puppets represent its founding idols. Though massacred in a quasi-Freudian murder ritual by their successors, they maintain their totemic power as portraits on the wall. Under their commanding gaze their titanic heirs morph into a bunch of scrambling, squeaking animals led by rooster conductor Karajan's cockadoodledoos. Not mentioned in the play, though known to everyone, were the fates and fortunes of those "famous" artists who perished during the Nazi regime. Bernhard often introduces names for their associative resonance without further elaboration. The political subtext has to be supplied by the spectator. In this early work, it is drowned out in the cacophony of animal noises. Not so in Jelinek, who cuts right to the chase. Her stage legends of the Burgtheater (whose real life counterparts were still alive when the play was written) are fascist egomaniacs, if blabbering fools at the height of their stardom during the Nazi regime.

The legendary actress, her famous husband and popular brother-in-law spout bits and pieces of Nazi-speak intersecting with lines from their roles on stage and in films (notably one infamous Nazi-propaganda movie *Die Heimkehr* that prepared for the enthusiastic acceptance of Hitler's invasion of Poland). Kaethe, the matriarch, is easily recognized as Paula Wessely, who rose to fame at the Salzburg Festival playing Gretchen in Max Reinhardt's legendary production of Goethe's *Faust.* The icon of soulful German femininity manhandles her three daughters (who would grow up to become well-known actresses) and their maid, her husband's impoverished sister. All speak an overblown, artificial Viennese dialect, a "foreign language" even to Germans. It magnifies and distorts the many diminutives so characteristic of Austrian dialect that contributes to the myth of the Austrians' endearing *Gemütlichkeit.* Jelinek's mangled prepositions and displaced compound nouns inflate the quaint charm into shrill dissonances. Scrambling to reinvent themselves as Hitler's victims before the Russian army arrives, the actors keep slipping on the Freudian bananas of their incurable Nazi babble. While Bernhard's language, even if passed on through generations, still constructs characters — it's their speech habits that make them so familiar — Jelinek radically defamiliarizes any recognizable speech patterns. The scrambled syntax and distorted dialect exemplify the disintegration of character. There is nothing beyond language. Barthes talks of speaking cadavers. They cling to bits and pieces of undying myths. Fascism is one such undying myth. Woman is another.

Jelinek's next two plays *Wolken. Heim* and *Krankheit oder moderne Frauen* tackle each myth, respectively. *Wolken. Heim* (Clouds. Home) — the title suggests Aristophanes' cloud-cuckoo-land, Heidegger's notion of home and homeland and the fascist utopia it engendered — has no designated speaker. The appropriated texts include Hölderlin, Hegel, Heidegger, Fichte, Kleist and letters of members of the Red Army Faction, the radical West German group responsible for assassinations and bombings in the 1970s. The drama is embedded in the assemblage of quotes and deliberate grammatical disruptions, all centered on the plural personal pronoun "we" that cuts across ages and maintains the nationalistic, xenophobic dynamic in German thought. The director needs the skills of an archeologist to dig up the artifacts inside the speech, as it were, the unspoken images that tell the history contained in the rubble of words. In *Krankheit oder moderne Frauen* (Illness or modern women), Jelinek personifies her feminist literary project in the female vampire. The model for the living dead is the woman writer. Emily Brontë is the inspiration for the bloodsucking nurse Emily who transforms the good childbearing housewife Carmilla into a lesbian vampire (borrowed from Sheridan *La Fanus'* story), who sucks the blood even of her own children. The women's "illness" mirrors the author's, who drains the life from the texts she needs for her hybrid literary products. In the end both women morph into one single unshapely, two-headed creature that gets shot and has its blood sucked by the men in their lives. The twin-monster of childbearing domesticity and female genius was Jelinek's controversial answer to the romantic feminism that was at its height in the mid-1980s. To the Marxist feminist, the notion of an autonomous woman is a monstrous delusion. So is any ideological utopianism. There is no way out of the bourgeois patriarchic language chain.

Jelinek's more recent play *Totenauberg* (1991)[7] links the Green Party's ecological rhetoric to Heidegger's exhortation of nature that weaves through the Nazi's blood and soil nativism to contemporary xenophobia. Jelinek's enraged dance of the undead makes Bernhard's staging of the dead look like a funny old grandpa's theater ("Opas Theater," as another Austrian, the young Peter Handke, famously sneered at the theater of the early 1960s). Bernhard's theater, peopled with its misanthropic, misogynist "Opas," all absurd relics of Western civilization, still allows for a certain nostalgic, if ironized indulgence in the past achievements of a dying culture. The melodramatic, deadly endings of his plays suggest closure. His leitmotif image of marionettes allowing for the final cutting of the strings is undermined by Jelinek's undead women, the lusty puppeteers who keep the old patriarchs (male or female) dancing, their broken limbs forever dangling from the tattered strings. The unnamed old man (Heidegger) of *Totenauberg* (named after Todtnauberg, the philosopher's Black Forest mountain retreat), is held together as much as trapped in a frame, the literal representation of Heidegger's concept of *Gestell* as both technological enframing and manifestation of Being. Scenarios of human limbs, gnawed on, eaten by fellow-humans, abound in her plays, the remnants of past and present wars, genocides and global capitalist sports mania. The vampire twin-creature chews on a child's bone. The alpine natives of *Totenauberg* gnaw on the broken limbs of dead skiers.

The Vienna Burgtheater production of her most ambitious project *Ein Sportstück,* in Einar Schleef's monumental staging, features the naked bodies of men hung upside down on one leg suspended on meat hooks. Both Jelinek and Bernhard are obsessed with the body, Bernhard with its sickness, Jelinek with a contemporary body cult that connects the fascist model to the joint interests of tourist and sport conglomerates. The two couples of *Raststätte* (Service Station) enter the food court outfitted in ultra chic sports clothing and state of the art gear to play out their *Cosi-fan-tutti* fantasy of anonymous sex with partners donning animal costumes in the restroom. The women had responded to a newspaper ad. But the strangers they encounter inside the elk and the moose are none other than their husbands. They end up in the parking lot, in an orgy of copulating humans and totem animals devouring body parts among shiny luxury cars. In Jelinek's millennial fin-de-siècle pastoral, Heidegger's exhortation of nature vis-à-vis the entrapments of technology asserts itself as a *grand guignol* of unreflected Being.

In *Stecken, Stab und Stangl,* written in response to the murder of four gypsies by an extremist group and set in the meat section of a supermarket, Heidegger's *Gestell* is replaced by pink crocheted coverings. Butcher and customers are busily crocheting a giant snake in which they get increasingly entangled. Some don crocheted animal masks. Sausages and chunks of meat are wrapped in doilies. The needlework, traditional emblem of feminine domesticity, enfolds the bloody merchandise, its handlers and the gruesome facts chopped up inside their language. Drawn from newsspeak, commercials, politicians' and media response to the murder in Burgenland, the text montage dramatizes the construction of popular speech (as myth) that softens, if not exonerates Austria's historic and most recent hate crimes. Derivations of Heidegger catch words (such as *nichten, wesen*) are added to the mix of sentimentalized, sensationalized media babble, along chatty references to the Holocaust, popular TV stars and sports idols, snippets of xenophobic commentaries, tabloid murder reports, such as babies thrown out the window, nurses killing elderly patients and other topical concerns known only to Austrians and tenderized by their native idiom. When it comes to mining etymological roots for interplaying meanings, Jelinek is Heidegger's master pupil and subversive clown. The title's *Stecken* and *Stab,* rod and staff, are borrowed from Psalms, 23.4: ". . . thy rod and thy staff they comfort me." *Stab* further suggests the diminutive *Staberl* that is also the pen name of Austria's most rabidly conservative (and popular) columnist in the tabloid *Kronenzeitung* (one of Bernhard's favorite targets), the paper with the largest readership. *Stangl,* which could be read as vernacular for *Stange,* a synonym for rod, was the name of the camp commander at Treblinka.

Historic memory, excised from de-politicized speech resurfaces on Jelinek's post-Marxist stage as a jumble of commodified signs on an open market of disembodied signifiers — an anonymous mass of producers and consumers trading in instant meanings. Her "planes of speech" are the panicked reconstructions of the Lacanian mirror stage, the infant's pre-linguistic illusion of an intact self, the imaginary "real," identical with "nature." Perhaps not surprisingly, both Bernhard and Jelinek indulge in infantile humor, recalling the mirror stage, as it were and the first impulse to smash it with the "symbolic," with language. According to Lacan's model, Jelinek's linguistic manipulations, not unlike Bernhard's monomaniacal hyperboles, stage the excesses of the imaginary "real" (appropriated from Heidegger's concept of nature and being) hitting against the boundaries of the "symbolic" (the language of myth as the Law).

Her method works on the page if only up to a point. Reading the texts without a logical syntactical progression, let alone a narrative, can be a nauseating experience. The physicality of the theater allows directors to inject their own visual narrative. In the case of East-German Einar Schleef, who draws on monumental images both of German culture leading up to the Nazi era and his own East-German past, the lines between critique and performative assertion get blurred. His eight hours mammoth production of *Ein Sportstück* was a hypnotizing tour-de-force, the postmodern sequel to the *Gesamtkunstwerke* of Wagner and Richard Strauss, whose opera *Elektra* he inserted in his mise-en-scène, expanding on the text's quasi auto-biographical figure of Elfi-Elektra. The director cast himself as the speaker of her lines. The choice foregrounds the question that drives all of Jelinek's writing (in Bernhard's wake): Whose voice is it anyway? As Heidegger put it after Novalis: Language speaks. Its voice is male. There is no way out of it. Jelinek herself is quite aware of her predicament. Quite consistently, she deconstructed her auto-mythology: Elfi Elektra, her mentally ill father's avenging daughter, on a rampage against Mother, parodying herself as the outspoken witness of all contemporary evils. St. Elfi flirts with Genet behind barricades of words in a clown show about the fall of patriarchy. Schleef, presenting himself in his work clothes as the author's double, foregrounds himself as the author of the mega-spectacle. Mass choruses, excerpts from Kleist's *Penthesilea,* Russian soldiers, fascist and Olympic tableaus and film clips showing the hell hounds chasing Orestes through the hellish splendor of the Burgtheater's entrance framed the massive waves of language in an orgy of vanities. Represented by a man — the director's authoritarian father figure, no less — Elfie/Elektra/Jelinek, the pioneering Austrian feminist seemed reconciled at long last with the voice of the Law: Father's good girl forever and a match to boot for his self-absorbed narcissism. The myth had been restored back in its/her place. What some critics faulted as the director's subverting of Jelinek's subversive agenda, might well have delivered the "real" Elfi, site-specifically enough in the city of Freud, only a few blocks from his home. The author in the body of her auteur/director replaced the twin lesbian vampire of *Krankheit oder moderne Frauen.*

Like Bernhard, albeit much later in her career, Jelinek owed her decisive breakthrough to a German director. Immediately after the fall of the Berlin wall, Schleef's younger East German colleague Frank Castorf took the surprised city by storm as artistic director of the Volksbühne am Rosa Luxemburg Platz, a bunker-like architectural monstrosity in the eastern part of the city. His productions deconstructed the Western theatrical canon and philistine assumptions both of bourgeois High Culture and a Marxist utopia by inserting improvisations, bits from other sources and popular music. His in-your-face directorial approach was similar to Jelinek's montage technique. Not surprisingly, his production of *Raststätte* rescued the play after a disastrous world-premiere at the Burgtheater. Bernhard would have sympathized. *Die Jagdgesellschaft* and *Die Berühmten* also flopped in Vienna. The former was rehabilitated in a Berlin production. *Die Berühmten* never really recovered from the initial fiasco. Ironically, Bernhard's definitive director Claus Peymann was responsible for the premieres of both *Die Jagdgesellschaft* and *Raststätte.* Earlier than Schleef and far more disrespectful than him, Castorf inserted the author as the missing subject in the shape of a monstrously oversized puppet with Jelinek's signature hairstyle and exposed giant breasts. Elfi emerged true to her own method and in the style of her anti-aesthetics, as an obscenely amusing ready-made. Apparently Jelinek took it in stride.

It is worth noting that both Bernhard and Jelinek benefited from German directors and actors. Bernhard mistrusted most Austrian actors not only for their emotional overacting but also for the Austrian lilt in their pronunciation even when speaking standard German. For her play *Burgtheater* Jelinek required that the Austrian dialect should not sound natural and best be spoken as a foreign language. Non-Austrian native German speakers would easily qualify. Since both writers are obsessed with the performative effects of language on character and culture, they needed their speakers' distance from it. Burgtheater audiences often resented that German actors distorted the famous musicality of Viennese German — the living proof of their Habsburg lineage — or violated their regional dialects. The effect was doubly estranging. It made familiar types into strangers, yet their strangeness was grotesquely familiar. German audiences, thrilled by academically challenging theater experiences and traditionally fascinated by Austrian speech habits, got an extra kick out of translating them.

Nevertheless, the problem of translation haunts Austrian playwrights from Raimund and Nestroy to Karl Kraus, Elias Canetti, Wolfgang Bauer, Peter Turrini and younger writers in the wake of Bernhard and Jelinek, such as Felix Mitterer, Marlene Streeruwitz and the late Werner Schwab who base their political and cultural critique of Austrian society on highlighting the close interaction between native speech and behavior. The drama of language motivates action and replaces psychology. Outside the original cultural context the critique of language as its prime agent is necessarily lost. In translation, the characters come across as uprooted strangers, the opposite of their original counterparts. The problem of both Jelinek and Bernhard as well as of their stage characters is that though estranged from their culture they remain irretrievably entrenched in it. As Wittgenstein postulated, one can't step outside the picture (of language).

Notes

[1] Quoted by Peter von Becker, "Die Unvernünftigen sterben nicht aus: Über Thomas Bernhards *Vor dem Ruhestand*," *Theater Heute* (August 1979): 4–6.

[2] Thomas Bernhard, *Heldenplatz* (Frankfurt: Suhrkamp, 1989), 69–70. See also Thomas Bernhard, *Heldenplatz,* trans. Gitta Honegger, *Conjunctions* 33 (1999).

[3] Anke Roeder, Elfriede Jelinek "Ich will kein Theater — Ich will ein anderes Theater," in *Theater Heute* 8 (1989): 30, 31. For a comprehensive study of Elfriede Jelinek see Marlies Janz, *Elfriede Jelinek* (Stuttgart: Metzler, 1995).

[4] Roland Barthes, *Mythologies,* trans. Annette Laver (New York: Hill and Wang, 2000), 142.

[5] Elfriede Jelinek, *Clara S. Theaterstücke* (Reinbek bei Hamburg: Rowohlt, 1992), 81.

[6] Ria Endres, *Am Ende angekommen* (Frankfurt: Fischer, 1980).

[7] Elfriede Jelinek, *Totenauberg* (Reinbek bei Hamburg: Rowohlt, 1991). Jelinek's title suggests her theme: Death in nature through technology, pollution and tourism. At the time the play was written, there were massive demonstrations in the *Auen,* the wetlands along the Danube, against the operation of a hydroelectric plant.

Andrew Webber

Costume Drama: Performance and Identity in Bernhard's Works

THIS ESSAY WILL CONSIDER the function of costume and performance in Bernhard's writing, focusing on dramatic works and shorter narratives where items of clothing take on a ritual, even fetishistic role. More particularly, it will discuss Bernhard's short narrative text "Ist es eine Komödie? Ist es eine Tragödie?" that features an unconventional and yet, I will argue, characteristic use of costume. Discussions of what Sebastian Neumeister has called Bernhard's dandyism have shown what store the author sets by codified styles of dress and social behavior.[1] Adolf Haslinger, in particular, has suggested that the obsessive concern with modes of dress has to be understood as a distinctive form of textual behavior, tightly bound to Bernhard's idiosyncratic *Sprechgestus* (gesture of speech).[2] The writer's attachment to repetitive habits of clothing is seen as a correlative of the narrative act of speech, of patterns of iteration and reiteration.[3] My argument here will consider this correlation more closely by focusing on those types of clothing that are associated in one way or another with acts of transgression, such as imposture, murder, and suicide, which characterize Bernhard's fiction and dramas. Styles of clothing and of speech are conventionally taken as the distinguishing features of a personal identity. Here, though, by their implication in these transgressive acts, they challenge radically the sustainability of any stable notion of identity. In this way, the investigation of identity through clothing performs a key function in Bernhard's ontological and epistemological inquiry.

The essay takes its cue from the alignment of dress and style of writing that Ingeborg Bachmann notes in her draft essay on Bernhard. Bachmann cites, as an example of Bernhard's extraordinary attention to styles of dress, the diatribe from *Watten*[4] on the profound lack of "Erstklassigkeit" or first-class quality in industrialized clothing.[5] It is, therefore, not by chance that she describes the paradoxical quality of Bernhard's style of writing by analogy with elegance of dress. On the one hand, his is a style which is folded into itself, "sozusagen ein Stil der Unauffälligkeit — nach dem alten Satz, wer am besten gekleidet ist, ist unauffällig gekleidet."[6] At the same time, it bears the idiosyncratic marks of his "Eigenheit" which Bachmann recognizes in the compulsive repetition of a vocabulary of apostrophe and of terror. If the general style of the writing is one of unostentatious grooming, then these compulsive features also profoundly disturb it. Bachmann appears to recognize the tendency for Bernhard's discursive clothing to be disrupted by marks of the sort of bodily trauma which so often breaks through in her own texts, when she includes the term "Stigmatisierung" in the inventory of his stylistic compulsions.[7] A key feature of Bernhard's rhetoric is its stigmatization of individuals, institutions, and practices, but his discourse is also subject to stigmatization in the sense of wounding and scarring. This form of stigmatization will indeed be seen to be a feature of the relationship between physicality and the leitmotif of clothing in Bernhard's writing.[8]

What I aim to show is that the concern with personal styling touches on the most fundamental aspect of identity in Bernhard's works: its performative character. Performativity, here, has a double level of meaning. The first is the routine sense of theatrical enactment. Whether in the dramatic or narrative genres, the structural logic of Bernhard's writing is insistently and self-consciously one of performance in this sense. At the same time, performativity extends to the meaning given to the term by speech act theory,[9] one subsequently adapted by theorists of identity, foremost amongst them Judith Butler. In this second sense, the performative is that style of speech that enacts or produces conditions of being through its enunciation. Bernhard's idiosyncratic voice is uniquely attached to this mode of utterance. The speakers in his texts are always seeking to establish states of affairs beyond doubt or to achieve different states of affairs by their acts of speech. While the first mode of theatrical or histrionic speech might appear to correspond to what speech act theory would call the constative, rather than the performative, constatation merges with performativity here; it becomes performative in both the theatrical and the linguistic sense of the word. Where constative speech is marked by excess of enunciation, say through hyperbolic or repetitive formulations, it projects into performativity. Constatation of fact, the discursive domain of the various types of *Genauigkeitsfanatiker* (perfectionists) who dominate Bernhard's works, is turned into performance, imitating the theatrical discourse of that other principle persona, the *Übertreibungskünstler* (artist of exaggeration). At the same time, an exaggerated insistence on constatation appears to imply a resistance to what it enunciates. It seems to be less concerned with a precise description of things than with their construction as one thing or another. Where constatation fails to be registered by the implied interlocutors of the author's narrative voices, the performative intervenes. The performative voice demands to be read or heard as citing an essentialist law or a truth which will brook no opposition and has established ritual forms of words for pronouncing states of being into that being.

Bernhard's performative voice might be better described as counter-performative, in that it seeks to contradict and upstage the conventional pronouncements of the prevailing ideology. This counter-performative function can be seen in *Gehen,* where Austria is seen to demand constant performative recognition that it is a "sogenannter Kulturstaat."[10] The state requires "daß er bei jeder Gelegenheit als solcher bezeichnet wird."[11] The dissident voices are thus engaged in a constant, repetitive counter-performance, an exposure of this act of state imposture. In this role, the speaking subject seems to assume the possibility of arrogating total control, and the texts frequently seem to be driven by a fantasy of this kind. After Foucault, however, theories of the performativity of identity serve to question that form of fantasy. They assert that the identity status and the power of the subject over objective conditions, achieved in the performative mode, are profoundly, even violently, controlled. The subject is given license to speak as an agent of social conditions, but that license is granted at a price. The speech acts of the subject are prescribed by social convention and subjected to the proscriptions which convention exacts. In the case of Bernhard, the individual voice, the voice seeking to achieve autonomy from the corrupt compromises of social being, is insistently re-subjected by the discourse it aims to expose. Like Hollensteiner, the Austrian dissident cited in *Gehen,* Bernhard is "an dieses Land gefesselt" (E, 434), even as he rails against the state that inhabits that land with its ideology.

Bernhard's speech and writing is always seeking to be oppositional to the standards of the dominant discourses of his culture. The lesson of his vitriolic oppositional voice is, however, that opposition is a slippery business. To find an individual style means to define the self in binary opposition to the other, but the categories of binary opposition that are engaged in Bernhard's texts are subject to switching and confusion. The structure of performance allows the texts to mimic the voices it would expose as corrupt, but it also establishes an arena of operation that relies on a sense of theatrical projection. In this arena the possibility of achieving a true voice is called profoundly into question. It is telling that the virtuoso impersonator of the title piece in the *Stimmenimitator* collection is unable to imitate his very own voice. The story "Ist es eine Komödie? Ist es eine Tragödie?" revolves around binaries that have a special attraction for Bernhard and commentators on his work. This question, framed in terms of the binary relation that regulates the structures of genre in the theater, echoes in different forms throughout Bernhard's narrative and dramatic writings. If this generic opposition is contested in this and other texts, then it can be seen to have a paradigmatic function for more general strategies of ordering through structures of opposition. Wendelin Schmidt-Dengler employs the comedy-tragedy opposition as a paradigm for one of his eleven axiomatic theses on the structures of Bernhard's writing. It represents for him the "Aufhebung der Gegensätze":

> Polare Paare, mit deren Hilfe sich am Werk Bernhards Kategorisierungen vornehmen ließen, kreist der Autor mit seiner Sprache so ein, daß die darin enthaltene Möglichkeit des Gegensatzes aufgehoben wird: "Ist es eine Komödie? Ist es eine Tragödie?" bleibt als Frage unbeantwortet.[12]

The "Aufhebung" or sublation of contraries in Schmidt-Dengler's formulation demands to be read in the full, dialectical sense of the word. The debate over comedy and tragedy serves as a model for a more general dialectical process, whereby Bernhard at once suspends or lifts the conventional distinctions between these categories and preserves and recreates them by lifting them to another level, where they provide a framework for his whole project of social and cultural judgment.

Tragedy and comedy are taken out of the theater and out of the discourse of poetics to become the arena for dealing with the most fundamental realities of life. The debate as to the viability of the oppositional categories of dramatic genres translates, in its turn, into one about the opposition between theater and life. Bernhard appropriates the time-honored topos of the world as theater, one that has held particular sway in the Austrian literary tradition, in order to show that the practice of performance is pervasive in the social, political, and cultural life of his world. For Bernhard, as for so many of those writing in the German-speaking countries in the wake of the Second World War and the Holocaust, the suffering of the victims is only properly imaginable for dramatic representation in the mode of tragedy. Yet the inevitable failure of ethical truth in the retrospective working through of this brutal heritage twists tragedy remorselessly towards the comic. For Bernhard, as for Dürrenmatt, the only genre that seems appropriate for the depiction of the aftermath of the War and the Holocaust is the hybrid genre of tragicomedy. And this uncomfortable generic hybridity appears to be especially attuned to Bernhard's view of the Austrian situation, to the particular kinds of dreadfully laughable theater, the trivializing operetta, which he sees in the political culture of Austria in the postwar period. The logic of the hybrid genre extends to the relationship between drama and narrative in Bernhard's oeuvre, the inclination of his dramatic works towards the epic mode of narrative reconstruction and the inclination of his narrative works towards the mode of the dramatic monologue or dialogue. The dramas refuse to transport their audiences into an arena of ready identification and conventional plot dynamics; and the narratives are insistently bound to the transcription of dramatically conceived voices. In both narrative and theatrical works, Bernhard's version of the *theatrum mundi* is most characteristically registered in the conjunction of two theatrical elements which form the basis for the issue of identity in this essay: styles of clothing and styles of speech. In either case, style is a function of repetition, and repetition gravitates between the possibility of establishing a tenable identity and the probability of compulsive circularity.

Clothing, in its ambivalent relation to identity, has a focal role in most of Bernhard's texts. In the framework of his dramas, clothing intrinsically functions as costume. Rather than hiding this function in the conventional manner, these texts expose and foreground it. Invariably the dramas have a self-reflexive relationship to the institution of the theater, and, within this structure, clothing is styled by analogy with the theatrical speech of the characters, by means of a sort of theatrical quotation. A prime example of this theatrical use of dress is the miniature dramatic trilogy *Claus Peymann kauft sich eine Hose und geht mit mir essen*. Peymann, as the new director of the Burgtheater, needs a new pair of trousers. The play revolves around the theatrical act of the "Hosenprobe" as a kind of dress rehearsal. As part of its structure of citation, the play incorporates two texts that deal with the performance of identity and clothing. Bernhard borrows the coat of Keller's *Kleider machen Leute,*[13] a text that has proverbial status in its exposure of false appearances and inauthentic social order through counterfeit costume. Keller's novella is itself a text engaged in intertextual games, citing conventions of formulaic appearance, the discourse and clothing of popular romantic writing. Bernhard's appropriation of its proverbial title "Clothes make people" is, in this sense, an imitation of strategies of imitation. And, in a similar manner, Bernhard borrows the trousers of another text which is also confected out of the clothes of other works, Büchner's *Leonce und Lena:* "wie mit Leonce und Lena ist es mit der Hose."[14] The trousers, a leitmotif of *Leonce und Lena,* are in characteristic fashion tailored out of a form of word-play and serve as much to expose as to clothe the fantasy of the text.

As both *Kleider machen Leute* and *Leonce und Lena* stage their political analysis of the human comedy through a parodic motley of Romantic textual clichés, so Bernhard uses citations to analyze what for him is the most fabricated of all forms of that comedy: contemporary

Austria. His drama of the director's new clothes serves as an exposure of the theater's attachment to appearances and, by extension, of the false new clothes that the Austrians adopt as a cover for the naked realities of their history. They dress up for the tragedy of Austria when their country, as they have performed and perform it, is in fact only the stuff of comedy.[15] The search for integrity in a pair of trousers, which accounts for the play's banal and farcical plot, functions as a grotesque counterpoint to the bad faith displayed by the national "theater." An obsession with clothing has a similar contrapuntal function in the most self-reflexive of Bernhard's Burgtheater plays, *Heldenplatz*. Trying on a pair of trousers extends the grotesque comedy of death here to the ritualistic preparation of the clothing of a dead man. The stage action is transposed backstage to the dressing room of an actor, as the theatrical identity of Professor Schuster is ritually enacted by his servants in a litany of imitative acts of speech and clothing. The Professor's character is conjured up on stage through an elaborate structure of citation in language and behavior, specifically in the handling of clothing. The beloved clothes of Schuster, the "klassische Schuhfetischist," represent the fetishistic vestiges of the body, incorporating its substance.[16] Indeed, their investment with the smell and the blood of their wearer — "Ich hätte den Anzug nicht in die Putzerei geben sollen" (H, 57) — gives them a special status as props in a sort of necrophiliac theater of mourning. As Frau Zittel re-enacts the Professor's ritual of shirt-folding, she cites his thoughts on the vampirism of the theater: "und wer einmal Blut geleckt hat im Theater / der kann ohne Theater nicht mehr existieren" (H, 25).

Heldenplatz uses clothing as the metaphorical material for rituals of identity performance. The uniform rituals of the Professor's dress habits are performed as an ironic counterpart to the sort of uniform fetishism that characterizes the theatrical performance of fascism. In particular, it corresponds intertextually to the SS uniform in *Vor dem Ruhestand*, which is also introduced through a performative ritual of ironing. The obsessive passions and phobias of dress are bound up with the spectacular mass passion and hatred of National Socialism. The Jewish Professor figures himself in the borrowed clothes of the essentialist language of fascist ideology as "der geborene Mantelhasser" (H, 40). He appears to be born into the condition of hating coats according to a grotesque principle of eugenic purity which is parodied by his brother's essentialist theory of the Austrian birthright of anti-Semitism: "der Judenhaß ist die reinste die absolut unverfälschte Natur des Österreichers" (H, 114). In this manner, clothing, as a metonymic substitution for the identity of its wearer, becomes marked by the coercion of ideological hatred. The stigmatized clothing of the suicide serves not only to re-enact Schuster in a performance of mourning but also to reconstruct the historical trauma of the Jews who did not escape. As in a whole series of Bernhard's texts, clothing is material for identification with its focus on labels, insignia, or other distinguishing features.[17] It serves in the assertion of an individual or collective identity and in the identification with the other. But, whether it functions as ideological uniform, as eroticized fetish, as evidence of violence, or as a ritual object of mourning, the forms of identification afforded by clothing are invariably troubled.

As uniform, clothing marks ideological belonging and the ideological exclusion of those deemed not to belong. This fact forms the basis of the repeated attempts of the narrator in "Die Mütze" to identify the owner of the cap into which he steps. The cap as "Schildmütze" carries the badge of the community that violently opposes the narrator's attempts at integration. The cap's purpose is to identify sameness and exclude otherness, and the narrator can only assimilate by adopting the communal practice of wearing the cap, but with a criminal sense of his own otherness. "Die Mütze" is haunted by an implication of criminality, and the piece of clothing functions in some sense as its evidence. At first, the cap appears to point to some communal crime. However, when the narrator begins to wear it, it bears witness against the narrator's own identity. He perceives it as an animal cadaver when he first treads on it and thereby enters into an uncanny relationship with the butcher community for whom the cap is a trademark. As with most of the texts under consideration here, the piece of clothing acts as a metonymic representation of a *corpus delicti*. It becomes a thing of obsessive attachment and returns insistently as evidence of more or less unidentifiable crimes.

Most commonly, clothing, as in *Heldenplatz,* is associated with sudden death, often suicide, and implies a pattern of repetition and circular violence. The eponymous coat in "Der Wetterfleck," identified by its distinctive buttons as that of the narrator's uncle, is washed up after his death by drowning only to pass on to the funeral clothier who re-enacts the presumed suicide. As the narrator eventually collects it from the "Bestattungswäschegeschäft," he seems set to continue the coat's suicidal relay by following literally the logic of "Kleider machen Leute." The coat also returns intertextually in the short text "Der Lodenmantel" from the *Stimmenimitator* where Bernhard appears to imitate as much his own pathological voice as that of a newspaper report.[18] Here, the washing up of the coat, which in itself is securely identified, only leads to a repeated failure to solve the case that it identifies, a mystery that is "wieder nicht aufgeklärt."[19] The coat passes as a token of serial violence from text to text, leading to degrees of identification, but not to any solution or resolution of the cases to which it bears witness.

The coat of a victim of drowning, for instance, appears, albeit in a different fashion, in the text that can be understood as paradigmatic for the representation of problematic identity, namely Bernhard's "Ist es eine Komödie? Ist es eine Tragödie?" This element of "costume drama" in Bernhard's works, his peculiar attention to clothing as the material crux for the performance of identity, indicates the possibility of an encounter between text and theory in a reading of Bernhard through the gender and queer theory of Judith Butler. The initial basis for this encounter is provided by a no less strange, not to say queer, encounter: the nocturnal meeting between men in a park, the one dressed for the theater, the other dressed in women's clothing and apparently accustomed to such importuning of young men.

"Ist es eine Tragödie? Ist es eine Komödie?" can be seen as an emblematic text in a sense beyond that which Schmidt-Dengler highlights when he sees it as a dialectical encounter between theater and reality, tragedy and comedy of life.[20] The text's marking of clothing as costume and of speech as script, as functions of an ongoing sense of existential performance, is also emblematic of the more general process of performative identity production in Bernhard's writing. It is of particular significance here that this emblematic function should be achieved through a scenario that has the appearance of an encounter that queers the normative behavior of gender and sexuality. The questioning of binary opposition between the master genres of the theater is cast in a drama, or what Bernhard might categorize as "Dramolett," that also questions the binary opposition of gender. The Platonic dialogue between men as they walk together is an archetypal structure in Bernhard's texts, one which also incorporates the homoerotic element of the Platonic tradition.[21] This scenario also lends itself to Bernhard's understanding of sexuality as a sort of universal human comedy played out in a variety of roles: "Sexualität spielt bei jedem Menschen eine ungeheure Rolle, gleich wie er sie ausspielt."[22] The peculiar version of the dialogue between men in "Ist es eine Komödie? Ist es eine Tragödie?" proves to be paradigmatic, that is, exemplary insofar as it is excessive or exceptional. The text can be viewed as a sort of outing through a type of drag act of the pervasive performance of homo-social or homo-intellectual bonding which sustains Bernhard's world.

It is certainly difficult to imagine Bernhard, or one of his key narrative personae, walking and talking with Judith Butler. It has generally been accepted that women in Bernhard's works are, if not the object of outright misogyny, then certainly a blind spot. The most notable encounter between his writing and a feminist critic became something of a *cause célèbre in 1980,* when Ria Endres published her drastically critical *Am Ende angekommen: Dargestellt am wahnhaften Dunkel der Männerporträts des Thomas Bernhard.*[23] For Endres, the man's world of Bernhard's texts is at once a totalizing fantasy of phallocratic power and its apocalyptic endgame. She sees the Bernhard text as a monstrous male body, made up of extravagant repetitions and citational layering. This text aims at absolute authority, but achieves only a massive cover-up for the colossal impotence of the phallocratic order. It is telling that Bernhard's predictably acidic response to this critique is framed in terms of the "natural" order of gender: "Eine Frau, die wirklich natürlich ist, also das, was man unter einer Frau versteht, würde nie so einen Blödsinn schreiben und verzapfen."[24] His voice here mimics that of many of his protagonists who appeal to the category of nature in order to support their judgments of the ills of culture. It is also countered by the more sophisticated understanding of the natural as a contradictory construction that is voiced by the same and other protagonists. A case in point would be the assessment of the homosexual relationship between the two woodsmen in *Amras,* where the notion of nature's naturalness is deconstructed in a series of shifts between negation and affirmation: "es ist nicht widernatürlich (ja, wie die Natur widernatürlich), nein" (E, 62). The sexist voice of Bernhard's counter-critique of Endres has to be heard against such more differentiating judgments.

The pronouncement of naturalness or unnaturalness is one of the most insistent forms of performative speech act in Bernhard's writing. Yet, as the example from *Amras* shows, it establishes a paradigm for the performative that incorporates a contradictory counter-voice. This type of performativity may allow for a more productive encounter between feminist and anti-feminist strains of thought than Endres's Bernhard model might suggest. Endres in her impassioned assault upon the citational character of the Bernhard text, views it as a massive machinery of phallocentric falsification. Contemporary feminism of the Butlerian type would have different ways of looking at this obsessive citational strategy. It might well conclude, along the lines of Endres, that its purpose is ultimately a form of fetishism, serving as a diversion from the lack of original power in the male author and his order. However, it would also consider in a more sophisticated manner the structures of textual transmission as, precisely, performative. Endres counters the essentialist in Bernhard with a similarly essentialist feminism, and Bernhard responds with more of the same essentialism. A dialogue with Butler might do more justice to the constructionist voice underlying Bernhard's essentialist rhetoric. In *Gehen,* for example, the lack of original authority in discourse is exposed in the form of an italicized citation: "*Im Grunde ist alles, was gesagt wird, zitiert*" (E, 420). This self-reflexive citational principle subverts the very grounding of the idea of the natural when Oehler begins to cite Karrer's citation of the concepts "*Menschliche Natur* und *Natur*" (E, 420).

A more viable model for the encounter with Butler might be Ingeborg Bachmann. If, as we have seen, Bachmann registered key features of the way in which Bernhard's texts are clothed, then he in turn responded to her texts and her clothing. What is distinctive about this response is its inclination towards forms of cross-dressing. For Bernhard, Bachmann is an exception that proves the rule of the essential masculinity of the intellect.[25] In the figure of the "Perserin" in *Ja,* who appears to be modeled in part on Bachmann,[26] a woman is granted the privilege of walking and talking, or communing, with the narrative persona. In order to perform this function it seems that she has to be dressed up in a motley mix of the feminine "Pelzmantel" and the effects of manhood, the "Männerhut" and "Männergummistiefel" borrowed from the innkeeper (E, 534). Similarly, the poet Maria, the Bachmann persona in *Auslöschung* is deemed suitable for a textual dialogue with such a canonical man of the German philosophical tradition as Schopenhauer. She figures most distinctively in Murau's dream, where she appears in a sort of operatic or pantomimic transvestism. She wears the breeches and jerkin, at once masculine in style and with extravagantly feminized accessories, which Bachmann herself wore in her own performative display of the "crazy" female writer:

> Maria ist aus Paris zu uns gestoßen in einem verrückten Hosenanzug, sagte ich zu Gambetti. Sie sah aus, als wollte sie gerade in die große Oper gehen oder als käme sie gerade aus der großen Oper zurück. Eine schwarze Samthose, Gambetti, die mit großen Seidenmaschen unterhalb ihrer Knie befestigt war, dazu eine kardinalrote Jacke mit einem türkisfarbigen Kragen.[27]

She goes on to engage in a cross-dressing dance with Eisenberg, exchanging her ballet shoes for his long black boots. Only in the context of a dream, it seems, can a man and a woman exchange their clothes in a pleasurable, transgressive performance of this kind. And even here, a masculine protest and censorship rudely interrupts the fantasy of such an exchange as the innkeeper intervenes to deny the fantasy any public space. In the context of the dream, it seems that the cardinal-red jacket can be read as encoding the patriarchal garb of Catholic authority that figures so significantly in the novel. Maria wears the clothes of patriarchy but in a theatrical style that seems to represent both her own operatic "madness" and the institutional madness of the male order that she mimics and provokes.

This conjunction of gender roles and institutional authorities is the point at which a Butlerian analysis appears appropriate. If Butler analyzes gender identity as a product of the performative enactment of discursive scripting, then the pronouncement of cross-dressing as "crazy" is a key example of such enactment. A dissident misappropriation of gendered styles of clothing can be understood as an act of performance which provokes the authority of the dominant ideology by pronouncing it mad or queer and so beyond the pale. Cross-dressing serves as a symbolic territory where systems of control and counter-control perform their contest. In proper Butlerian fashion, dress is therefore subject, like the performance of speech, to the codified power practices, the citational structures, of the law. Gender performance and the law converge in "Ist es eine Komödie? Ist es eine Tragödie?" The question of generic assignment in the title points to a more general problematics of categorization. The protagonist is, characteristically for Bernhard, a scholar figure, but one who is split by hybrid interests. Even before we learn of the impassioned ambivalence of his treatise on the theater, the discursive field in which he officially moves, that of medicine, is conceived as a space for performance. In the scholarly privacy of his room, he plays a dramatic monologue, where the formula "sagte ich mir" is rendered into a mode of performance.

In this performance, the theater is excoriated with theatrical hyperbole: "das Theater ist eine einzige perfide Ungezogenheit, eine ungezogene Perfidie" (E, 154). The narrator is, so to speak, on a stage with fore- and background and the performer is split between these stage settings: "mir ist nicht ganz klargeworden, im Vorder- oder Hintergrund des Medizinischen" (E, 154). The theater preemptively enters into the discourse of medicine and in turn reflects upon the pathology of the discourse of the theater. Medical study turns into a study of the theater. Indeed, the theater enters every physical and discursive space in the narrative. The narrator's room and the outside park become settings for a meta-theater, an arena where the characters' performances are always citing the institution of theater as an ambivalent authority. Bernhard's protagonists are, like those of Kafka, irresistibly cited and situated before the Law.[28] Here, though, the building of the Law has become the Burgtheater,[29] and its structures recede ever inwards in a Kafkaesque *mise-en-abyme:* "DIE SCHAUSPIELER IN DEN SCHAUSPIELERN DER SCHAUSPIELER usf" (E, 155). At the same time, like Kafka's ubiquitous, self-replicating and self-citing Law, the elaborate structures of the institution of theater with its "BÜHNENEXZESSE" proliferate outwards into the theater of the theater-goers observed by the protagonists at the entrance of the theater. And so the protagonists themselves proceed to perform, dressed as they are, in different ways for the theater.

The analogy with Kafka's emblematic text "Vor dem Gesetz" is not arbitrary, for the theater of Bernhard's text moves from the discourse of medicine to that of the law, from pathology to criminology. When the narrator tells the time to a man requesting it, he does so in a way that acts as a cue to their own performance: "das Theater hat angefangen" (E, 156). This line is at once a constatation of the actual play having started and a form of performative pronouncement marking the beginning of an alternative theater on the fringe of institutional theater. This performative cue leads to a dramatic interaction focusing on the performative authority that the discourses of medicine and law share as discourses able to pronounce people sick or guilty of crimes.[30] The driving logic of the drama that unfolds is performative because it is a re-enactment, following a ritualized and scripted sequence of such re-enactments. It is also performative in the sense that it appeals to the ritual judgments of courtroom drama, specifically the psychiatric judgment that might mitigate the crime. The man in women's clothing calls for a diagnostic pronouncement from his interlocutor, the student of medicine: "Verrückt, nicht wahr?" He duly responds: "ein Verrückter? dachte ich" (E, 157–58). At the same time, the "madman" judges the world that would judge him mad and a murderer. Accordingly, the world, like Kafka's world, is not just tantamount to a penal institution, "ein Zuchthaus," but a total reproduction of the discourse of the law: "Die ganze Welt ist eine einzige Jurisprudenz" (E, 162). It is a world that, in its theatricality, is dominated by structures of ritual juridical performance. The juridical discourse interjects the subject into its structures, calling him into an identity that, in its constant state of performance, is as much a citation of the law as a theatrical script.

The murderer's enactment follows coordinates of space and time that are precisely prescribed. The number of steps he takes in his alternative pairs of shoes and the number of days since his last performance are marked by the "genau" of the juridical pedant or "Genauigkeitsfanatiker." Like a master criminal or criminologist, he is uncannily attuned to the operations of the police: "Seit mehreren Tagen meidet die Polizei den Volksgarten und konzentriert sich auf den Stadtpark, und ich weiß, warum" (E, 159). At the same time, the theatrical citation of his crime is an act of impersonation. By playing the double role of criminal and victim he submits to judgment. The act of imposture is at once registered as a transgression, a gender crime, and serves as a form of criminological reconstruction. The transvestite embodies and performs another form of the *corpus delicti* familiar from other texts. The women's clothes that he wears are performative of the sort of reaction of "Übelkeit" or disgust that his crime is supposed to elicit. While the cross-dressing of Maria in *Auslöschung* represents a form of cultivated madness, a challenge to conventions of performance, which the male narrator can embrace as a fantasy, the reverse performance produces a more ambivalent form of fascination. The drag performance, as Butler has shown, exposes the arbitrarily imposed character of gender performance and on another level associates this form of performativity with the more general, existential condition of performing an identity according to the prescriptions of social law. The criminal must transgress gender law in a repeated performance in order to subject himself repeatedly as "unnatural" to the master discourse of jurisprudence.

The ending of the story also offers a kind of theatrical closure. The re-enactment has finally been completed in the sense that the murderer's interlocutor has sustained the dramatic dialogue to the point of confession. However, it also fails to close the case. The logic of re-enactment would look for the actor dressed as the victim to be killed by the other or by himself. It is a scenario, in other words, akin to that of Josef K.'s theatrically mounted execution at the end of Kafka's *Der Process* and, like that scenario, it fails to follow its script. The narrator refuses to respond to the directions that he should leave, and the drama ends differently, following another type of prescription, that of a continued performance of living punishment. It returns from the institution of the law, the world as "Zuchthaus," to that of the theater, the world as a performance of the discourse of the law. The narrative ends with a different kind of judgment, one that denies the possibility of the cathartic closure of crime through punishment in tragedy. The self-indicted criminal closes the narrative in a type of performative speech act that is exemplary for the whole system of judgment in Bernhard's world. He pronounces the play being performed in the theater, whatever its genre in constative terms, a comedy, "*Tatsächlich* eine Komödie" (E, 162), and in doing so, produces it as one.

This performative production of a comedy leaves the story, its drama, and its case open even as it goes through the performance of closure. The declaration which is asked for in the title imitates the "it is a" form of what Butler has established as the primal scene of performativity, the assignment of a gender identity at birth. But the genre of comedy in this citation does not correspond to one gender or the other, any more than to one or other of the officially sanctioned genres of the theater. Rather, it stands for the disjunctive comedy intrinsic to unworkable systems of binary organization like those of gender or of genre. As Butler has argued, the primal, ritual pronouncement "It's a boy" or "It's a girl" which elides the constatation of the subject's biological sex with the first performance of its gender identity, also prepares the ground for the performative to fail, for sex and gender to mismatch.[31] It is this sort of gender trouble that the transvestite drama enacts. The exaggerated proliferation of the supposedly unproblematic epithet "der Mann" when the transvestite figure first appears and the narrator's resistance to recognizing the figure's clothing as feminine indicate an anxiety which haunts the primal performative pronouncement "It's a boy" and its production of gender.[32] Against the grain of his more essentialist pronouncements, Bernhard shows here the susceptibility of "natural" categories like gender to forms of masquerade.

The theater of cross-dressing, apparently to be replayed again and again, crosses a whole series of binaries other than male/female. It dresses opposing personae like tragedian and comedian, actor and spectator, perpetrator and victim in each other's clothes and denies any possibility of categorical identification. In the words of the self-proclaimed criminal, the human condition is a constant comedy of errors: "Das Merkwürdige an den Menschen ist, daß sie sich selber andauernd mit anderen Menschen verwechseln" (E, 160). The particular genre that the narrative performs is therefore Bernhard's favored version of the human comedy, the *Verwechslungskomödie* or comedy of error. It is a comedy of mistaken identities that works through the switching of the mistakable materials of clothing.[33] If we can apply a genre label to the human drama of Bernhard's works, then it would have to be pronounced, after this model, a comedy of errors in the performance of identity. In accordance with the view of the narrative persona in *Watten,* it is a comedy which operates by means of *Verwechslung* in that it is always ready to switch into the domain of tragedy which is coextensive with it: "Man kann in Verzweiflung, sage ich, . . . von einem Augenblick auf den andern aus der Tragödie (in der man ist) in das Lustspiel eintreten (in dem man ist), umgekehrt jederzeit aus dem Lustspiel (in dem man ist) in die Tragödie (in der man ist)" (E, 318).

Notes

[1] Sebastian Neumeister, *Der Dichter als Dandy: Kafka, Baudelaire, Thomas Bernhard* (Munich: Fink, 1973).

[2] Adolf Haslinger, "Mütze, Mantel, Wetterfleck: Kleiderthematik und poetisches Verfahren bei Thomas Bernhard," *Bernhard-Tage Ohlsdorf 1994: Materialien,* eds. Franz Gebesmair and Alfred Pittertschatscher (Weitra: Bibliothek der Provinz, 1995), 23.

[3] Haslinger, 28.

[4] Thomas Bernhard, *Watten. Ein Nadleß* (Frankfurt: Suhrkamp, 1969).

[5] Ingeborg Bachmann, "[Thomas Bernhard:] Ein Versuch: Entwurf," *Werke,* vol. IV, eds. Christine Koschel, Inge von Weidenbaum, and Clemens Münster (Munich, Zurich: Piper, 1993), 361–64; here 362–63.

[6] Bachmann, 362.

[7] Bachmann, 362.

[8] One example, among many, would be the blood on the jacket of the narrator of "Die Mütze."

[9] For a foundational discussion of speech act theory, see J. L. Austin, *How to Do Things with Words* (Oxford: Oxford UP, 1961).

[10] The "Kulturstaat" as "sogenannt" or "so-called" is a key case in the more general category of "Sogenanntes" exposed later in the text. Things like the "Kulturstaat" are performatively called into being, but they seek to posit their identity as actual and integral, rather than so-called.

[11] Thomas Bernhard, *Die Erzählungen* (Frankfurt: Suhrkamp, 1979), 433; hereafter quoted in text as E.

[12] Wendelin Schmidt-Dengler, *Der Übertreibungskünstler: Studien zu Thomas Bernhard* (Vienna: Sonderzahl, 1989), 108.

[13] Thomas Bernhard, *Claus Peymann kauft sich eine Hose und geht mit mir essen: Drei Dramolette* (Frankfurt: Suhrkamp, 1990), 32.

[14] *Claus Peymann,* 29.

[15] *Claus Peymann,* 40.

[16] Thomas Bernhard, *Heldenplatz* (Frankfurt: Suhrkamp, 1988), 129; hereafter quoted in text as H. The name Schuster (shoemaker) has a performative character, helping to present the Professor's identity as shoe fetishist. Similarly, in "Die Mütze," the narrator's fetishistic attachment to an item of clothing is prefigured by his attachment to the forestry theories of a Dr. Mantel (*Erzählungen,* 138).

[17] This meticulous attention to clothing is, for instance, given in the inconclusive evidence of the "Schneidersiegel" in the story "Der Wetterfleck" (*Erzählungen,* 367).

[18] The "autoreferentielle Vertextung," the imitative relations that Eybl identifies between the various voices of *Der Stimmenimitator* extends intertextually to Bernhard's other narrative voices. Franz M. Eybl, "Thomas Bernhard's *Stimmenimitator* als Resonanz eigener und fremder Rede," *Kontinent Bernhard: Zur Thomas-Bernhard-Rezeption in Europa,* ed. Wolfram Bayer (Vienna: Böhlau, 1995), 31–43; here 35.

[19] Thomas Bernhard, *Der Stimmenimitator* (Frankfurt: Suhrkamp, 1978), 96.

[20] "Dieser Text Bernhards dürfte, so meine ich, einmal allegorisch auf das Gesamtwerk übertragen werden." Wendelin Schmidt-Dengler, "Komödientragödien: Zum dramatischen Spätwerk Bernhards," *Bernhard-Tage Ohlsdorf 1994: Materialien,* eds. Franz Gebesmair and Alfred Pittertschatscher (Weitra: Bibliothek der Provinz, 1995), 74–98; here 78.

[21] As noted by Reiter in her discussion of gender relations in Bernhard's work, particularly in the case of the pedagogical relationship between Franz-Josef Murau and his pupil Gambetti in *Auslöschung:* "Die Männerfreundschaften kennzeichnet eine Erotik des Intellekts." Andrea Reiter, "Die Bachmann . . . war halt eine gescheite Frau," *Die Rampe* (1992), 2, 17–43; here 26.

[22] Quoted in Kurt Hofmann, *Aus Gesprächen mit Thomas Bernhard* (Vienna: Löcker, 1988), 60.

[23] Ria Endres, *Am Ende angekommen* (Frankfurt: Fischer, 1980).

[24] Hofmann, 95.

[25] "Die Bachmann hab' ich sehr gern mögen, die war halt eine gescheite Frau. Eine seltene Verbindung, nicht?" Quoted in Hofmann, 96.

[26] See Hans Höller, *Thomas Bernhard* (Reinbek: Rowohlt, 1993), 92–93.

[27] Thomas Bernhard, *Auslöschung* (Frankfurt: Suhrkamp, 1986), 215. Höller reproduces a photograph of Bachmann in this pantomimic costume (93).

[28] That Bernhard may be in dialogue with Kafka's novel is suggested by its inclusion in the readings Murau recommends to his student Gambetti in *Auslöschung.* Butler, too, is drawn before Kafka's Law as a paradigm for the interpellation of the subject in the performance of identity. There is a consistent Kafkaesque subtext in her discussions of citation.

[29] These two institutions, the Burgtheater and the metaphorical prison, are further related through a textual relay with the parliament building and its law-making theater.

[30] Variations on this conjunction of the theater with the discourses of psychiatry and the law arise in two of the texts from the *Stimmenimitator* collection, namely "Unmöglich" and "Empfindung." In the second of these, a playwright, who has called his tragedies comedies and vice versa, as a response

to them being performed in a theater he calls a "Narrenhaus" (*Stimmenimitator,* 117) is cited before the law by an insulted spectator. The theater-hating judge, though, pronounces him innocent and thereby ratifies the performative authority of the playwright's judgments.

[31] Judith Butler. *Bodies That Matter: On the Discursive Limits of "Sex"* (New York & London: Routledge, 1993), 7–8.

[32] In the same way, Bachmann's reference to the narrative as "eine einfache Geschichte: über das Theater" in which "zwei Männer gehen miteinander zweimal auf und ab und sprechen über das Theater, in das sie nicht gehen" overlooks the gender performance and the way in which the piece does go to the theater. It is precisely these performative features that make this story a paradigm for the representation of "die Verstörung, in der sich jeder befindet" (Bachmann, 363–64).

[33] In the film-script *Der Italiener* (Salzburg: Residenz, 1971) the confusion of life and the theater is represented by an inventory of stage costumes, including "Ein Seidenumhang, wie er für eine Verwechslungskomödie paßt" (32).

Bernhard's Social Worlds

Photo courtesy of Erika Schmied

Gitta Honegger

Language Speaks. Anglo-Bernhard: Thomas Bernhard in Translation

> The stupidity of entrusting oneself to the German language, my dear Doctor — absurd! And not only the German language, I think, but still the German language above all.[1]

MANY OF THOMAS BERNHARD'S characters, disgruntled Austrians, spent a period of their lives in England. In Austria's postwar culture in which Bernhard came of age, Anglo-culture offered an alternative to the Austrians' self-image as born guilty, trapped in the provincialism of a tiny Alpine enclave and stuck with a language that had lost all credibility. London, Oxford, Cambridge are codes for rational versus speculative thought, worldliness as opposed to parochialism, a cosmopolitan open-mindedness versus Viennese provincialism, Anglo-composure as opposed to Central-European histrionics. Many of Bernhard's characters are descendants of Austrian gentry and nobility. It is as if the disenfranchised heirs of one collapsed Empire find comfort in the ambience of another, still existing monarchy.

In his self-representations, Bernhard metamorphosed from rough peasant outsider to cosmopolitan country squire.[2] Early photographs show him in the traditional costume of rural Austrians. He appears with *Lederhosen, Steirerhut* — the Alpine equivalent to the Stetson — heavy knit knee socks and hiking boots while hanging out with the local guys who help remodel his farmhouse. He took pride in his tractor license and the title to his farm, which acknowledged him as "Farmer of Nathal." Later in life when he spent more time in Vienna, he dressed immaculately with that casual elegance associated with old class rather than new money. Like many upper class Austrians who rejected the native, rural look once favored by the Nazis, he sported the tailor-made, timeless elegance of British clothing.

It seems that the translations of his works follow a similar path. Unlike Peter Handke, who was fortunate enough to have the brilliant Ralph Mannheim translate nearly all of his major prose works, Bernhard had several translators, both in the United States and in England. It was only when David McLintock took on the translations of his later works, starting with his memoir *Gathering Evidence* to his last work *Extinction,* that Bernhard finds his voice in the English language and his narrators acquire the flair of the Englishman, if not born then at least bred as such, validating all those years they spent studying in London.

The opening sentence of *Beton* (*Concrete*) in the English publication, offers a good example of what happens in the transition from a choleric Austrian to a miffed Brit, the latter's ennui tempered by the syntactical restrictions of the English language:

> Von März bis Dezember, schreibt Rudolf, während ich, was in diesem Zusammenhang gesagt sein muß, große Mengen von Prednisolon einzunehmen hatte, um meinem zum dritten Mal akut gewordenen *morbus boeck* entgegenzuwirken, trug ich alle nur möglichen Bücher und Schriften über Mendelssohn Bartholdy zusammen, suchte alle möglichen und unmöglichen Bibliotheken auf, um meinen Lieblingskomponisten und sein Werk von Grund auf kennenzulernen und, so mein Anspruch, mit dem leidenschaftlichen Ernst für ein solches Unternehmen wie das Niederschreiben einer wissenschaftlichen Arbeit, vor welcher ich tatsächlich schon den ganzen vorangegangenen Winter die größte Angst gehabt habe, alle diese Bücher und Schriften auf das sorgfältigste zu studieren, war mein Vorsatz gewesen und erst darauf, endlich, nach diesem gründlichen, dem Gegenstand angemessenen Studium, genau am siebenundzwanzigsten Jänner um vier Uhr früh diese meine, wie ich glaubte, alles bisher von mir die sogenannte Musikwissenschaft betreffende von mir aufgeschriebene Veröffentlichte sowie Nichtveröffentlichte weit zurück und unter sich lassende, schon seit zehn Jahren geplante, aber immer wieder nicht zustandegekommene Arbeit angehen zu können nach der für den Sechsundzwanzigsten bestimmten Abreise meiner Schwester, deren wochenlange Anwesenheit in Peiskam selbst den geringsten Gedanken an eine Inangriffnahme meiner Arbeit über Mendelssohn Bartholdy in seinen Ansätzen sogleich zunichte gemacht hatte.[3]

In German, the opening sentence consists of 197 words. The English version cuts this breathless overture into three sentences and a total of 237 words:

> From March to December, writes Rudolf, while I was having to take large quantities of prednisolone, a fact which I am bound to record here, against the third acute onset of my sarcoidosis, I assembled every possible book and article written by or about Mendelssohn Bartholdy and visited every possible and impossible library in order to acquaint myself thoroughly with my favorite composers and his work, preparing myself with the most passionate seriousness for the task, which I had been dreading throughout the preceding winter, of writing — such was my pretension — a major work of impeccable scholarship. It had

> been my intention to devote the most careful study to all these books and articles and only then, having studied them with all the thoroughness the subject deserved, to begin writing my work, which I believed would leave far behind it and far beneath it everything else, both published and unpublished, which I had previously written in the field of what is called musicology. I had been planning it for ten years and had repeatedly failed to bring it to fruition, but now I had resolved to begin writing on the twenty-seventh of January at precisely four o'clock in the morning, after the departure of my sister, who was due to leave on the twenty-sixth, and whose presence in Peiskam had for weeks put paid to any thought of my starting work on Mendelssohn Bartholdy.[4]

Through the specific gestures of language, the Austrian-baroque excesses of inspired self-indulgence disappear behind an Anglo-aristocrat's stiff upper lip. But even in this anglicized version, the computer's automatic grammar check mercilessly underlined the entire paragraph in translation. According to its style format, Bernhard remains a foreigner.

What fades in the British version is the performative element of Bernhard's language that is so characteristic even of his prose texts, especially his later ones. Austrian writer Elfriede Jelinek, Bernhard's literary successor as the country's most prominent scourge and author of aggressive, marathon speech acts, once observed that Bernhard's texts read as if he spoke them out loud into the typewriter.[5] He performed himself in the act of writing. The early interjection "writes Rudolph," rather than distancing the speech-act, stages its performance. It suggests that the narrator is watching his subject in the act of writing. This motif is repeated later on in the text when Rudolf, unable to sit down at his desk to write, imagines himself sitting at the desk, writing. In German, the speaker's self-absorbed monologue and furor is sustained over one single sentence that extends for one and a half pages. The broken-up English version takes on a more conversational, rational quality. Actors would find that there is a solid motivation for the opening sentence to be that long. This is a man who has tried for years to write the opening sentence for his study on Mendelssohn Bartholdy. Now that he begins to write, he better not stop.

The novel's English title adds a telling resonance that is absent in the German *Beton*. *Concrete* suggests the process of this particular work. Rudolph sets out to write a theoretical study and ends up writing about a concrete experience: his brief encounter with a desperate young widow in Mallorca who would eventually commit suicide. He finds her buried in the same concrete burial block where her husband was interred after he jumped from the balcony of their hotel room the year before. In German, *Beton* means only one thing: the heaviest building material. Some might say, this is an apt description of the weightiness of Bernhard's language, as evidenced in his interminable sentences.

Bernhard himself is fully aware of the traps and trappings of German syntax. The narrator of his last novel *Extinction* performs a hilarious comedy routine on the problems his overweight native tongue poses to the German writer:

> German words hang like weights on the German language, I had said to Gambetti, and constantly drag the mind down to a level that can only be harmful to it. German thought and German speech soon become paralyzed under the intolerable weight of the language, which suppresses any thought before it can find expression. Under the German language, I said, German thought had developed only with difficulty and never come to full efflorescence, as Romance thought had under the Roman languages — as witness the centuries of effort that the Germans had invested in their thinking. Although I have a higher regard for Spanish than for Italian, because I am more familiar with it, Gambetti that morning illustrated yet again the lightness, effortlessness, and infinite versatility of Italian, which bears the same relation to German as a child reared in complete freedom, in a happy and prosperous home, bears to one who has been cowed and beaten into low cunning in the poorest of poor families. How much more highly then must we rate the achievements of our philosophers and writers? I asked. Every word inexorably drags their thought down, every sentence forces to the ground whatever they venture to think, and thus forces everything to the ground. That's why their philosophy and their writing are so leaden. Using my hands to simulate a balance, the left representing the German scale and the right the Italian, I quoted a sentence from Schopenhauer's The World as Will and Idea, first in German and then in Italian, and showed Gambetti how the German scale sank and the Italian sprang up. For his amusement, as well as my own, I recited a number of sentences from Schopenhauer, first in German and then in an extempore Italian translation, weighing both versions in my hands and making what was first an object lesson into a kind of bizarre game, concluding with some sentences from Hegel and an aphorism from Kant.[6]

It is not clear whether Bernhard includes himself in this problematic tradition or whether, as an Austrian he sets himself apart, as Austrians love to do, with their own, idiosyncratic — and as many pride themselves — superior ways with the German language. The English version moves the Austrian born and bred narrator, a writer, who studied in England and lives in Italy, outside his native language. In his presentation to Gambetti, he can maintain the more discursive mode of the poised professor who is above the problem he articulates. In German, he has to tackle it head on. And Bernhard does it with gusto. His verbal inventions have entered the German vocabulary. His constructions of interminably interlocked clauses and sub-clauses stretch the German language to its limit. Note how Bernhard tears into Goethe, the *Übervater* or superpatriarch of Teutonic *Dichtung:*

> Von Spadolini war ich dann merkwürdigerweise auf Goethe gekommen: auf den Großbürger Goethe, den sich die Deutschen zum Dichterfürsten zugeschnitten und zugeschneidert haben, habe ich das letzte Mal zu Gambetti gesagt, auf den Biedermann Goethe, den Insekten — und Aphorismensammler mit seinem philosophischen **Vogerlsalat**, so ich zu Gambetti, der natürlich das Wort Vogerlsalat nicht verstand, so habe ich es ihm erklärt.[7]

Lost in translation is a chain of associations linked to the German *Vogerlsalat,* which is replaced with the English *mishmash. Vogerlsalat* is a type of lettuce with very small leaves. It looks a bit like watercress. *Vogerl* is the diminutive term for *Vogel:* birdie. *Einen Vogel haben,* literally "to have a bird," means being crazy. The verb *vögeln* translates into "fuck." Heidegger's excessive manipulations of word roots pop up in Bernhard's texts in various etymological stand-up-routines.

And Bernhard keeps working his linguistic *Schrebergarten,* pulling up every bit of its comic possibilities in further elaborations on Goethe:

> **A:** Insgesamt habe ich zu Gambetti gesagt, ist das Goethesche Werk ein philiströser philosophischer Schrebergarten. In nichts hat Goethe das Höchste geleistet, sagte ich, in allem nur das Mittelmaß zustande gebracht. Er ist nicht der größte Lyriker, er ist nicht der größte Prosaschreiber, habe ich zu Gambetti gesagt, und seine Theaterstücke sind gegen die Stücke Shakespeares beispielsweise so gegeneinanderzustellen, wie ein hochgewachsener Schweizer Sennenhund gegen einen verkümmerten Frankfurter Vorstadtdackel. Faust, hatte ich zu Gambetti gesagt, was für ein Größenwahnsinn! Der total mißglückte Versuch eines schreibenden Größenwahnsinnigen, hatte ich zu Gambetti gesagt, dem die ganze Welt in seinen Frankfurter Kopf gestiegen ist. Goethe der größenwahnsinnige Frankfurter und Weimarianer, der größenwahnsinnige Großbürger auf dem Frauenplan. Goethe, **der Kopfverdreher der Deutschen**, der sie jetzt schon hundertfünfzig Jahre auf dem Gewissen hat und zum Narren hält. Goethe ist der Totengräber des deutschen Geistes, habe ich zu Gambetti gesagt.[8]
>
> **B:** Goethe's work as a whole is a philosophical truck farm. Goethe never reached the heights in any sphere, I said. He never rose above

> the mediocre in anything he attempted. He isn't the greatest lyric poet, he isn't the greatest prose writer, and to compare his plays to Shakespeare's is like comparing a stunted dachshund from the Frankfurt suburbs with a tall Pyrenean mountain dog. Take Faust, I said — what megalomania! A totally unsuccessful experiment by a megalomaniac whose ambition went to his head and who imagined that this head could encompass the world. Goethe, the Frankfurter with big ideas who moved to Weimar, the megalomaniac patrician in the world of women. **Goethe, who turned the German heads** and made fools of them and had them on his conscience for a hundred fifty years. Goethe is the gravedigger of the German mind, I told Gambetti.[9]

Here is an absurd case where geography is lost in translation. *Goethe auf dem Frauenplan* simply refers to Goethe's Weimar address (which still exists and can be found on a map of Weimar). Maybe the translator looked for more layers of meaning. *Frauenplan* means something like woman's square ["Plan"= "Platz"] and the address might fortuitously evoke Goethe's relationship to women — something that would not have been lost on Bernhard. This might have misled McLintock to turn *Goethe auf dem Frauenplan* into *Goethe in the world of women*. (Even more misleading than this choice are frequent references in scholarly writings to the title of Bernhard's play *Heldenplatz* as *Hero's Square*. This would be the equivalent to translating New York's Times Square into the German *Zeitplatz*). Goethe, the *Kopfverdreher der Deutschen* turns into *Goethe who turned German heads*. The latter is a much more levelheaded description of something that happened in the past, compared to the still active verb in the noun *Kopfverdreher,* turner of heads, which indicates that Goethe is still messing with the Germans heads, still appealing to their *Schrebergarten* mentality. This again highlights the conscious performativity of Bernhard's understanding and use of language. Iteration here, rereading Goethe through generations, keeps producing Goethe's reality, the German reality of petty bourgeois homeliness.

In the juxtaposed German and English passages, the English *parochialism* substitutes for *Schrebergarten*. A *Schrebergarten* is similar to a victory garden. These gardens are tiny allotments of land that usually line railroad tracks. Later on, the translator uses "truck farmer" for *Schrebergärtner* (one who owns and tends a *Schrebergarten)* which turns Goethe into a muscular peasant with much greater mobility than the meticulous clerk and hobby gardener conveyed by Bernhard's term. Lost is the picture of the pedantically designed, miniscule layout of a *Schrebergarten* that can only accommodate the kind of miniature vegetable evoked by the leaves of a *Vogerlsalat.* Both suggest narrow-mindedness and parochialism, which in English is stated directly rather than through the confluence of two outrageously absurd images. Furthermore, there is an old comedian's adage that certain words evoke immediate laughter on stage. In English those are words with two k's (Hackensack), according to Cole Porter. *Schrebergarten* and *Vogerlsalat* have that sort of auditory effect that is further augmented by the quaintness of their visual associations.

The performativity of this passage also works in purely theatrical terms. Encouraged by Gambetti's laughter, the narrator enjoys his rage more and more. It turns into a virtuoso performance that further inspires inventiveness in the contraction of nouns. The words sound like thunder: *Kopfverdreher*. It is an active word, a theatrical word — a performative word. The loss of the verb in the noun, takes out the most important element in the theatricality that is at the heart of Bernhard's later prose texts. "What's my action" asks the Stanislavsky trained actor. Bernhard's language is active that way. While Murau, the narrator of *Extinction,* speaks of Goethe as the still active *Kopfverdreher* of the Germans, he himself messes with Gambetti's, his pupil's head. Goethe, the man who turned German heads, separates the actor from the activity. On the surface, it is a small sacrifice for the sake of lucidity. But it has an important side effect: It exorcises Heidegger's ghost from Bernhard's verbal inventions. The German language, which allows the transformation of verbs into nouns, enables Heidegger to insist that there is no such thing as a subject other than the sum total of his activities. Language speaks, says Heidegger, borrowing from Novalis.

Take the whimsically Heideggerian title: *Holzfällen,*[10] cutting wood — which in David McLintock's elegant translation turns into *Woodcutters.*[11] There is another translation, by Ewald Osers with the more accurate, if clumsier title *Cutting Timber.*[12] Osers should know. He translated Rüdiger Safranski's biography of Martin Heidegger.[13] To begin with, what is eliminated in the term *woodcutters* is the process of cutting wood, which is essentially the action of the text. Bernhard brandishes words like an axe that chops the pretenses of Austria's aging artists (including himself) like so much brittle kindling wood. And there is, of course, the Heideggerian moment of the actor's epiphany at the conclusion of the infamous artistic dinner in his honor. After much drinking and phony talk about an actor's existence, the state of the arts and the theatre, the actor suddenly speaks of cutting wood deep in the forest:[14]

A: In den Wald gehen, tief in den Wald hinein, . . . ***sich gänzlich dem Wald überlassen,*** das ist es immer gewesen, der Gedanke, nichts anderes, als selbst Natur zu sein. ***Wald, Hochwald, Holzfällen,*** das ist es immer gewesen, sagte er plötzlich aufgebracht und wollte endgültig gehen.

B: ***To go into the forest, deep into the forest*** **. . . to yield oneself up to the forest,** that has always been his ideal — to become part of nature oneself. ***The forest, the virgin forest, the life of a woodcutter*** — that has always been my ideal, he said with sudden excitement, as he made to leave.

C: To walk into the forest, deep into the forest, said the Burgtheater actor, completely surrender to the forest, that's what it had always been, the idea, no more, of being nature oneself. ***Forest, tall forest, cutting timber, that's what it has always been,*** he said suddenly excited and finally tried to leave.

The translators differ on their respective choice for *Hochwald,* a resonant term that does not exist in the English language. It connotes an old forest of tall trees, usually firs that had been groomed for many years by clearing the underbrush. What is implied in the term is an ongoing process of civilization that works in tandem with the cyclical processes of nature. The cutting of timber makes room for new trees. A *Hochwald* ready to be cut down holds the promise of the new. The cut wood or timber is not dead matter. Heidegger, who lurks in this *Hochwald,* would point to the Greek term for wood, *hyle.* It suggests potentiality, the raw material for cultural constructions, for processes rather than (waste) products. Osers, opting for a literal rendering, chops the prefix off the noun. The result is the description of a picture, something static, while *Hochwald* suggests a process as it is also implied in other terms that use *hoch* as a prefix, such as in *hochwachsen* (to grow tall), *hochkommen* (to come up) etc. McLintock's virgin forest introduces an entirely different kind of forest that triggers a chain of associations related to penetration, a return to the womb as a (self-) sacrifice (*yielding oneself up to the forest*) and a staying there (the oddly lifeless *life of a woodcutter* replaces the dynamic of Bernhard's *cutting wood*).

Bernhard's sequence *Wald, Hochwald, Holzfällen* (Osers, literally correct, albeit tone-deaf: *forest, tall forest, cutting timber*) suggests the natural cycle of a forest growing into a tall forest until it is time to cut it down, thus preparing for the growth of a new forest and the creative transformations of the old. Osers, faithful to the original, loses the rhythm and alliterations of Bernhard's cadence that suggest a cyclical movement. McLintock's *forest, virgin forest, the life of a woodcutter* introduces a binary split between nature and man. His elegantly idiomatic term *virgin forest* suggests the standard identification of woman with nature, whereas his woodcutter appears as an intruder. Tellingly, his speaker wants to become *a part* of nature in contrast to Bernhard's actor who wants *to be* nature. (Osers' clumsier rendering "of being nature oneself" comes closer to the point). Woodcutters do not make an appearance in Bernhard's text, which is concerned only with the process of cutting wood. The action serves as a metaphor that, like wood, offers the matter for multiple constructs. The book itself can be considered a product of cutting timber. Cutting down his generation of artists, they yield the stuff for Bernhard's narrative. McLintock's individualized woodcutters remain nevertheless oddly faceless. At best, they yield a generalized, nostalgic representation of a sentimentalized way of life, the cliché image of rural simplicity. No wonder McLintock's speaker considers his notion of becoming a part of nature an *ideal* (a male fantasy one might add) rather than a *Gedanke* or thought (an *idea* in Osers' translation) and as such a philosophical action. It is on that level that he earns the narrator's respect:[15]

A: **Der anfängliche Schwätzer,** der nur durch seine faulen Witze und abgestandenen Anekdoten Eindruck hatte machen wollen zu Beginn, war im Laufe dieses künstlerischen Abendessens auf einmal zur interessanten, ja sogar zur philosophischen Figur dieses künstlerischen Abendessens geworden, dachte ich. . . .	B: **This man, who had at first seemed merely a portentous driveler,** seeking to create an effect with his feeble jokes and stale anecdotes, had in the course of the artistic dinner turned into **a fascinating figure,** even ***a philosophical figure,*** I thought.	C: **The initial prattler,** who had at first wanted to make an impression with his feeble jokes and stale anecdotes, had suddenly, in the course of the artistic dinner become **an interesting, even *a philosophical figure*** of this artistic dinner, I reflected. . . .

True to the cliché arcadia introduced by McLintock's woodcutter fantasy, his narrator appreciates the actor as a *fascinating* figure before he discovers him as a *philosophical* figure. Bernhard's observation, accurately reflected in Osers's translation, is a more rational gradation from interesting to philosophical.

The actor's philosophical moment took the narrator by surprise. He examines it closer:

A: Aber als der Burgschauspieler schon mehr getrunken gehabt hat, als ihm im Grunde zuträglich, war er auf einmal interessant geworden durch seine Veränderung, durch ein plötzlich aus ihm zum Vorschein gekommenes **merkwürdig Altphilosophisches** genau da, wo er angefangen hatte, fortwährend die Wörter **Wald, Hochwald** und **Holzfällen** auszusprechen, die, wie ich jetzt weiß, nicht nur seine, sondern vieler solcher Menschen wie der Burgschauspieler und Millionen Anderer Lebensstichwörter sind; plötzlich ist mir am Ende dieses künstlerischen Abendessens zu Bewußtsein gekommen, was der Burgschauspieler mit diesen seinen Lebensstichwörtern sagen wollte, sich selber immer wieder sagen, den Anderen sagen, ja allen sagen wollte und ich habe angefangen, ihm aufmerksam zuzuhören;[16]

B: But after a few glasses of wine a change had come over this actor from the Burgtheater: all at once he had become an interesting person, **with a philosophical cast of mind** that suddenly revealed itself when he uttered the **words *he forest, the virgin forest, the life of a woodcutter.*** I have since learned that these are catchwords used by many others like him, by millions of others. At the end of the artistic dinner I suddenly became aware of what the actor meant by using these catchwords, what he was trying to say to himself and others, what he was trying to tell all of us, and I began to listen to him attentively.[17]

C: But when the Burgtheater actor had drunk more than would have been basically good for him he had suddenly become interesting through his transformation, through a strange ***old-age philosophical element*** that had suddenly appeared in him just when he began to utter the words **forest, tall forest and cutting timber** continually, words which, as I now realize, are not only his life cues but those of many such people as Burgtheater actors and millions of others; suddenly, at the end of the artistic dinner, I realized what the Burgtheater actor had intended with these life cues of his, intended to say to himself again and again, to say to the others, indeed to everyone, and I began to pay careful attention to what he was saying;[18]

(Bernhard's italics, my emphasis)

Bernhard's *merkwürdig Altphilosophisches* becomes *a philosophical cast of mind* in McLintock without consideration of the prefix "old." Osers's *old-age philosophical element* suggests a geriatric symptom. Indeed, the narrator had been going on about old age and the actor prattling like an old man. But old-age philosophy is not what Bernhard has in mind here. Rather, *Altphilosophisches* (Bernhard's invention, appropriated from the familiar term *Altkatholiken*) suggests arcane philosophy (emphasized by the adjective *merkwürdig* (odd), something that evokes a romantically Teutonic mediaevalism in its forest imagery of darkness and mystical oneness with nature as extolled by Heidegger. Not to worry, Bernhard is not a disciple, but a trickster. *Holzfällen* produces *Holzwege* or timber trails, which is also the title of one of Heidegger's books, a collection of essays and papers. Those timber trails do not just serve as a simile for the paths of thinking, which might stop suddenly without leading anywhere or might, as unexpectedly, lead to a clearing. In popular idiom *auf dem Holzweg sein* means barking up the wrong tree which can be said of all the artistic dinner guests in Bernhard's novel. McLintock's no-nonsense British woodcutters eliminate all that underbrush of meanings.

Note that *Lebensstichwörter* are translated as *catchwords* by McLintock and as *life cues* by Osers. *Stichwort,* cue, in its theatrical sense is the signal for the other to go on — again, this is an existentially very active term: if the actor misses his cue, he drops his line. Without language, on stage, as in Heidegger's *Weltbild,* there is no existence. McLintock's *catchword* is smooth, elegant, without the existential implications of the theatrical term. Osers's term *life cue* is not only clumsy, but it misses the active element of living. It is lifeless in more than one sense.

Bernhard's narrator spent most of his adult life in England. McLintock's translation certainly shows the transformative effect of language. This narrator has adopted the elegant straightforward irony of an Englishman. It sets him apart much more distinctly from the party crowd he observes from his wing chair. Bernhard stages this distance by placing the narrator in the wing chair that faces the sitting room like a stage. Sharing the language of the other guests makes him much more part of the scene, part of the betrayal of their youthful ideas, which he attacks so ferociously. In German, he cannot extricate himself. The translation lets him off the hook as someone who has clearly chosen another path, one that led out of the woods, and that is no longer a *Holzweg,* no longer a self-delusion. On the other hand, he might also be just barking up the wrong tree. In Osers's attempt at a faithful translation, the narrator remains a pedantic grumpy old German professor, who never learned much from his host country. Osers uses "I reflected" for *dachte ich,* whereas McLintock chooses "I thought." The remark is interjected repeatedly throughout the narrative, to bring the attention back to the narrator. What the narrator or Bernhard does not do is reflect, in the sense of "mirroring," of giving back what is seen. Thinking, for Bernhard, is a staging, a generative act of constructing a hyper-reality inside the head, a theatrical experience. The term "reflecting" blocks the motion, whereas McLintock's "I thought," like Bernhard's *dachte ich,* is a more apt rendering of what is at stake: The author as narrator is the playwright, director and audience of his *mise-en-scène* of cutting timber.

There are terms among Bernhard's verbal inventions based on local Austrian idioms that require translation even into straightforward "German" German. *Kronenkraxler* is one of them. Bernhard applies it to the host of the artistic dinner of *Woodcutters.* He is a lowly born aspiring composer who marries a woman boasting aristocratic ancestry, albeit from the lowest ranks of former Austrian nobility. Both have enormous social and artistic aspirations that in Austria traditionally go hand in hand. Literally, these *Kronenkraxler* are people who climb up crowns. McLintock settles for the factual, globally recognizable "social climber." Osers struggles with "coronet climber." But Bernhard's inventions are not as farfetched as they may seem. Quite the contrary, they are as close to home as they can get. Aside from the historic connection to post-Habsburgian social nostalgia, the term *Kronenkraxler* has a geographic foundation. Many mountains in Austria, also in the immediate vicinity of Bernhard's childhood environment, refer to the Emperor, the Kaiser: *Wilder Kaiser* (The Wild Emperor), *Kaiserscharten* (The Emperor's Crevasse). *Hochkönig* (High King) or *Bischofsmütze* (The Bishop's Cap) refer to other high ranking dignitaries in the Imperial hierarchy. The sharp-edged silhouettes of the alpine peaks named after them have the shapes of craggy crowns. So, in the Austrian Alps you find yourself literally climbing up Kaisers and kings and bishops and crowns of rock.

Finally I want to discuss two Bernhardian terms, *Lebensmensch* and *naturgemäß*, the former his own coinage, the latter his revival of an archaic term. Both have become a permanent, prominent part of German vocabulary. They pose a huge problem for the translator. In *Wittgenstein's Nephew,* Bernard talks about the woman in his life, more than thirty years his senior, who inspired the term *Lebensmensch.* It is translated accurately, elegantly, without further circumlocution as *companion.*[19] Lost here, of course, is the inventiveness and the profound resonance of the term, a person, a *Mensch* (with all the connotations the term has in Yiddish) for life, who makes living possible. *Naturgemäß,* according to nature, in the nature of things, was a rarely used term until Bernhard made it popular. It remains an unresolved challenge for translators. They grapple with variations, from "naturally" to "in the nature of things" to leaving it out completely. Bernhard uses it with great precision and ease as shorthand for a philosophical or existential point. It appears most frequently in *Der Stimmenimitator* (translated literally as *The Voice Imitator*).[20] Considering Bernhard's theatrical sensibility, impersonator would have been the more idiomatic choice. The collection offers a series of brief anecdotes and reports in a terse, distanced style that is appropriated from newspaper briefs, court reports and stand up comedian routines. The translator, Kenneth Northcott uses "in the nature of things" throughout. As the term appears in most of the 104 anecdotes, it draws attention to itself as a linguistic tic, a heavy drumbeat, grammatically often awkwardly out of place. Bernhard's *naturgemäß* (one word against five!) is slipped into the sentence almost surreptitiously, where it lurks both as a question and assertion and puts the stylist's ironic spin on our understanding and usage of the terms "nature" and "naturally."

The point here is neither to bemoan what is lost in translation nor to contribute once again to the argument about a translator's fidelity or freedom toward the original text and the preference of one over the other. What is of particular interest in Bernhard's performative prose texts, which are so driven by the temperament of one archetypal character, is how language transforms his narrators. All of them painfully experience themselves as strangers in their country. That sense of alienation takes on a different meaning in translation. On the one hand, the language that is foreign to the Austrian born and bred narrator reinforces his cultural estrangement. On the other hand, as in the English translations of *Woodcutters,* the narrator who has spent many years in England now speaks the language of the culture of his choice. Unlike the original, the translation shows the "British part" of him in action. Both English versions of *Woodcutters,* through the performative force of language, stage the radical act of his distancing himself from his native culture and suggest the degrees of difficulty involved. McLintock's translation brings out the savvy cosmopolitan. Anchored in his irony and driven by his rage, he is at home everywhere and nowhere. Osers's narrator, it appears, never really has found his place abroad. His English gives him away. He sticks to his continental syntax as stubbornly as to his obsessive reiterations of past betrayals. While McLintock's translation suggests Bernhard's mastery of style, Osers might come closer to his character. Read in tandem with the original they bring out what an actor would call the subtext, the attempted identification with British culture as a way out of the Austrian alienation.

In conclusion, let me quote Bernhard's take on translators (in my own translation) from his play *Der Weltverbesserer,* which has not yet been translated into English. The problem begins, once again, with the title. Literally world-improver, utopian comes to mind as a more idiomatic alternative. Lost in the latter is the stubborn insistence that's hammered in by the sound of the German compound noun, which gives some clues to the character himself. Bernhard offers little comfort:

Einem Übersetzer kann nicht geholfen werden
Der Übersetzer muß seinen Weg allein gehen
Sie haben meinen Traktat entstellt
Total entstellt
Die Übersetzer entstellen die Originale
Das Übersetzte kommt immer nur als Verunstaltung auf den Markt
Es ist der Dilettantismus
Und der Schmutz des Übersetzers
Der eine Übersetzung so widerwärtig macht
Das Übersetzte ist immer ekelerregend
Aber es hat mir eine Menge Geld eingebracht.[21]

A translator can't be helped
A translator has to go his way alone
They distorted my treatise
Completely distorted it
Translators distort the originals
Translations always hit the market as distortions
It's the dilettantism
And the dirt of the translator
That makes a translation so repulsive
Translations are always disgusting
But they brought me a lot of money.

Photo courtesy of Erika Schmied

Notes

[1] Thomas Bernhard, *Gargoyles,* trans. Richard and Clara Winston (Chicago: U of Chicago P, 1986), 104.

[2] See photo illustrations (1) at the beginning of this essay, and (2) above. These photos have been reprinted with the kind permission of Erika Schmied.

[3] Thomas Bernhard, *Beton* (Frankfurt: Suhrkamp, 1982), 7.

[4] Thomas Bernhard, *Concrete,* trans. David McLintock (Chicago: U of Chicago P, 1986), 1.

[5] Personal conversation with author, Vienna, December 1994.

[6] Thomas Bernhard, *Extinction,* trans. David McLintock (New York: Alfred A. Knopf, 1995), 4.

[7] Emphasis mine. Inspired by Bernhard's example of Schopenhauer, I tried to visualize the weight of his sentences in German and in English. The English version consists of 65 words against 60 in German. However, the character count in German is up to 361 against 324 in English, which would prove Murau/Bernhard's claim correct. German words consist of more characters and are therefore heavier.

[8] Thomas Bernhard, *Auslöschung* (Frankfurt: Suhrkamp, 1986), 576–77.

[9] *Extinction,* 290–91. The German predilection for compound nouns allows the term *Lebensopportunist* whose English counterpart breaks down into the four-word phrase "man on the move." The outrageous *Gesteinsnumerierer* translates into a dry, three-word explanation: *classifier of stones. Seelenmarmelade* disintegrates into spiritual jam and *Haushaltsgläser* turn into household canning jars.

[10] Thomas Bernhard, *Holzfällen* (Frankfurt: Suhrkamp, 1984).

[11] Thomas Bernhard, *Woodcutters,* trans. David McClintock (New York: Alfred A. Knopf, 1987).

[12] Thomas Bernhard, *Cutting Timber. An Irritation,* trans. Ewald Osers (London, New York: Quartet Books, 1988).

[13] Rüdiger Safranski, *Martin Heidegger: Between Good and Evil,* trans. Ewald Osers (Cambridge, MA: Harvard UP, 1998).

[14] A: *Holzfällen,* 302; B: *Woodcutters,* 169; C: *Cutting Timber,* 138–39. Bernhard's italics, my emphasis.

[15] A: *Holzfällen,* 305; B: *Woodcutters,* 172; C: *Cutting Timber,* 140. Bernhard's italics, my emphasis.

[16] *Holzfällen,* 305.

[17] *Woodcutters,* 171.

[18] *Cutting Timber,* 139–40.

[19] Thomas Bernhard, *Wittgensteins Neffe* (Frankfurt: Suhrkamp, 1982). Thomas Bernhard, *Wittgenstein's Nephew,* trans. David McLintock (New York: Alfred A. Knopf, 1989).

[20] Thomas Bernhard, *Der Stimmenimitator* (Frankfurt: Suhrkamp, 1978). Thomas Bernhard, *The Voice Imitator,* trans. Kenneth J. Norton (Chicago and London: U of Chicago P, 1997).

[21] Thomas Bernhard, *Der Weltverbesserer* (Frankfurt: Suhrkamp 1979), 28.

Jonathan Long

Ungleichzeitigkeiten: Class Relationships in Bernhard's Fiction

IN RECENT DECADES, LITERARY CRITICISM has become increasingly preoccupied with questions of ideology. Critics have devoted attention to the politics of narrative texts in order to show that questions of class conflict are always present in novels, even if the texts themselves attempt to contain or conceal them. This is no less true of Thomas Bernhard than of any other writer. We shall see in the course of this essay that devices such as character configurations and structures of focalization serve to encourage identification with representatives of the upper echelons of postwar Austrian society. At the same time, however, other elements of the texts can be seen to call these class hierarchies into question. This happens in two distinct ways according to the class status of the main character in the novel concerned. In section one, I analyze three novels whose protagonists and/or narrators are descendants of the Habsburg aristocracy and continue to live, stripped of their titles, in the Austria of the postwar period: *Verstörung* (1967), *Korrektur* (1975) and *Auslöschung* (1986). In section two, I turn my attention to two texts whose main characters are members of Austria's *Großbürgertum* (grand bourgeoisie): *Beton* (1981) and *Der Untergeher* (1983). The thematic and structural differences between these two groups of texts entail distinct critical approaches. Section one is concerned primarily with the means by which class oppositions exceed the binary terms within which they are ostensibly constituted, while section two analyzes the means by which the explicit class hierarchies and value systems of the texts are implicitly called into question.

A preliminary general point that needs to be made is that Bernhard's novels are set in a world that is barely recognizable as that of the late twentieth century. With few exceptions his characters either walk from one place to another, or they take the train, the dominant symbol of industrialization and modernity in the culture of the nineteenth century rather than the twentieth.[1] Other modes of transport may be mentioned, but journeys by, for example, car or airplane are seldom actually represented. In the rare instances where motor vehicles are mentioned, they are frequently agents of destruction (*Ja, Auslöschung*).

In addition, long-distance communication takes place not by telephone, but by mail or wire.

There is also virtually no representation of the urban environment in Bernhard's novels. While several of them do have a specifically Viennese setting, the city is reduced to a limited number of internal spaces: Irina's *Blumenstockgassewohnung* (apartment in Blumenstockgasse) and a series of cafés in *Wittgensteins Neffe,* the Auersbergers' flat in *Holzfällen,* the Kunsthistorisches Museum (art history museum) in *Alte Meister.* The one major exception to this is an episode from *Frost* in which the narrator recalls his lunchtime strolls between lectures in Vienna.[2] However, solely the middle classes sauntering at their leisure through the shopping streets people the city here. Although the narrator is invaded by a sense of profound loneliness in the crowd, this kind of urban experience is another topos of late nineteenth-century literature, the paradigmatic example being Baudelaire's *flaneur.* It appears decidedly out of date in comparison with the more radically anomic experience of the city in the novels of Kafka, Döblin, Kubin, and others. This has important consequences for the representation of class relationships. Most importantly, it precludes portrayal of the urban proletariat. As Norbert Langer has pointed out in a discussion of "Auslöschung im Kontext der österreichischen Schloßromane nach 1945": "die moderne, industrialisierte Welt [gerät] aus dem Blickfeld . . . . Sie paßt nicht ins Österreichbild, wie es die von bürgerlichen Autoren für ein bürgerliches Publikum geschriebenen Schloßromane vermitteln."[3] The rural setting of Bernhard's texts entails a concentration on the upper echelons of the bourgeoisie and the aristocracy, and on members of the *Kleinbürgertum* or petty bourgeoisie. The relationships that Bernhard's texts construct between these antithetical groups form the central subject of this article.

Anachronistic Aristocrats

The main characters in the three novels *Verstörung, Korrektur* and *Auslöschung* are the descendants of aristocratic families of the defunct Habsburg monarchy. In *Verstörung,* most of the text consists of the monologue of a former Habsburg Prince. The narrator himself is reduced to a mere agency of quotation whose presence is signaled by a small number of brief interventions and the fact that he reports much of Saurau's speech in the subjunctive. *Korrektur* is likewise based on the technique of quotation. In the first half of the text, the narrator tells the story of his relationship with the recently deceased Roithamer, a relationship that is characterized in terms of fascination. In the second half of the text, he quotes extensively from Roithamer's posthumous papers that he has been given the task of editing. The notable fact about the narrators of both *Verstörung* and *Korrektur* is their failure or inability to comment on the words they quote. In terms of narrative technique, this failure has the effect of aligning the narrator's perspective with that of the protagonist in a tacit gesture of collusion. This collusion in turn also encourages the reader to accept the perspective of the quoted character as authoritative.

Auslöschung, on the other hand, falls into the category of what Willi Huntemann has termed "'authentische' Selbstdarstellung."[4] Rather than quoting another character's words, Franz-Josef Murau, the narrator of *Auslöschung*, provides a narrative of his own life. As with most first-person texts, the alignment of central figure and narrator impels the reader to see the world from the narrator's point of view, and, in principle at least, accept his judgments. *Auslöschung* is admittedly more complicated because Murau is a self-critical narrator who frequently draws attention to the unreliability of his judgments and the inevitable perspectivism of any representation.[5] This feature, however, can also be seen as a neutralizing device whose function is to restrict and curtail the scope of the reader's criticism. This critique is a premeditated function of Murau's discourse, and so even in dissent the reader is in fact acquiescing.

The structures of quotation and focalization in these texts establish a clear class hierarchy, for the reader is encouraged to see the represented world through the eyes of aristocrats, identifying with their interests and accepting their interpretations of the world. In addition, the texts mobilize other strategies for containing and neutralizing the potential for class conflict. The narrator of *Verstörung* is the son of a country doctor who accompanies his father on his rounds one late-September Saturday.[6] The text is divided into two long sections. The first, untitled, narrates a series of visits to patients who are all more or less chronically, if not terminally, ill. The second section, which accounts for roughly two thirds of the novel, takes place at the castle Schloß Hochgobernitz and is entitled "Der Fürst." The eponymous prince bears the name Saurau, and the second section consists primarily of a transcription of his extended monologue. The first section of *Verstörung* sees the narrator and the doctor driving steadily further into a ravine, whereas in the second section they climb up to the lofty Hochgobernitz with its panoramic views.

Critics are largely in agreement about the meaning of spatial relationships in *Verstörung*. In terms of pathology, they represent a shift from physical to mental disease. Historically speaking, the topography of the text symbolizes the contrast between the Second Republic and the Habsburg Monarchy. The opposition between the bourgeoisie or proletariat, and the feudal aristocracy informs the text's political dimension.[7] Spatial relationships thus tend to be interpreted allegorically, as does the figure of Saurau himself. He has often been diagnosed by critics as schizophrenic,[8] and Hermann Helms-Derfert reads this as a metaphor for postwar Austria and its problematic relationship to the past: "Überspitzt formuliert, bildet der Wahnsinn des Fürsten das biographische Korrelat zur 'Schizophrenie' der Zweiten Republik, wo — in der Metaphorik des Romans gesprochen — kleinbürgerlicher Geschäftssinn Leichenschändung am toten Erbe der Geschichte treibt."[9] In a similar vein, Josef König sees him as embodying the decline of feudal "Altösterreich" and the "Identitätskrise der Tradition."[10]

While the studies by König and Helms-Derfert elevate the question of history to a central position, they appear themselves to be in one sense unhistorical, for they do not consider why an aristocrat can still function as an allegory of Austria in 1967, or why a representative of *Altösterreich* is the central figure of a text produced almost half a century after the Austrian aristocracy had been officially abolished. To read Saurau as an allegory of the Second Austrian Republic leaves one fundamental question unanswered: how is it that a Prince, a member of the landed classes, can retain an ideological hold over Austrian society long after the material power of those classes had evaporated? By 1918 at the latest, after all, the conditions on which the power of the landed interests was based — the dominance of agriculture, the link between personal wealth and the land, the favorable structure of politics — had ceased to exist.

The answer is to be sought in the political character of postwar Austria.[11] This political landscape was long dominated by the Social Partnership and the "Paritätische Kommission für Lohn und Preisfragen," a commission regulating wage and price disputes. The latter entails the cooperation of the state, industry, and the unions, and led to high and sustainable growth in the early decades of the Second Republic. One of its effects was to transform class struggle into bureaucracy. Class conflict was neutralized and sublimated into negotiation between interest groups. Robert Menasse terms this "Klassenkampf am grünen Tisch." He goes on to argue that the Social Partnership removes power-relations from public control, which means that they cannot be changed by democratic initiative. No matter which government is in power, the decision-making process remains the same. Furthermore, it favors economic growth over the redistribution of wealth, and the latter disappears from public discussion.[12] Menasse's analysis of the Social Partnership culminates in the striking paradox that Austria is a country of low economic power, but possesses the world's most highly-developed form of social organization: "enormes Wirtschaftswachstum, niedrigste Lohnabschlüsse und erstaunlicherweise gerade deshalb sozialer Friede. Tatsächlich: welche kapitalistische Organisationsform hat sich jemals besser bewährt?"[13]

The phenomenon to which Menasse alludes here is best described by the term *Ungleichzeitigkeit*. The concept of *Ungleichzeitigkeit* was first elaborated by Ernst Bloch in his 1935 book *Erbschaft dieser Zeit*. Both Bloch and subsequent Marxist critics such as Andreas Huyssen or Fredric Jameson tend to apply the term to two related but distinct phenomena. The first is the simultaneous existence within a society of archaic and ultra-modern modes of production: in Bloch's time, peasant farming alongside manufacturing giants such as Krupp or Siemens, and in our own day, cottage industry alongside the great multinationals. The second is the discrepancy between the "base" and "superstructure" of classic Marxism. "Superstructure" here may consist of modes of consciousness or cultural production that are perceived to be *ungleichzeitig* or non-synchronous with economic development.[14]

The second type of *Ungleichzeitigkeit* is clearly more important for a consideration of Bernhard's work. Firstly, Menasse sees Austria's economy as lagging behind its exceptionally advanced organizational system. Secondly, there is a non-synchronous relationship between Austria's capitalist democracy and the status of Austrian culture. Cultural politics in the early years of the Second Republic were motivated by a largely restorative impulse, and tended to institutionalize the idea of Austria as a museum caring for the treasures of the Habsburg past.[15] Thus considerable value accrued to the cultural products of the Habsburg era, even though the economic and political conditions supporting that cultural value no longer obtained.

The reason for Saurau's central role in *Verstörung*, then, is not merely that he personifies the cultural past of which postwar Austria was the proud guardian; it is also the fact that he represents the non-convergence of cultural hegemony and political power. His schizophrenia in fact signifies the incongruity between cultural significance and the real structures of power.[16] Saurau's numerous denunciations of the Austrian state take a form that appears to reflect a specifically aristocratic and feudal consciousness. The state is a ridiculous "pseudodemocracy" which fails to act to prevent agricultural disaster. Saurau ends up making the same point as Menasse concerning Austria's backwardness: "In Österreich . . . ist allerdings alles von einer perversen Rückständigkeit. Zweihundert Jahre auf fast allen Gebieten zurück" and goes on to accuse the state of ruining everything (V, 98, 100–101). At the same time, the people, the "masses," come in for particular criticism: "das Volk ist blöd und stinkt" (V, 97). These criticisms appear to be unmotivated until we read them in conjunction with certain of Saurau's other comments. At one point he accuses the state of senseless expropriation: "Um und um wird enteignet, sage ich, überall unter mir wird enteignet, aus den fadenscheinigsten Gründen. Sie Politiker enteignen hin und her. Hin und her wird enteignet" (V, 97). The passives and objectless constructions in this speech ostensibly obscure the fact that it is Saurau himself who fears expropriation. When he later exclaims, "Die Masse interessiert niemanden mehr, weil die Masse schon an der Macht ist" (V, 171), it becomes explicit that the reasons for his earlier criticisms of the state are based on economic self-interest.

In order to detract from this fact, however, his antagonism toward the state is transferred to a personal aversion or animosity toward the Gemeindesekretär Moser. During his lengthy monologue, Saurau refers in great detail to a dream whose subject is a letter written by his son shortly after his, Saurau's, projected suicide. The letter unveils the son's desire to liquidate the entire Hochgobernitz estate and to leave everything at the mercy of nature. But there is no textual evidence to suggest that the son does indeed harbor such desires. The destructiveness implied by the dream is attributable solely to Saurau himself. During the dream, Moser walks up to Schloß Hochgobernitz in order to persuade Saurau's son to allow the local inhabitants to harvest the year's agricultural produce before it rots in the ground. Moser is acting in the interests of the *Gemeinde,* interceding on their behalf in order to secure six months' worth of food supplies for several thousand people. Saurau's son, however, refuses.

While the son claims to see Moser as a representative of the state, the failings he enumerates are of a purely personal nature. He obfuscates the fact that he is withholding food from those who need it by describing Moser in terms of "Gemeinheit und Niederträchtigkeit." He writes of Moser's "Geistesverfassung, in welcher sich das ganze Böse seiner auf das Abscheuniveau heruntergezogenen Kategorien zu einem einzigen ununterbrochenen gemeingefährlichen zu vereinigen schien" and terms him a "Gewohnheitsverbrecher" (V, 120). The son thus imputes to Moser criminal inclinations, and this accusation recurs. Moser's gait and general demeanor resemble that of imprisoned convicts and he is always on the lookout for others whom he can drag into criminal activity. Not only is Moser castigated in purely personal terms. As a Gemeindesekretär, he is merely a functionary and hence a basically powerless figure. The tirades that Saurau levels at Moser via his absent son represent the aggression of a disempowered class, the aristocracy, toward the petty bourgeoisie. This agonistic character configuration, however, produces an apparent power gap at the heart of the text, as Saurau fails to touch on the genuine locus of power, the interests of capital. It is here that *Ungleichzeitigkeit* manifests itself once again. The text constitutes class conflict as an opposition between the aristocracy and the petty bourgeoisie, while repressing the real structures of economic and political hegemony. This repressed conflict can be seen as corresponding to the structures of power within Social Partnership, one of whose effects is to preclude confrontation in the public sphere. Because all decisions are made by consensus behind closed doors, power relations are obscured, disarming genuine opposition. Nevertheless, Saurau's denunciation of Moser raises the question why he so vehemently defends his own interests, conceived largely in cultural terms, against social forces that appear powerless to challenge them.

A basic contradiction within Saurau himself suggests an answer to this question. In a further example of *Ungleichzeitigkeit,* Saurau's attitudes toward the feudal order of the Habsburg era and the capitalist democracy of the Second Austrian Republic are far from being consistent. Indeed, a profound rift characterizes them. Saurau's status as a feudal relic within a capitalist society can be seen in his attitude toward tradition. Hochgobernitz, we learn, once flourished as a center for the arts as actors, magicians, musicians, writers and philosophers converged there. Now, however, tradition has become "eine perfekt gespielte, aber doch unerträgliche Komödie, die, weil sie so unverständlich ist, unser Gelächter einfrieren läßt" (V, 177). The lament for a tradition that continues even though those who perpetuate it are aware of its redundancy, is augmented by Saurau's bewailing the disintegration of the relationship between masters and men that obtained under the Habsburgs. "Das harmonische Herr-Knecht-Verhältnis," as Norbert Langer writes, "ist ein traditioneller Bestandteil der Österreichideologie."[17] It manifests itself in *Verstörung* in the figure of old Saurau who decides to liquidate the estate but changes his mind when he thinks of all the workers who depend on him for their livelihood. Similarly, the Krainer family are characterized not as working for Saurau, but as "brav" and "dem Saurau ihr ganzes leben lang dienend" (V, 70). These passages conjure up a nostalgic image of loyal underlings happily serving their benevolent master. Moser is vilified precisely because he does not conform to this anachronistic arrangement of social relations.

Saurau's position as a representative of the old order, however, exists side by side with the ideology of private enterprise. He states, "das ist kein Staatsbetrieb, das ist ein Privatunternehmen" (V, 91), thereby emphasizing that the entrepreneurial spirit that governs Hochgobernitz is of capitalist provenance. He has fulfilled his aim of doubling the extent of his property according to the capitalist ideology of economic growth and the accumulation of wealth, contrary to European and global political trends: "der ganzen politischen Entwicklung in Europa, der ganzen Welt entgegen"(V, 118). It is clear, however, that while he claims to have asserted himself against history, his expansion has mobilized precisely the economic and ideological forces that he claims to despise. In addition, the expansion is brought about through radical simplification of the estate's administrative system, thus being an example of the instrumental rationality that has been one of Marxism's perpetual targets in its critique of capitalism. It is significant that of the three forest managers Saurau interviews on the day of the visit by the doctor, the one he employs, Henzig, is preferred because of his "moderne Arroganz und Wissenschaftlichkeit" (V, 98).[18]

The same contradiction emerges when Saurau states: "Die Modernität in einem Gehirn erfrischt mich, die innere Modernität," sagte er, "die äußere stößt mich ab" (V, 147). The revulsion at outward modernity manifests itself in the numerous tirades against the economic and political organization of modern Austria. Inner modernity, on the other hand, emerges in the mechanistic or industrial metaphors Saurau uses for the human mind such as "Geistesmechanik," "Gehirnmechanismus," and the description of the brain as a "Kraftwerk" (V, 102, 146, 143). As Hans Höller has pointed out, however, the notion of man as machine is a component of Marx's critique of labor under capitalism, according to which "nicht der Arbeiter die Arbeitsbedingungen, sondern umgekehrt die Arbeitsbedingungen den Arbeiter anwenden."[19] Saurau's apostrophizing inner modernity merely clarifies the extent to which he has internalized the tenets of the economic order against which he vituperates. *Ungleichzeitigkeiten* or incongruities in *Verstörung,* then, are manifested in Saurau's own contradictory situation. On the one hand, he is a representative of cultural values that still obtain even though they seem to have lost their meaning. On the other hand, he has internalized precisely those historical and economic developments that he claims to despise but from which he has profited considerably. While Saurau appears to be defending a cultural dominance whose provenance is aristocratic, he is actually defending the economic interests of capital. It is for this reason that the narrator aligns himself with Saurau's point of view. As a student of mining science, he is himself destined for a managerial role within enterprise. Ultimately, his interests and those of the Prince coincide.

Korrektur narrates the story of Roithamer, a member of the landed classes and of aristocratic lineage, who has long left Austria to pursue an academic career in Cambridge. Despite being his father's second son, he is bequeathed the family estate of Altensam. The title of the novel is drawn from Roithamer's manuscript "Über Altensam und alles was damit zusammenhängt unter besonderer Berücksichtigung des Kegels." Roithamer's repeated corrections reduce the initial 800 pages of the treatise to 300, then to only 80, before he undertakes the ultimate correction by committing suicide. Before doing so, however, he plans and constructs, over a period of six years, a vast conical dwelling for his sister. It is intended to correspond precisely to her nature and bring about her "höchstes Glück," but she dies soon after its completion without ever having lived in it.

A note is discovered on Roithamer's corpse stating that the narrator is to be charged with editing his *Nachlaß* or literary estate. The first chapter of *Korrektur* tells of the narrator's preparation for his editorial task, and the second consists of a fragmentary collage put together from Roithamer's posthumous papers in random order. Whereas the protagonist of *Korrektur,* Roithamer, is an aristocrat, the narrator himself is once again the son of a country doctor and hence a member of the bourgeoisie. Their childhood friend Höller is, like his father before him, a taxidermist, a craftsman who belongs to the petty bourgeoisie. This triple constellation is of fundamental importance to an examination of class relationships within this text.

It becomes apparent in both theme and structure of *Korrektur* that the narrator identifies with Roithamer. There are also numerous passages that make clear the parallelism between Roithamer's life and that of the narrator. He re-lives Roithamer's initial visit to Höller's attic as it had been described to the narrator several years before. When the latter descends to dine with the Höller family, he fills in the role of an ersatz Roithamer, occupying a position which became vacant upon the latter's death. Frau Höller bangs on the dining room ceiling to summon the narrator, just as she had done with Roithamer:

> ich dachte, die Höller verhalten sich mir gegenüber wahrscheinlich jetzt so wie sie sich Roithamer gegenüber verhalten haben, in dem Augenblick, in welchem ich die höllersche Dachkammer bezogen hatte, war ich in dem Mechanismus ihres Verhaltens gegenüber Roithamer eingeschlossen gewesen, wahrscheinlich ist jeder . . ., der nach Roithamer die höllersche Dachkammer bewohnt, in dem Verhaltensmechanismus eingeschlossen, der in Gang gewesen war, wie Roithamer in der höllerschen Dachkammer gelebt hat.[20]

More significant than this, however, is the fact that the narrator is saturated in Roithamer's system of thought. The narrator refers to "Gefangenschaft, wenn nicht Kerkerhaft des roithamerschen Gedankengefängnisses" (K, 38) and claims to have entered a room in which it is impossible not to think like Roithamer. At the level of lexis, too, the narrator weaves into his own speech verbal formulations that originate in Roithamer's *Nachlaß*. One consequence of this is a convergence of the narrator's attitudes with those of Roithamer, and this includes attitudes to class.

As in *Verstörung*, class conflict emerges in interpersonal relationships. In *Korrektur*, the aristocracy-petty bourgeoisie dichotomy again forms the terms within which that conflict is played out, but the representative of the petty bourgeoisie in this case is Roithamer's mother, a butcher's daughter from Eferdingen. She is described in exceptionally negative terms, being prematurely old and a master of emotional blackmail. She is suspicious of everyone and superficial in both her own existence and in her love of culture (K, 248–56, 265, 292–93). Everything negative about Altensam is ascribed to the influence of Roithamer's mother. Höller's wife, on the other hand, represents the antithesis of "die Eferdingerin." She possesses, as Helms-Derfert points out, "alle Eigenschaften, die eine von der Kirche abgesegnete, patriarchal-repressive Gesellschaft an Mutter und Gattin stellt: Gehorsam, Familiensinn, Häuslichkeit und aufopfernde Hingabe werden unverblümt als weibliche Tugenden gepriesen."[21] The idealization of Frau Höller as a perfect, submissive wife and mother finds its correlative in the idealization of the agricultural laborers with whom Roithamer converses during the music festival in Stocket on his twenty-third birthday.[22] Roithamer and the narrator initially turn up as objects of curiosity and the locals bombard them with questions about their lives in England. Later, they stay up into the early hours in the company of farmers and miners they knew in their childhood. Roithamer is described as a master of the storytelling style of the local farmers, the "Bauernburschen," and familiar with their whole way of life, offering a further example of the harmonious relationship between masters and men that continues to characterize the Austria ideology within the Social Partnership (K, 74–75).

Once again, critics have tended to read class relationships in *Korrektur* as compressed historical allegory. Josef König suggests that Roithamer's father's first marriage to a lawyer's daughter is a representation of the Austrian aristocracy's "Verbindung mit der Verwaltungs- und Jurisprudenzschicht" toward the end of the Habsburg monarchy, and the fact that the union resulted in a miscarriage is highly significant. Helms-Derfert argues that Altensam sees itself as a "komprimiertes, bisweilen verzerrtes Spiegelbild der österreichischen Geschichte."[23]

It is once again clear, however, that these readings fail to address the problem of *Ungleichzeitigkeit* raised by *Korrektur.*

Altensam clearly symbolizes Habsburg culture that relies exclusively on the external trappings of wealth for its representative function, having lost the link with power politics that initially legitimized that function. Roithamer's father devotes his life to the management of his forests and agricultural land, and indulges his passion for hunting, while neglecting his family. When a member of the petty bourgeoisie invades this existence, the invasion likewise takes place at the level of representation. Because Roithamer's father himself possesses no genuine power, the "Eferdingerin" cannot usurp it. She merely adopts the lifestyle of the aristocracy in an attempt to gain legitimacy for herself. Once again, however, the text leaves the real power relations in postwar Austria untouched.

Helms-Derfert is right to characterize *Korrektur* as an attempted restoration of Habsburg power, but whereas he attributes this restoration to Roithamer and his cone-building project, it is clear that it dominates the ideology of the text at a much more profound level. Class mobility, such as that attempted by Roithamer's mother, is damned as deleterious not in a specifically economic sense, but in terms of cultural values. Class conflict can be resolved at the level of personal relationships, provided that the behavior of individuals is correct. In this manner class relationships remain stable, hence the idealized representations of the Höllers' petty bourgeois marriage, and of the local farm hands and miners. By representing the basic class dichotomy as existing between the petty bourgeoisie (and, to a limited extent, the working classes) and the aristocracy, however, the narrator represses the interests of capital from his account. The real locus of economic power in *Korrektur* remains elsewhere, intact.

The ideology of *Korrektur* unites both gender and class assumptions in its implication that women and the lower classes should remain in their pre-ordained position of inferiority and powerlessness. But the construction of class positions in terms of values that derive from the Habsburg ideology ultimately do not serve the scions of the defunct aristocracy: both Roithamer and his father die, thereby signaling the end of the family line. Rather, by replacing class conflict by an antagonism between the aristocracy and the petty bourgeoisie, the narrator, a representative of the genuine bourgeoisie, can leave his own socioeconomic position utterly unchallenged.

Like Roithamer in *Korrektur,* the narrator of *Auslöschung,* Franz-Josef Murau, unexpectedly becomes the heir of an extensive ancestral property, Wolfsegg, when a wire arrives at his home in Rome to inform him of the death of his parents and his elder brother Johannes in a car accident. The text of *Auslöschung* is Murau's monumental attempt to come to terms with the past that Wolfsegg represents, and to dispose of the estate on which he has definitively turned his back. In terms of class, *Auslöschung* can be seen as uniting the thematic concerns of both the novels discussed above. Again, class relationships in *Auslöschung* are intimately tied up with questions of gender. Murau justifies his own patriarchal and aristocratic attitude by casting his mother, a representative of the petty bourgeoisie, in the role of the outsider. She is analogous to the mother in *Korrektur,* a petty-bourgeois upstart whom Murau's father married hastily for the sole purpose of producing an heir. The terms in which she is portrayed are already familiar: the daughter of a greengrocery wholesaler, she is sexually rapacious, as manifested in her barely concealed affair with Spadolini, and she is a cruel mother who unjustly punishes Murau and treats her daughters like puppets. As in the earlier texts, however, class interests are partially disguised in terms of personal qualities. Murau's mother is described as "Die treibende Kraft des Bösen" who turns everyone into "böse Menschen" (A, 298–99). Class antagonism becomes thereby a question of personal aversion, as Murau's mother's social position is partially transposed into the metaphysical issue of evil.

Auslöschung also portrays the duality between an aristocratic self-perception and capitalist modes of production. Rather than existing within the same schizophrenic character, however, the duality manifests itself in the contrast between Murau and his father and brother. Murau represents aristocratic values in *Auslöschung.* He works as a teacher of German literature in Rome, but he is not dependent on this work for his living. Indeed, he has only one pupil, Gambetti, and he charges Gambetti's parents exorbitant fees even though he does not need the money. The main duality established by Murau is that between *Geist* (spirit) and *Verstand* (rational intellect), the former being divorced from practical concerns and the latter representing the instrumental reason that is a common target of Marxist critiques of capitalism. Like the protagonists of *Verstörung* and *Korrektur,* Murau yearns for a return to an earlier age, but in his case it is less nostalgia for harmonious master-servant relations than for the former relationship between wealth and culture that emerges in the course of his historical account of Wolfsegg. In one of his many conversations with Gambetti, Murau mentions that the original builders and inhabitants of Wolfsegg had established five libraries, had a "natürliches Bedürfnis nach Geist and Denken," and had elevated "Denken" (as opposed to instrumental "Verstand") to a central position in their lives (A, 263). The narrative of historical development as implied by *Auslöschung* and systematized by Andreas Gößling is one of decline. The two main caesurae separating *Geist* from *Verstand* are the industrial revolution and the Nazi period.[24]

At the end of this phase of decline stands Murau's father, a clear example of *Verstand*.[25] He is motivated by profit, always wanted to be nothing but a farmer, and even writes like "ein Handelsgehilfe [. . .] aber nicht [wie] der Herr von Wolfsegg" (A, 522). Furthermore, he has no interest in culture, valuing art solely in terms of its exchange value, the degree to which it can be converted into money. His life exhausts itself in a daily routine of tractor driving and writing business letters among the numberless files that encumber his office, a striking symbol of administrative rationality. "Eine so ungeheure Natur," writes Murau, "und ein tatsächlich so ungeheurer Besitz, und der Vater hat eine solche erbärmliche Schreibtischexistenz geführt" (A, 605). Whereas in the earlier texts the incommensurability of capitalist modes of production and an aristocratic demeanor is largely contained, the conflict between the two becomes utterly intractable in *Auslöschung* because the main protagonist attempts to cultivate a lifestyle with absolute disregard for the accumulated wealth on which its values depend. The fact that he finally donates the entire estate of Wolfsegg to the Israelitische Kultusgemeinde (Viennese Jewish Community) can be seen as an attempt to make good his own parents' implication in the injustices of National Socialism. Structurally speaking, however, it offers a formal solution to the conflict between aristocratic cultural values and capitalist economy not by reconciling the two but by annihilating the problem altogether. The title *Auslöschung*, to which much critical attention has been paid,[26] thereby reveals yet one more aspect of its polysemy. Giving away Wolfsegg resolves the problem of *Ungleichzeitigkeit* by negating it.

The Bourgeoisie and Its Other

Alongside the texts with aristocratic protagonists, Bernhard also returned time and time again to the problems faced by intellectuals of independent means who devote their lives to artistic or scholarly projects. In the main, economic questions are excluded from these texts and the narrative interest is concentrated on the existential and epistemological issues which the main characters face. *Das Kalkwerk*, *Ja*, and *Die Billigesser* all circle around this thematic nexus. Only in the first of these three does money play a significant role. In *Das Kalkwerk*, Konrad has progressively sold all his furniture and taken out large loans in order to finance his scholarly project. His final visit to the bank manager, however, reveals that his assets are no longer sufficient to cover his debts, and the economic independence on which the study depends dissolves.[27] This both causes and parallels, at the level of finance, the existential impasse to which Konrad's monologues testify. Intellectual activity is seen to be inseparable from financial independence. At first glance, *Beton* and *Der Untergeher* seem to draw on the same thematic material. The main characters in these texts are wealthy bourgeois who devote themselves to their artistic projects and seem not to question the assumptions on which their highly elitist conceptions of art are based. And yet the novels' character configurations include two female characters whose narratives emerge toward the end of the texts and cast radical doubt on the values that the narrators appear to presuppose.

Rudolf, narrator of *Beton*, has spent ten years gathering material in preparation for a monumental study of Felix Mendelssohn-Bartholdy. Like Konrad in *Das Kalkwerk*, Rudolf faces the fundamental problem of beginning. Whereas in the earlier text this problem was quite literally a matter of life and death, *Beton* rehearses the same issues in the mode of comedy or irony. At the root of Konrad's difficulties is the fact that he lacks "Furchtlosigkeit vor Realisierung."[28] This lack of fear in turn is due to the fundamental incommensurability of his desire for totality and the necessary specificity of language.[29] Rudolf's problems, on the other hand, are of a banal and quotidian nature. He sets himself a date and a time, January 27 at four in the morning, at which he is going to commence the writing of his magnum opus.[30] But in his anxiety that his sister, who has just left after an extended stay, could return, he is plagued by insomnia. When he finally does doze off, of course, he oversleeps the decisive moment and his attempts to start writing the study fail.

The majority of the text consists of Rudolf's solipsistic, hypochondriac outpourings which primarily concern his own illness, the pernicious influence of his sister, the hypocrisy of Austrian high society and the Catholic Church, the need for both isolation and human contact, and the anti-intellectualism ("Geistesfeindlichkeit") of Austria. At the same time, Rudolf is aware of the absurdity of his situation. He had, for example, asked his sister to come to Peiskam, which undermines his claims to detest her presence. He also quotes her mockery of him without ever contradicting her accusations. He frequently repeats words to himself and then ends up laughing aloud at his own behavior, and all these devices betray a consciousness of his own ridiculousness. Rudolf's observations are made from a position of total financial security. He belongs to the landed bourgeoisie and is free from the need to earn a living:

> ich [könnte] noch zwanzig Jahre leben, ohne einen Groschen verdienen zu müssen und dann bliebe mir immer die Möglichkeit, nach und nach eine Parzelle nach der andern, ohne das Grundstück wesentlich in Mitleidenschaft zu ziehen und dadurch zu entwerten, zu verkaufen. (B, 57)

However, Rudolf is not as oblivious to the hardship of others as Konrad happens to be in *Das Kalkwerk*. Once installed in his hotel room in Palma, capital of the Balearic Island of Mallorca, Rudolf writes:

> Ich habe hier nicht den Eindruck, von den Einheimischen isoliert zu sein, obwohl mich, der ich tatsächlich in einem solchen großzügigen Zimmer in Luxus lebe und die in der Altstadt unter mir gerade im Gegenteil von diesem Luxus, doch fast alles von ihnen trennt. Aber meine Krankheit, so denke ich, entschuldigt diesen Luxus. Aber im Grunde habe ich keine Skrupel mehr. Am Lebensende sind Skrupel das Lächerlichste. (B, 172)

Here, the awareness of the discrepancy between his own living standards and those of the working classes is at once acknowledged and justified. Once the illusion that he is somehow in touch with the local population collapses, Rudolf first tries to persuade himself that his illness justifies the luxury in which he lives. Then this luxury is put down to his own lack of scruples, but the final aphorism "Am Lebensende sind Skrupel das Lächerlichste" is a means by which he attempts to elevate his own failings to a general principle. This pattern of acknowledging class conflict and then seeking to retract or relativize the awareness is related in the story of Anna Härdtl that challenges the narrator's position.

Sitting on a wicker chair in the Molo in Palma, Rudolf closes his eyes and recalls his chance encounter with Anna Härdtl eighteen months prior at the same location. She had married a Nuremburg engineering graduate and despite the fact that they had a young child, she more or less forced him to open an electric appliance shop in Trudering, a suburb of Munich, in the conviction that it would afford them a better living than an office job as a civil servant. While she had been obsessed with "Selbständigkeit" (independence), her husband turned out to be unfit for independence, "der ungeeigneteste für jede Art von Selbständigkeit" (B, 185). The business fails because suppliers deliver the wrong goods or damaged goods, refusing the Härdtls further credit. As a means of escape, Anna suggests a holiday in Palma, which, however, turns out to be disastrous in every respect. On the fifth day, she wakes up to discover that her husband had fallen over the seventy-centimeter-high balcony railings and plunged to his death on the concrete below. The results of this tragedy involve not only considerable legal expenses but the Härdtl's insurers refuse to honor the policy and an American manufacturing firm institutes incipient court proceedings. Totally preoccupied by this story, Rudolf finds himself unable to concentrate on Mendelssohn-Bartholdy. After a sleepless night, he visits the cemetery that he had previously visited with Anna Härdtl to view her husband's grave. On his arrival he discovers that the inscription on the concrete tomb now bears her name as well. An attendant informs him that she had committed suicide.

The above summary of *Beton* is not entirely representative, since Rudolf's monologue dominates the majority of the novel. Once he begins the narrative of Anna Härdtl's life, however, his tirades virtually cease, and whenever they begin they are curtailed and interrupted by Härdtl's story, which dominates the remaining thirty-six pages of the text. This structural imbalance is a facet of the text that has been largely ignored by critics. Its effect is to call into question the system of values subtending Rudolf's solipsistic pursuits. Anna Härdtl's financial hardship, mental anguish, and ultimate physical suffering reveal Rudolf's intellectual endeavors and health concerns to be trivial luxuries affordable only to those who have attained the independence for which Anna yearns. It is interesting to note that Rudolf attempts to explain the Härdtls' misfortune in terms of individual failings:

> Ihr Unglück ist, sagte ich mir, daß sie den jungen Härdtl, ihren Mann, zur Aufgabe seiner Ingenieurslaufbahn und in ein zu ihm gar nicht passendes Geschäft gezwungen, und ihm dann auch noch, aus was für einem Grund immer, die Mallorcareise eingeredet hat. Eine fürchterliche Idee, dachte, ich, Ende August nach Palma zu fahren! (B, 210–11)

It has already become clear by this point, however, that the reasons for the Härdtls' lack of success is in part determined not by their own personal incompetence, but by the structures of the market in which small businesses are at the mercy of large concerns who pursue their own interests, no matter how trivial, across countries and continents. Ascribing Anna Härdtl's fate to her own doing is Rudolf's belated attempt once again to suppress his awareness of the injustices of an economic system of which he is the indirect beneficiary.

Der Untergeher has as its central subject the friendship between the narrator, Wertheimer and Glenn Gould, a triple configuration of characters around which the text circles with characteristic insistence. Gould represents, for Wertheimer and the narrator alike, a nonpareil standard of artistic performance, and the recognition of this comes to play a decisive role in the development of their lives. Both Wertheimer and the narrator are initially highly promising concert pianists, the former having been an "außerordentliches Talent" and the latter "einer der besten Klavierspieler Österreichs, wenn nicht Europas."[31] But Gould is the only one to go on to enjoy a successful musical career; the others give up because the distance between Gould's perfection and their own playing renders their efforts pointless and absurd. The narrator decides more or less immediately never to touch another piano, and gives away his Steinway to the daughter of a music teacher in Neukirchen bei Altmünster. Wertheimer, on the other hand, gives a few concerts before following the narrator's lead and auctioning off his piano in the Dorotheum. The narrator then embarks on a process of slow decline, his "Verkümmerungsprozeß," and devotes himself to writing a study of Glenn Gould. Wertheimer lives with his sister and occupies himself with the production of vast quantities of aphorisms. When his sister leaves him and marries a Swiss industrialist, Wertheimer commits suicide.

On one level *Der Untergeher* is clearly about art and the artist. The very epitome of the artist ostensibly put forward by the text is Glenn Gould. As Manfred Mittermayer points out, Gould represents "Präzisionsstreben und Selbstdisziplin, Isolationsdrang und Ordnungsfanatismus," qualities possessed or striven for by many of Bernhard's other characters.[32] Gould can be seen as the ideal, self-sufficient artist who wants nothing to do with his audience, desiring instead to withdraw from the concert platform and, indeed, all forms of social interaction. In fact, Gould's "Klavierradikalismus" (U, 10) in *Der Untergeher* takes the notion of dedication to one's art to even further extremes: he expresses a wish to rid himself entirely of the trappings of nature and depersonalize himself to the extent of actually becoming the piano: "Das ideale wäre, ich wäre der Steinway, ich hätte Glenn Gould nicht notwendig, sagte er, . . . Glenn Steinway, Steinway Glenn nur für Bach" (U, 119).

Critics who have analyzed the development of Bernhard's writings stress the elements of self-criticism that manifest themselves in the texts after *Korrektur*.[33] At one level, of course, the narrator of *Der Untergeher* is self-critical to the point of debilitating himself. He gives up playing the piano because he cannot attain Gould's level of performance. In another sense, however, he is not as explicitly self-critical as, for example, Rudolf in *Beton,* for he never calls into question the absolute standards that he and Wertheimer demand, and Glenn Gould achieves. At the same time, there are other elements of the text that do imply a critique of those values. Herbert Gamper, for example, shows that in taking up an oppositional stance toward society, Bernhard's artist figures end up reconfirming precisely what they sought to avoid. Employing an analytic method that owes much to Adorno, Gamper suggests that by adopting a stance of deliberate artificiality in opposition to the involuntary artificiality ("Marionnettismus") of society, these characters paradoxically reproduce that which they had sought to counter. The excision from their lives of anything that does not serve their artistic purpose reproduces the instrumental thought ("Zweckdenken") of the practically-minded "Vorteilsmenschen" for whom they feel nothing but contempt and from whom they wish to dissociate themselves.[34] This kind of analysis that has so far been ignored by critics focuses on the relationship between artistic production and economic circumstances.

The abstruse intellectualism of the main characters in *Der Untergeher* depends, more explicitly than in *Beton,* on character configurations that exclude or marginalize representatives of the working classes. Gould, Wertheimer and the narrator are all themselves offspring of exceptionally wealthy bourgeois capitalists. We learn that the narrator's great grandfather had succeeded in business, presumably during the so-called *Gründerzeit* in Austria, an era of industrial expansion and high economic growth between 1850 and 1873. Wertheimer is the son of wealthy parents and was born into a "riesiges Vermögen" (U, 28, 143). Gould's family fortune is the result of the fur trade. Art thus becomes divorced from the necessity of making a living. The text's three main figures are cut off from economic concerns, and it is this circumstance that enables them to cultivate such impossibly high standards. In *The Political Unconscious,* Fredric Jameson points out that narrative texts employ strategies of containment in order to manage, at a formal level, objective social contradictions. He also suggests that most types of critical practice are reliant on analogous containment strategies.[35] Both these contentions clearly apply to *Der Untergeher* and its critical reception. The character configurations of the text itself are designed to divert attention from socio-economic issues, and the critical literature has consequently tended to concentrate on the relationship between Wertheimer, Gould and the narrator, at the expense of other aspects of the text.[36]

At the same time, however, it becomes apparent that intellectualism in general and artistic production in particular are dependent on the labor of the working classes. The role of the landlady within the economy of the text is to illustrate this very point. As in *Beton,* it is the narrative of a female character, occurring late in the text, that calls into question the purpose of such intense artistic self-questioning that dominates the lives of Wertheimer and the narrator. The inn, we learn, had fallen into her ownership following the murder conviction of the previous proprietor, her uncle. She had married a worker from the local paper factory, who died four years later in an industrial accident ("er [ist] in die Papiermühle hineingefallen und war weg" [U, 171]), leaving her with a child. Dependent on the inn for her livelihood, she now faces the possibility of having to wind up the business because the state-owned paper factory, on whose workers she relies for her custom, is threatened with closure.[37] A comparison with the landlady in *Frost* is instructive in this case. The latter is represented as sexually rapacious, violent, deceitful, and acquisitive, whereas the landlady in *Der Untergeher* is a considerably more sympathetic figure. Her narrative, which is concerned with basic human survival, relativizes the concerns of the narrator and his friends, and implies that art is produced on the back of exploitation and human suffering, as if to illustrate Walter Benjamin's famous dictum that every document of culture is at once also a document of barbarism.[38]

The problem of art in *Der Untergeher,* then, is not merely a thematic question of artistic perfection and its destructive, even fatal, effects on those whose inadequacies it exposes. The formal issue of the text's character configurations suggests that such considerations are relevant only to those who move in the rarified atmosphere of musical virtuosity. The presence of the landlady in the text, on the other hand, betrays a profound concern also with class. The values of art are juxtaposed with the social conditions of those whose economic circumstances depend on their own labor and the vicissitudes of the market. These conditions in turn call into question the values that the world of art seems to represent. *Ungleichzeitigkeit* characterizes not only the represented world of Bernhard's texts, but can also be seen as a feature of his oeuvre as a whole. As the above discussions have shown, texts produced at the beginning, middle and end of Bernhard's career contain representations of class relationships that are in some sense anachronistic and exist alongside other texts whose class consciousness is more genuinely contemporary. There is a simultaneous presence in his work of the aristocratic Habsburg ideology and the real circumstances of life under market capitalism.

The narrators of *Verstörung* and *Korrektur* are members of the bourgeoisie who portray within their narratives class antagonism between aristocrats and the petty bourgeoisie. By constituting class conflict in these terms, and by focusing specifically on the traits of individuals, they obscure their own class interests and deflect attention away from the genuine class issues in postwar Austrian society. In *Auslöschung,* a novel whose narrator is himself an aristocrat, the social contradictions, which the narrators of the earlier novels succeed to contain, prove to be insoluble. The only resolution is the death of the protagonist and the "Abschenkung" of his estate. *Auslöschung* provides a solution to the problem of *Ungleichzeitigkeit* only by negating it. *Beton* and *Der Untergeher* deal with bourgeois protagonists who are engaged in a lifelong intellectual pursuit. In contrast to the other novels by Bernhard that cover similar thematic ground, however, these texts also contain stories told to the narrators by female characters, and these narratives provide a critical perspective on the value-systems which the narrators attempt to establish. Their cerebral existence is made possible at the expense of the working classes from whose labor they ultimately profit. While the phenomenon of *Ungleichzeitigkeit* makes it difficult to speak of development or progress in Bernhard's representation of class, it is possible to discern an increasing inability of Bernhard's protagonists and/or narrators to manage the class conflict that they cannot help but inscribe in their texts.

Notes

[1] See, for example, such diverse cultural products as Thomas Hardy's novels, Hauptmann's *Einsame Menschen,* Zola's *La bête humaine,* Frank Norris's *The Octopus,* J. M. W. Turner's painting *Rain, Steam, and Speed,* and the numerous impressionist canvasses of Paris stations.

[2] Thomas Bernhard, *Frost* (Frankfurt: Suhrkamp, 1972), 157–58.

[3] Norbert Langer, "Die Schwierigkeit, mit Wolfsegg fertig zu werden: Thomas Bernhards *Auslöschung* im Kontext der osterreichischen Schloßromane nach 1945," *Antiautobiografie: Zu Thomas Bernhards Auslöschung,* ed. Hans Höller and Irene Heidelberger-Leonard (Frankfurt: Suhrkamp, 1995), 197–214; here 204.

[4] Willi Huntemann, *Artistik und Rollenspiel: Das System Thomas Bernhard* (Würzburg: Königshausen und Neumann, 1990), 99–117.

[5] See *Auslöschung: Ein Zerfall* (Frankfurt: Suhrkamp, 1986), 105, 106, 135, 248–49, 304; hereafter quoted in text as A.

[6] See *Verstörung* (Frankfurt: Suhrkamp, 1967), 7, 19, 63; hereafter quoted in text as V.

[7] See Hermann Helms-Derfert, *Die Last der Geschichte: Interpretationen zur Prosa von Thomas Bernhard* (Köln: Böhlau, 1997), 41; Josef Donnenberg, "Gehirnfähigkeit der Unfähigkeit der Natur," *Thomas Bernhard (und Österreich): Studien zu Werk und Wirkung 1970–1989* (Stuttgart: Heinz, 1997), 25–52; here 32, 34; Nicholas J. Meyerhofer, *Thomas Bernhard* (Berlin: Colloquium, 1985), 31.

[8] See Jürgen Petersen, "Beschreibung einer sinnentleerten Welt: Erzählthematik und Erzählverfahren in Thomas Bernhards Romanen," *Bernhard: Annäherungen,* ed. Manfred Jurgensen (Bern: Francke, 1981), 143–76; here 145; Renate Fueß, *Nicht fragen: Zum Double-bind in Interaktionsformen und Werkstruktur bei Thomas Bernhard* (Frankfurt: Lang, 1983); Bernhard Sorg, *Thomas Bernhard,* 2nd edition (Munich: Beck, 1992), 77.

[9] Hermann Helms-Derfert, 65.

[10] Josef König, *Nichts als ein Totenmaskenball: Studien zum Verständnis der ästhetischen Intentionen im Werk Thomas Bernhards* (Frankfurt: Lang, 1983), 57–68; here 60.

[11] For accounts of postwar Austrian history, see Peter Dusek, Anton Pelinka and Erika Weinzierl, *Zeitgeschichte im Aufriß: Österreich seit 1918: 50 Jahre Zweite Republik* (Vienna: Jugend und Volk, 1995); John Fitzmaurice, *Austrian Politics and Society Today: In Defense of Austria* (New York: St. Martin's Press, 1990); Barbara Jelavich, *Austria: Empire and Republic 1800–1986* (Cambridge: Cambridge UP, 1987).

[12] Robert Menasse, *Überbau und Underground: Essays zum österreichischen Geist* (Frankfurt: Suhrkamp, 1996), 19–22.

[13] Menasse, 23–24.

[14] See Ernst Bloch, *Gesamtausgabe 4: Erbschaft dieser Zeit* (Frankfurt: Suhrkamp, 1977), 104–26.

[15] On postwar cultural politics in Austria, see Klaus Amann, "Vorgeschichten: Kontinuitäten in der österreichischen Literatur von den dreißiger zu den fünfziger Jahren," *Literatur der Nachkriegszeit und der fünfziger Jahre in Österreich,* eds. Friedrich Aspetsberger, Norbert Frei and Hubert Lengauer (Vienna: Österreichischer Bundesverlag, 1984), 46–58; here 47; Kurt Bartsch, "Die österreichische Gegenwartsliteratur," *Die Geschichte der deutschen Literatur. Band 3,* ed. Viktor Zmegac (Königstein: Athenäum, 1984), 695–825; here 695–700; Michael Mitchell, "Restoration or Renewal? Csokor, the Austrian PEN Club and the Re-establishment of Literary Life in Austria, 1945–55," *Austria 1945–1955: Studies in Political and Cultural Re-emergence,* ed. Anthony Bushell (Cardiff: University of Wales Press, 1996), 54–83; and Wendelin Schmidt-Dengler, *Bruchlinien: Vorlesungen zur österreichischen Literatur 1945 bis 1990* (Salzburg: Residenz, 1995), 11–23.

[16] For this reason, Hugo Dittberner's article on *Verstörung* misses the point: "Die heimliche Apologie der Macht: Kritisches zu Thomas Bernhards *Verstörung,*" *Thomas Bernhard Text+Kritik 43,* 2nd edition, ed. Heinz Ludwig Arnold (Munich: text+kritik, 1982), 46–53.

[17] Langer, "Schloßromane," 202.

[18] I owe many of the insights in this paragraph to Helms-Derfert, 57–58.

[19] Höller, *Kritik einer literarischen Form: Versuch über Thomas Bernhard* (Stuttgart: Heinz, 1979), 10.

[20] Thomas Bernhard, *Korrektur* (Frankfurt: Suhrkamp, 1975), 115; hereafter quoted in text as K.

[21] Helms-Derfert, 127.

[22] Idealization of workers, particularly agricultural and manual laborers, occurs frequently in Bernhard's work, from *Frost* onwards.

[23] König, 95–96; Helms-Derfert, 126.

[24] Cf. Andreas Gößling, *Die 'Eisenbergrichtung': Versuch über Thomas Bernhards Auslöschung* (Münster: Kleinheinrich, 1988), 11.

[25] *Eisenbergrichtung*, 10–11.

[26] See in particular Silke Schlichtmann, *Das Erzählprinzip Auslöschung: Zum Umgang mit der Geschichte in Thomas Bernhards Roman Auslöschung. Ein Zerfall* (Frankfurt: Lang, 1996).

[27] *Das Kalkwerk* (Frankfurt: Suhrkamp, 1973), 177–83.

[28] *Das Kalkwerk*, 211.

[29] On the reasons for Konrad's failure, see especially Heinrich Lindenmayr, *Totalität und Beschränkung: Eine Untersuchung zu Thomas Bernhards Roman Das Kalkwerk* (Königshausen: Athenäum, 1982), 69–89.

[30] Bernhard, *Beton* (Frankfurt: Suhrkamp, 1988), 7; hereafter quoted in text as B.

[31] Bernhard, *Der Untergeher* (Frankfurt: Suhrkamp, 1988), 152, 158; hereafter quoted in text as U.

[32] Manfred Mittermayer, *Thomas Bernhard* (Stuttgart: Metzler, 1995), 121.

[33] See, for instance, Bernhard Sorg, *Thomas Bernhard* (Munich: Beck, 1992), 111; Huntemann, *Artistik und Rollenspiel* 41; Mittermayer, *Thomas Bernhard*, 94–121; Hugo Dittberner, "Der Dichter wird Kolorist: Thomas Bernhards Epochensprung," *Thomas Bernhard Text+Kritik* 43, 3rd edition, ed. Heinz Ludwig Arnold (Munich: text+kritik, 1991), 11–21; Annegret Mahler-Bungers, "Die Antiautobiographie: Thomas Bernhard als 'Antiautobiograph?'" *Über sich selber reden. Zur Psychoanalyse autobiographischen Schreibens* (*Freiburger literaturpsychologische Gespräche* 11), ed. Johannes Cremerius (Würzburg: Königshausen und Neumann, 1992), 121–33; here 122.

[34] How Bernhard's Gould differs from the real Glenn Gould becomes very apparent when reading Otto Friedrich's authoritative biography *Glenn Gould: A Life and Variations* (London: Elm Tree, 1990).

[35] See Frederic Jameson, *The Political Unconscious: Narrative as a Socially Symbolic Act* (London: Routledge, 1989), 52–53. Jameson's own critical project is an attempt to uncover the class antagonisms and contradictions that the text represses.

[36] The exception to this is Ingrid Petrasch. She rightly sees the landlady's story as mirroring that of the narrator, but does not point out that her narrative also has a potentially critical effect. See *Die Konstitution der Wirklichkeit in der Prosa Thomas Bernhards: Sinnbildlichkeit und groteske Überzeichnung* (Frankfurt am Main: Lang, 1987), 223–25.

[37] This is a veiled reference to the increasing lack of competitiveness in Austrian nationalised industries in the 1980s; see Jelavich, *Modern Austria*, 313.

[38] Walter Benjamin, "Über den Begriff der Geschichte," *Illuminationen: Ausgewählte Schriften I* (Frankfurt: Suhrkamp, 1977), 251–61; here 254.

Willy Riemer

Thomas Bernhard's *Der Untergeher*: Newtonian Realities and Deterministic Chaos

> Wertheimer war nicht imstande, *sich selbst als ein Einmaliges* zu sehen, wie es sich jeder leisten kann und muß, will er nicht verzweifeln, gleich was für ein Mensch, er ist ein einmaliger, sage ich selbst mir immer wieder und bin gerettet.[1]

THREE MUSIC STUDENTS, aspiring virtuosos all, become acquainted at a master class of the celebrated pianist Horowitz. The brilliant performance and career of one of them, named after the Canadian pianist Glenn Gould, leaves the ambitions of the other two, Wertheimer and the narrator, in shambles. *Der Untergeher* consists of complex loops of ruminations in which the narrator tries to come to terms with his role in Wertheimer's suicide and with his own precarious existence after the encounter with Glenn Gould. As with all of Thomas Bernhard's prose, fact and fiction form an explosive composite in a setting notable for its constructedness. An agglomerate of sharp-edged fragments, recognizable and sometimes wildly exaggerated bits of the real world, are designed to appear in the matrix of the text, ready to burst and cut. Comparing venerable institutions to bordellos and their dignitaries to pimps, for example, makes for piquant copy and controversy. In no small measure Thomas Bernhard's notoriety in the popular press stems from realistic readings of such passages in his books.

Bernhard's Glenn Gould provides the realistic focus for *Der Untergeher*. He has so much in common with his famous namesake that some reviews have the real Glenn Gould die at his Steinway while playing Bach's *Goldberg Variations* — the dramatic death of Bernhard's fictive Gould. In fact, Gould suffered a stroke and died some days later when the life support systems were shut off.[2] Some biographical works on Gould mention this "novel of sorts"[3] for the sake of documentary completeness or to buttress an enthusiasm for Glenn Gould's accomplishments as a concert pianist.[4] Less referential approaches tend to foreground Wertheimer as a tragic figure who fails to achieve artistic perfection.[5] In their quest for meaning, such interpretations illuminate salient aspects of the narrative without, however, engaging its conspicuous structure. Uwe Betz compiles a table of characteristics for the three figures to show that the narrative is constituted of the permutations of their differences and similarities.[6] Such analysis undoubtedly has validity, but it is not clear that it helps the reader in understanding the text better. The evident musicality of Bernhard's language has invited comparison to musical forms, but according to Christian Klug there is not a great deal to be gained from such analysis.[7] Distancing themselves from the realistic readings that have fueled scandals and legal standoffs, some critics insist on the art and artifice of Bernhard's texts.[8] This approach is productive and in keeping with Wendelin Schmidt-Dengler's call to return to the text itself.[9] But the narratives of Bernhard are nothing if not also a diffracted representation of the real. In my approach to *Der Untergeher* I will use concepts from the theory of deterministic chaos to explore whether some aspect of Bernhard's brand of realism can also be found in the structure of the narrative.

The narrator's swirling monologue traces out intricate patterns of embedded details, some of which are also found in Bernhard's biographical writings and interviews. Much as the narrator of *Der Untergeher,* Bernhard attended the Mozarteum, but then with diploma in hand vouched never again to have anything to do with that institution.[10] Bernhard mentions his yearning for acceptance by the common folk, all the while realizing the futility of such a wish; he mentions his dislike of applause.[11] The dead, he claims, leave one with an immense burden of guilt.[12] As he does in the narrative, he criticizes the paper factories for practices that result in workers being crippled on the job. Indeed, Bernhard claims that reality is much worse than anything he could possibly invent.[13] Yet the structure of the narrative makes it clear that the real world serves as little more than a quarry for details to be combined into complex patterns. This is immediately evident from the time line of the narrative and from its eviscerated characters.

The few moments that the narrator takes to cross the threshold of an inn are stretched and successively twisted and folded to take up two thirds of the book. In his convoluted ramblings he reminisces and traces and retraces events of the twenty-eight years since the encounter with Glenn Gould. And as the vortex of memories and rationalizations grows ever tighter, a small set of motifs appears again and again with the question, what to make of life and at its end: death. Although the narrative often provides markers for the twenty-eight years of remembered time, they do not constitute a linear frame or vector along which the narrative develops. Once the primary themes have been introduced in three short passages of a sentence each, there are no paragraphs or chapters to structure the flow of fragmented thoughts and memories. It is as if the temporal details of the narrator's life have been mapped and dispersed onto a textual matrix. An essential ingredient of realism — time — is denatured.

Der Untergeher is awash with signifiers, yet it is difficult to imagine very much in concrete detail. Things are named, rather than described. The performance of music, for example, is central to the narrative and repeatedly mentioned, but not once is it described in other than evaluative terms. There is nothing to be learned about Glenn Gould's remarkable rendering of Bach's *Goldberg Variations.* The sparse landscapes, cities and countries are ridiculed; they lack a fullness of impression, as do the three main characters. Not much is known about their appearance and their bodies, apart from their pulmonary ailment. And even this condition is relativized, as if it were a second art form. Bernhard adapts two well-known idiosyncrasies of Glenn Gould's stage manner. As can be heard in some of his recordings, Gould sometimes softly hummed along as he played; the narrative gives him a stronger singing voice (U, 10). Glenn Gould became attached to a small piano chair made by his father; he continued to use it over the years, even when the fabric was worn away to expose the wooden slats underneath. His unusual posture at the keyboard is exaggerated by Bernhard: "Kaum saß er am Klavier, war er auch schon in sich zusammengesunken gewesen, dachte ich, er sah dann aus wie ein Tier, bei näherer Betrachtung wie ein Krüppel, bei noch näherer Betrachtung aber dann wie der scharfsinnige, schöne Mensch, der er gewesen war" (U, 34). Bodies, it seems, are deficient husks to be shed for the magnificent intellect and genius within. In his devotion to music, the fictive Gould strives to overcome the gap between the perfect idea of Bach's music in his mind and the imperfect rendering at the keyboard. Becoming one with the instrument, "*Steinway und Glenn in einem sein*" (U, 119), would be a first step. Gould, Wertheimer and the narrator are constructs with only a vestigial physical presence. As they are put through their paces, they function as text generators for an elaborate game about life and death, and about reality.

Both time and physicality of *Der Untergeher* derive from a reduced set of the real that nonetheless is complex in its structure. By contrast, the three characters face their actual environment:

> Unsere Ausgangsbasis ist immer nur die, daß wir von nichts etwas wissen und nicht einmal eine Ahnung davon haben, sagte er [Wertheimer], dachte ich. Schon gleich, wenn wir etwas angehen, ersticken wir in dem ungeheueren Material, das uns zur Verfügung steht auf allen Gebieten, das ist die Wahrheit, sagte er, dachte ich. (U, 96)

The pulmonary ailment that afflicts all three characters serves as a metaphor for their difficulty in coming to terms with an overwhelming reality. They adopt various strategies for simplifying and reducing reality, following what could be called the Newtonian paradigm: reality is taken to be a linear mechanism and therefore manageable in its reduction. At least in principle such a model promises the kind of control and analysis that is possible with machines.

In *Der Untergeher* references to "Berechnung," "Kalkül" and "Maschine" abound. Glenn Gould is said to have made himself into a "*Kunstmaschine*" (U, 132), with his studio functioning as a "*Verzweiflungsmaschine*" (U, 57). Once again, Thomas Bernhard adapts a detail to his purpose. The historic Glenn Gould had mastered the skills of post-performance editing; his recording sessions generally included numerous takes, followed by extensive editing and tape splicing, all under his supervision.[14] He enthusiastically welcomed "the overwhelming sense of power which editorial control makes available" to the performer.[15] For Gould, technology enhances art; in *Der Untergeher* machines dehumanize the artist. More generally, Wertheimer regards life itself as a horrible machine, "diese Existenzmaschine" (U, 64), into which he had been tossed by his parents. He is trapped in an "Untergeher- und Sackgassenmenschenmechanismus" (U, 211). The machine paradigm is important for the narrator's life as well. For example, as he plans his convalescence at the coast, he remarks, "ich werde mich durch mathematisch ausgeklügeltes Einatmen der Atlantikluft regenerieren" (U, 105). The three male characters persist with their Newtonian strategy, even though their every step reveals its inadequacy.

Both Wertheimer and the narrator engage in a game that takes into account the anticipative behavior of the other. They each infer that the other will commit suicide and that they will be at the other's funeral. The narrator claims that the end of Wertheimer as well as that of Gould could long ago have been predicted. Indeed, the motto of the book informs the reader that Wertheimer's death was "lange vorausberechneter Selbstmord" (U, 7). Even small details are calculated for effect: "Wenn [Wertheimer] jammerte, war es nicht Sentimentalität, sondern Berechnung, Kalkül" (U, 50). He dictates, for example, his sister's every move. All three characters pursue their goals with discipline and ruthless self-denial. They practice day and night; they torture themselves with the presumption of total control. The narrator concedes that perhaps, unlike Glenn Gould, he was not the born concert pianist after all; he tenaciously continues with his studies nonetheless. Endless hours of practice on the best instruments, prestigious conservatories, and finally the master class with Horowitz were to ensure a brilliant career. He planned and calculated to achieve artistic excellence by doing all the right things, by perfecting his skills and acquiring an appropriate aura. Ambiguity and imprecision are anathema to all three characters.

Perfectibility in its absoluteness implies a Newtonian view of reality in which every detail can have its correct place. The quest to achieve perfection frequently appears in the work of Thomas Bernhard. After twenty-two years of practicing Schubert's "Trout Quintet," Caribaldi in *Die Macht der Gewohnheit,* for example, dreams of the unattainable: "ein einziges Mal eine perfekte Musik."[16] When Wertheimer and the narrator visit Glenn Gould in America, he plays a passage from the *Goldberg Variations* for them: "Sein Spiel war jetzt genauso perfekt wie damals" (U, 36). The stress is on performance, not interpretation. For the narrator the piano had become something of a pinball machine, with Gould having mastered the secret for a perfect music score. The Newtonian view of reality is here applied to music as well. The real Gould as media artist was much more enterprising in his creative activities: "By taking advantage of the post-taping afterthought . . . one can very often transcend the limitations that performance imposes upon the imagination."[17] While perfectionism in performance ultimately destroys the careers of Wertheimer and the narrator, it leads the real Gould to a fruitful symbiosis with the producers and engineers of recording studios.

Alban Berg contends in his short essay on Schönberg that "jeder große künstlerische Wille — wende er sich dem eigenen Schaffen, der Reproduktion, der Kritik oder schließlich dem Lehrfache zu — das Höchste hervorbringen muß."[18] The narrator of *Der Untergeher* clearly accepts this demand as a radical imperative: he simply has to achieve the most sublime; he has to be the very best (U, 9). He casually dismisses renowned artists like Gulda and Brendel; they amount to nothing much. His Gould, however, is the most important concert pianist of the century or, in the words of Leonard Bernstein speaking of the real Gould: "He is the greatest thing that has happened to music in years."[19] The fictive Gould is the greatest and also the narrator's nemesis: "ich wollte *der Beste sein oder gar keiner,* so hörte ich auf" (U, 123). The narrator is talented and ambitious, but not genial; he is at risk of becoming a casualty of the Newtonian quest with its notion of perfectibility.

As Wendelin Schmidt-Dengler and Stephen Dowden have pointed out, Thomas Bernhard does not base his writings on the precepts of the philosophers that he happens to mention.[20] And he never mentions chaos theory. Nonetheless, I would like to suggest that some concepts of this paradigm might be useful in comprehending the structure of *Der Untergeher.* Contemplating Wertheimer's decision to put an antique desk where his Bösendorfer piano used to be, the narrator continues:

> Aber wir müssen ja auch nicht immerfort etwas studieren wollen, dachte ich, es genügt ja vollkommen, wenn wir nur denken, nichts als denken und dem Denken ganz einfach freien Lauf lassen. Daß wir der Weltanschauung nachgeben und uns dieser Weltanschauung ganz einfach ausliefern, aber das ist das Schwierigste, dachte ich. (U, 73)

To give free rein to his thoughts, however, is contrary to his Newtonian disposition with its methodical search for cause and reason. Unlike Wertheimer, the narrator in time succeeds in embracing this unspecified "Weltanschauung." He gives away his Steinway piano, the symbol of entrapment, and with a sense of liberation moves to Spain. He has become a "*Weltanschauungskünstler*" (U, 74). But to make it clear that he has not simply exchanged one oppressive system of thought for yet another, he bursts into laughter at his neologism. His new view of reality, most evident in the iterative structure of the book that he subsequently writes in Spain, can be taken as isomorphic with the approach of chaos theory, a discourse that retains deterministic features without requiring narrowly predictive constraints.

The discovery that seemingly chaotic events have structure and conversely that even simple deterministic systems can produce random behavior has led to a "new paradigm in scientific modeling,"[21] a "completely new orientation in science"[22] and a "true revolution in our view of the world."[23] Thomas Bernhard would say a new "Weltanschauung." This paradigm switch has been widely registered in cultural criticism, often in the context of postmodernism with its rejection of fixed origins and totalizing structures.[24] Katherine Hayles alludes to Gregory Bateson's *Steps to an Ecology of Mind* (1972) in arguing that scientific and literary theories constitute an ecology of ideas; they are isomorphic "because their central ideas form an interconnected network."[25] Chaos theory, however, has blossomed especially in the physical sciences.

The constructed realities of traditional or Newtonian science are special cases of orderly behavior. For given initial conditions and boundary values, relevant equations can be solved and causalities can be established. Reality in practice is usually not as accommodating. Even the simplest deterministic systems, such as three mutually attracting objects, may lead to wholly unpredictable motion. The reason for this difficulty lies in the strongly nonlinear equations that determine their behavior. By a recursive procedure, computers can model such nonlinear systems from some initial condition and produce a sequence or orbit of possible states. The algorithms employed in chaos theory require no interpretation; they are precisely defined procedures that remain stable between iterations. In contrast, literary texts involve signification and intertextuality, as well as the ambiguities and sonorities of the narrator's voice. By comparison to the usual practices of chaos theory, literary texts have few iterative cycles and even these tend to be blurred by narrative devices. I am therefore not setting out to establish tidy equivalences between literature and science. Rather I wish to show that some of the central ideas of chaos theory — iteration, nonlinearity, and the loss of origins — are useful for considering the narrative structure of *Der Untergeher.*

After initial failed attempts, the narrator discovers a possible beginning for his treatise on Gould. He does not explain what this new approach might be nor how he went about the writing project; it is not even clear that the finished project is the book in the hands of the reader. There are indications, however, that it has to do with his new "Weltanschauung," with his newly developed reading habit, "die Kunst, dasselbe immer wieder als etwas ganz anderes in mich aufzunehmen" (U, 60). Instead of following a Newtonian narratology with establishing sequence, development and closure, *Der Untergeher* evolves iteratively, without proper beginning or end. Bits of quotations, notes and reminiscences are worked into tangled layers and braids of text that are often repeated and varied. This unusual repetitiveness has been explained in different ways. Rüdiger Görner claims to see "die sinnentleerte Wiederholung" as a parody of the processes in life and the arts.[26] The repetition suggests the tediousness of it all. That is, an evaluative posture is attributed to Thomas Bernhard. For Oliver Jahraus the author's problem reduces to the insurmountable gap between "Außersprachlichem und Sprache."[27] Since the quest for referential authenticity must necessarily fail, the text turns into "eine Kreisbewegung der Wiederholung grammatischer und thematischer Strukturen."[28] For Jahraus it is as if in these repetitions the sentences come ever closer to some essential meaning to be expressed, to an end that can only be suggested by proximity. The narrator of *Der Untergeher,* however, seems very little concerned with the limits of language; the repetitive patterns involve people, situations, opinions and wholly unproblematic forms of attribution. Perhaps the difference in interpretation is best illustrated by the central motif of *Der Untergeher,* Bach's *Goldberg Variations.* It is not as if its variations are trying to reach some gleaming essence of a musical idea; the piece as a whole with all its variations constitutes Bach's composition. Similarly one may say that the message of *Der Untergeher* is conveyed in all of its recursive complexities as a whole.

How can iteration be used to shape a literary text? With his rambling workshop monologue *Wenn man mich so reden hört: Ein Selbstgespräch* (1993), Paul Wühr illustrates that his book and life in general turn on chaos and complexity.[29] He discusses in some detail two variants of the iterative process. For one book he worked with as many as thirty interlaced narrative planes. For an anthology of some fifty poems he periodically inserted the individual texts into new positions relative to each other. At each station they were then revised and given shape in their new context. That is, each poem changed by increments as it circulated through the anthology. This is, of course, not quite the methodical iteration found in applied mathematics, but it does follow a similar idea. Linear progression is replaced by a procedure that can be compared to the stretching and folding of puff pastry, a mundane metaphor that is widely used in explaining chaos theory. Wühr's volume of poems, once finished, is much like a completed fractal pattern. The sequence of iterative steps that generated the pattern is itself no longer in evidence.

We do not know how Thomas Bernhard constructed *Der Untergeher,* but the countless repetitions of "sagte er, dachte ich" in its variations function like little tabs on index cards which the narrator randomly presents at the inn and then on his way to Wertheimer's country retreat. These cards of the mind are filled with attempted explanations, penned up resentments, and remembered details. Even recent events lack completeness. When the narrator describes Wertheimer's funeral, for example, he concedes: "Es ist mir naturgemäß nur ein bruchstückhafter Bericht gelungen" (U, 172). Unlike the unified and coherent progression expected from a Newtonian report, the narrator's monologue is a torrent of fragments and increments. The iterations involve large motifs like death and artistic perfection, but they also are found in the small detail. Before the narrator leaves for Wertheimer's funeral, for example, he listens to Glenn Gould's recording of the *Goldberg Variations,* "immer wieder von vorne" (U, 70). It is not clear, whether he does so in order to grasp the essence of the performance or to solve the enigma of its supposed perfection. The obsession with iteration also characterizes the writing projects that had filled the days of the narrator and Wertheimer; here, however, the comments are more explicit.

Wertheimer had wanted to publish a book, but he kept revising it, "die Veränderung seines Manuskripts war nichts anderes, als das völlige Zusammenstreichen des Manuskripts, von dem schließlich nichts als der Titel *Der Untergeher* übriggeblieben ist" (U, 79). As he works to perfect his manuscript and progressively reduces and concentrates its subject matter, only a suggestive particle of the comprehensive topic of the book remains. He sets out to produce a Newtonian text, but ends up with countless bits and pieces. Wertheimer had become ein *Zettelmensch* (U, 79) or even more decidedly minimalist, ein *Aphorismenschreiber* (U, 93). Fragmentation into narrow disciplines has been the practice of the sciences and technologies. Problems are solved by identifying a small set of variables and procedures that produce valid results within this limited context. By analogy, Wertheimer also breaks down his large project into small pieces, each aphorism expressing some local insight. Reduced complexity can also be found in the tendency to categorize and substantiate actions and conditions. Wertheimer, for example, is variously called *Untergeher* (U, 26), *Asphaltgeher* (U, 41), *Der Gekränkte* (U, 45), *Lebens- und Existenzvernichter* (U, 58), *Nacheiferer* (U, 134) and *Schuhfetischist* (U, 65). In each case his complex life is squeezed into a minimalist identity, into a narrow definition that has some validity, but at the expense of neglecting both complexity and the possibility of change. Wertheimer, unlike the narrator, is not an *Ortsveränderer* (U, 65).

Since giving up his piano career, the narrator too has been preoccupied with his writing projects, accumulating outlines, countless sketches and notes. And he too strives for textual concentration and authenticity. Repeatedly he alludes to his interest in Wertheimer's notes, most frequently referring to them as *Zettel,* as fragments. At his country retreat he hopes to find stacks and heaps of such notes, mostly on mathematical and philosophical matters. That is, he does not expect a coherently structured book, but rather countless little theoretical attempts at its approximation. He seems resigned to the iterative approach: "Tausende seiner Zettel aneinandergereiht, dachte ich, und unter dem Titel *Der Untergeher* herausgegeben" (U, 79). The book that ultimately does appear indeed has this structure, but it is also evident that it contains material besides Wertheimer's notes. This feature then is the difference between them: while for Wertheimer the Newtonian writing quest disintegrates into countless particles, the narrator regards the assembly of these textual fragments as the representation of reality based on the paradigm of deterministic chaos. He must therefore also conclude that even such an assembly of notes is only provisional, without beginning or end. Even after he realizes his method of procedure, "*wie* die Schrift *Über Glenn* anfangen" (U, 108) and after completing the manuscript, he is determined to destroy it once he is back in Madrid. His *Glennschrift* is an iterative work-in-progress. It has to be rewritten yet again, not because it is less than perfect in the Newtonian conception, but because in principle it never can be finished or solved explicitly.

In solving equations, various orbits of solution are possible. For a range of initial conditions, some systems may run down and come to an end at a so-called fixed point. Fixed points thus seem to attract the orbits within the basin of their influence. Such systems are deterministic and predictable; they can be described as a whole. Glenn Gould with a mathematician's mind and as an artist obsessed with his music can in a metaphorical sense be considered in this context: "Wir gehen entweder als Ganzes in die Musik hinein oder gar nicht, hat Glenn oft gesagt" (U, 121). And Gould's reality as "Ganzes" certainly is complete in itself. In some remarks about the conductor Stokowski, the historical Gould makes a revealing observation: "Artists, I think, work best in isolation — in an environment where their knowledge of the world outside is always under editorial control, and never permitted to intrude upon the indivisibility of that unit formed by the artist's idea and its execution."[30] Once again, Bernhard greatly exaggerates details of Gould's reality in order to construct a character whose coordinates of existence and life's path then become calculable. According to the narrator, Gould had already perfected his performance of the *Goldberg Variations* at their first encounter in Salzburg. After perfection, there is no place else to go; Gould had reached the artistic fixed point, the end. The narrator thus concludes: "Er hatte den Gipfel seiner Kunst erreicht und es war nur eine Frage der allerkürzesten Zeit, daß ihn der Gehirnschlag treffen mußte" (U, 25). In time, after a number of years, he indeed does die, or rather: he has a natural death at the keyboard while playing — perfectly — the *Goldberg Variations.*

The fictive Gould does not have to develop theories in order to understand his life; he does not engage in writing projects. The historical Gould actually published numerous essays on a range of subjects; he received a Grammy award for the liner notes for a Hindemith recording, and he left a set of notes for a projected autobiography. His diverse and many contributions are in accord with an early self-image as "a sort of musical Renaissance Man, capable of doing many things."[31] In contrast, the Glenn Gould of *Der Untergeher* has become a scaled-down mathematical option equipped with the trappings that are relevant to this role. He does one thing and this he does extremely well. All the great philosophers who attempted to construct comprehensive world systems — including Kant and Schopenhauer — are reduced to puny caricatures. They went wrong in trying to impose a Newtonian view on reality: "Alle diese Leute haben sich an der Natur vergriffen" (U, 98).

And so did Wertheimer and the early narrator in their search for explanations.

After many attempts the narrator begins to understand what was wrong with his writing project: "ich habe sie [die Schrift] immer zu früh angefangen" (U, 109). That is, in his search for explanations he and Wertheimer always started with events in the past, with origins. Ignoring the inherent problems of attributing efficient cause, the narrator plays through numerous scenarios in his mind. The encounter with Glenn Gould, Gould's playing of the *Goldberg Variations,* the master class with Horowitz, their supposedly difficult childhood and a host of other possibilities are all reiterated and blamed for their aborted career and for Wertheimer's suicide. Origins and causes, however, only make sense in constructed linear worlds in which everything can be calculated. The events of reality occur not in linear fashion. From the narrator's monologue it is evident that, at least in his reminiscences, most events happened abruptly, that is, in nonlinear fashion. From one moment to the next he decides to become a concert pianist, then years later just as suddenly comes to hate his piano and gives up his career. His sentences lurch and jump between themes; they follow one line of thought and then without transition switch to an entirely different topic. While in the narrator's early Newtonian quest there is always the presupposition of a linear world with its fixed points, *Der Untergeher* flows along with the ripples, curls and vortices that are characteristic of complex systems. With such abrupt transitions the past is irretrievably lost. The narrator prospects in his memory, but the origins and causes are obliterated.

For complex systems the orbits of solutions are constrained within a region of possible states, but within this region they are entirely random. That is, the evolution of the system is unpredictable and subject to dramatic change. It is the study of such regions called strange attractors that is at the heart of chaos theory. Strange attractors are notable for their fractal form,[32] a textual variant of which is provided by the structure of *Der Untergeher.* The thematic orbits swirl and loop and in their iterations gradually reveal strange attractors. Again and again the narrator comes back, for example, to Glenn Gould and the *Goldberg Variations;* he refers to this motif as Wertheimer's *Lebensfalle* (U, 131), a metaphor that has the same dynamics as a strange attractor. The narrator's speculations suggest that Gould's performance of Bach's composition had a profound effect on him, but as he hedges and reasserts his position no simple causal relationship can be established. The orbits are without recoverable beginning. Both Wertheimer and the narrator try to control the development of the orbits, but the narrator must concede that this is not possible: "wir existieren ja nicht, es existiert uns" (U, 70).

Wertheimer, in his Newtonian mode, assumes that solutions and fixed points can be imitated; he would like to be the greatly admired Gould or Horowitz, and then later a "Zweitschopenhauer, Zweitkant, Zweitnovalis" (U, 155). Orbits of complex systems, however, are unique. The narrator gains this insight: "Wertheimer war nicht im Stande, *sich selbst als ein Einmaliges* zu sehen, wie es sich jeder leisten kann und muß, will er nicht verzweifeln, gleich was für ein Mensch, er ist ein einmaliger, sage ich selbst mir immer wieder und bin gerettet" (U, 133). He now no longer tries to force the complexities of his life into a Newtonian paradigm; instead he allows the iterative process to take its course as he assembles the variously dispersed bits and pieces of his reminiscences into the book that he finally does publish. Thomas Bernhard's realism thus has as much to do with the structure of the narrative, as it does with its occasionally exaggerated factual ingredients.

Notes

[1] Thomas Bernhard, *Der Untergeher* (Frankfurt: Suhrkamp, 1986), 133; hereafter cited in text as U.

[2] Otto Friedrich, *Glenn Gould: A Life and Variations* (New York: Random House, 1989), 326.

[3] Friedrich, 335.

[4] Wera Matheis, *Glenn Gould: der Unheilige am Klavier* (Munich: scaneg, 1987), 101.

[5] Manfred Mittermayer, *Thomas Bernhard* (Stuttgart: Metzler, 1995), 122. Eckhart Nickel, *Flaneur. Die Ermöglichung der Lebenskunst im Spätwerk Thomas Bernhards* (Heidelberg: Manutius, 1997), 22.

[6] Uwe Betz, *Polyphone Räume und karnevalisiertes Erbe. Analysen des Werks Thomas Bernhards auf der Basis Bachtinscher Theoreme* (Würzburg: Ergon, 1997), 287.

[7] Christian Klug, *Thomas Bernhards Theaterstücke* (Stuttgart: Metzler, 1991), 188–190.

[8] Mittermayer, 2; Lutz Köpnick, "Leben in der Hölle. Thomas Bernhards *Heldenplatz*," *New German Review* 7 (1991): 15–25; here 15.

[9] Wendelin Schmidt-Dengler, "Zurück zum Text: Vorschläge für die Lektüre von Thomas Bernhards *Frost*," *Thomas Bernhard: Beiträge zur Fiktion der Postmoderne. Londoner Symposion,* ed. Wendelin Schmidt-Dengler, Adrian Stevens, and Fred Wagner (Frankfurt: Peter Lang, 1997), 201–220; here 216.

[10] Brigitte Hofer, "Das Ganze ist im Grunde ein Spass," *Von einer Katastrophe in die andere. 13 Gespräche mit Thomas Bernhard,* ed. Sepp Dreissinger (Weitra: publication PNo 1, 1992), 49–62; here 52.

[11] Asta Scheib, "Von einer Katastrophe in die andere," *Von einer Katastrophe in die andere. 13 Gespräche mit Thomas Bernhard,* 136–53; here 142.

[12] Scheib, 150.

[13] Niklas Frank, "Ansichten eines unverbesserlichen Weltverbesserers," *Von einer Katastrophe in die andere. 13 Gespräche mit Thomas Bernhard,* 89–94; here 91.

[14] Andrew Kazdin, *Glenn Gould at Work: Creative Lying* (New York: Dutton, 1989), 28.

[15] Glenn Gould, "The Prospects of Recording," *The Glenn Gould Reader,* ed. Tim Page (New York: Knopf, 1984), 399.

[16] Thomas Bernhard, *Die Macht der Gewohnheit* (Frankfurt: Suhrkamp, 1974), 21.

[17] Gould, 339.

[18] Alban Berg, "Schönberg als Lehrer," *Die Wiener Moderne. Literatur, Kunst und Musik zwischen 1890 und 1910,* ed. Gotthart Wunberg and Johannes J. Braakenburg (Stuttgart: Reclam, 1981), 612–13; here 613.

[19] Quoted in Friedrich, *Glenn Gould: A Life and Variations,* 70.

[20] Schmidt-Dengler, *Londoner Symposium,* 219; Stephen D. Dowden, *Understanding Thomas Bernhard* (Columbia, SC: U of South Carolina P, 1991), xiii.

[21] James P. Crutchfield et al., "Chaos," *Scientific American* 255 (1986): 46–57; here 46.

[22] Heinz-Otto Peitgen and Peter H. Richter, *The Beauty of Fractals: Images of Complex Dynamical Systems* (Berlin: Springer, 1986), 31.

[23] David K Campbell, ed., *Chaos / XAOC* (New York: AIP, 1990), xi.

[24] Jean-François Lyotard, *The Postmodern Condition: A Report on Knowledge,* trans. Geoff Bennington and Brian Massumi (Minneapolis: U of Minnesota P, 1984), 60. Rainer Paslack, "'...da stellt ein Wort zur rechten Zeit sich ein.' Die Karriere des Chaos zum Schlüsselbegriff," *Kursbuch* 98 (1989): 121–39; here 122.

[25] Katherine N. Hayles, *Chaos Bound. Orderly Disorder in Contemporary Literature and Science* (Ithaca: Cornell UP, 1990), 184.

[26] Rüdiger Görner, "Gespiegelte Wiederholungen: Zu einem Kunstgriff von Thomas Bernhard," *Londoner Symposion,* 111–25; here 114.

[27] Oliver Jahraus, *Die Wiederholung als werkkonstitutives Prinzip im Oeuvre Thomas Bernhards* (Frankfurt: Peter Lang, 1991), 50.

[28] Jahraus, 39.

[29] Paul Wühr, *Wenn man mich so reden hört: Ein Selbstgespräch* (Graz: Droschl, 1993).

[30] Gould, "Stokowski in Six Scenes," *The Glenn Gould Reader,* 259.

[31] Bernard Asbell, "Glenn Gould," *Horizon* 4.3 (1962): 89.

[32] Benoit B. Mandelbrot, *The Fractal Geometry of Nature.* (New York: Freeman, 1983), 197.

Marlene Streeruwitz

My Latest Encounter with Bernhard[1]

I FOUGHT WITH A POLICE OFFICER. Once again after a long time. Like in the demonstrations from the 1970s, I felt the heavy, rough cloth of the police uniform. And the arms underneath it. The arms that kept pressing my companion against the wall.

My companion had said to the police officer, "you're not going to talk with me in this manner," since the officer had kicked him in the ass and yelled at him "Get up" in the tone of a military boot camp. Instead of replying to his "you're not going to talk with me in this manner," the police officer had immediately grabbed my companion and pressed him against the wall. Instantly. Without a word. I began pulling at the officer. I threw myself over the arms of the officer so that he would let go of my companion. It looked like a real fight. The two men were already heavily entangled with one another. I was hungry. I wanted to go out and eat. I didn't fell like spending the night at the police station. Statements and the like. And how they inflate themselves in front of you, making it clear to you that you are all alone with them. I wanted to leave. Leave the police officer behind who, as anyone could tell, was trying to make out what type of people we were. And whether he should really lunge at us. Or not. After long indecision. The police officer couldn't make up his mind. We finally got away. I pulled my companion away. Dragged him down the stairs from the balcony on the left in the Akademietheater. My companion is from Frankfurt. He does not know the power of the civil servant's oath here. The police officer had a lot of gold on his uniform. There were no witnesses. The man in the coat check area had immediately disappeared. Escape was the best solution. Particularly because of dinner.

This whole incident happened after a performance of Thomas Bernhard's *Claus Peymann kauft sich eine Hose und geht mit mir essen* at the Akademietheater. Recently. It must have been a so-called *Theaterpolizist* who responded to the sentence "you're not going to talk with me in this manner" with violence. That goes without saying. As if speaking and fighting were on the same level of language and that speaking was to be answered with fighting and fighting with speaking. Language and violence as compatible modes of communication.

While we were wrestling in the lobby, an enthusiastic audience applauded the actors and a play in which Thomas Bernhard's misanthropy combined with his contempt for authority exposes every representative of authority as a Nazi to the resounding laughter of the audience. The police officer, who sits in the theater, represents this scorned and ridiculed authority. He observes and protects the scorn and ridicule. This officer must be quite upset after a play like this one. Every laughter concerns him as well. That is understood. He does not have to understand anything. Yes. The less he understands, the more he is meant. Afterwards he is at a loss of words. Only his fists are left. Simple minds see in this the confirmation of such a play. Beneath it. At the bottom of such an incident, however, are much more complicated matters of interest that collide in this representative of the law.

And yet it all started off so well. How Bernhard and Peymann arrived in Vienna in their tailored suits. How Bernhard, in the Bräunerhof, quietly nodded assent to the question whether it was true. The Burgtheater? And how he answered the question, why he wanted it this way. Had he not hated the Burgtheater so much? One could read this and hear it from him at any time. How Bernhard looked astonished at this question and his female disciples nodded blissfully. The two of them had really wanted it. Peymann and Bernhard wanted to take over. To take over the Burgtheater. An occupation. To become important. To destroy the old and become the most famous ones. In doing so.

As with Bernhard's literature, things took a wrong turn. They had not considered that taking over the position of the father turns one into the father. That one would then become the father. And that Oedipal stunts of rebellion would not only appear ridiculous but become irresponsible. Irresponsible towards a dimension of politics that reaches deeper. Deeper than the uproar about deliveries of manure to the front entrance of the Burgtheater. Deliveries that turned out to have been ordered up by the director of the theater himself.

Bernhard brilliantly exaggerated the dilemma of the son who can't catch his breath due to his father/grandfather. He burdened his characters with the weight of Oedipal problematics and seduced them into the extinction of abstraction. He suffocates the topic of infertility in language through endless repetition. He always remains the disappointed son. The disappointing son. Under the debris of disappointments scorn rises, one that looks comical. But to laugh about this matter is an affirmation, like most laughter.

Bernhard never took a step out of the grave dug by patriarchy. He allows his characters to hate all that which was promised but never came. Life. Love. Lust. His characters comprise hatred by proxy. Move into hatred. Into the reader. The theater audience. Here Bernhard becomes reactionary. Bard of a contempt for life and people that leads us back to patriarchy. Keeps us imprisoned there where our culture traps our pursuits everywhere. Because tragedy is so beautiful. Seductive. We know it all too well. We can follow him in this respect. His text whines: Destroy yourself! You're not worthy! You'll never get it right! One can never get it right! The religious tenets of our Austrian culture.

The writer of such statements can feel himself as the master of hatred in writing them. Perhaps this was liberating for Bernhard. Alleviating. On occasion, it looked like that. The male and the female reader. The theater audience. In their pursuits of a dry and winding language, they become themselves the objects of contempt.

Therein lies the irresponsible short-circuit of an interpretation as given in the Akademietheater with Bernhard sliding into the mode of cabaret. The audience is invited to indulge via Bernhard's literature of contempt in their own contempt of the world. To channel their own contempt of the world in Bernhard and thereby gain height. In the theater, the hesitant mass of the audience deludes itself into a complicity with Bernhard. But. The invitation to self-destruction is precisely passed along in this fashion. The invitation to self-destruction that is written into the text. An interpretation that does not expose this invitation turns the play totally into a reactionary play. The theater audience becomes a laughing mass, laughing about an authority that it represents itself. The unemployed do not sit at the Akademietheater. It is the upper middle class that becomes complicit. Seeking alleviation in a laughter that demands reflection. Enough confirmation that it is once again other people. Scorn must find a different outlet. One who contradicts in this matter offers an ideal opportunity. A German is attacked. Asked who he is. He is threatened. He should behave himself. He is not at home here. Things are run differently here. — As if we didn't know it.

This brings us back to a fundamental question for the director of the Burgtheater. Why does the police sit in his theater? Why does the police sit in the Burgtheater? How could Peymann take over the Burgtheater, call himself left wing and only produce political theater, when in fact the censorship of authority is maintained. Yes, that it even goes so far that in the case of intensive anti-Peymann protests the police would have to defend Peymann's position. The director. The police would have to protect the man who has made it his task to ridicule authority and who brings his deceased and preferred author of the house back to life against his will. The police would have to defend a man. A man whose political program got stuck in an adolescent stage of protest would have to be defended by the police.

Yet political matters of the most basic kind could have been dealt with in this case. One could have looked into the basis of freedom, free speech and the power of authority in a democracy. Here a step could have been taken that could have changed more than fifty *Hermannschlachten*. Nobody, except seasoned Austrians, can imagine the presence of the police in a theater. (The companion from Frankfurt thought he was dealing with a fireman). And. The police should abandon this type of supervisory activity. They could demonstrate a lead in enlightenment spirit towards people active in the theater. For security we still have the fire department. For health the medical doctor hired by the theater. And there are also the ticket operators. The so-called law about mandatory police presence in the theater is a fairy tale. There are only government orders. The interior minister can at any time change all these orders.

But that would have been responsible political action. And. In the disparity between claim and reality, the power of patriarchy remains secured. As in the statement to honor a legacy and then not to fulfil the final will by the author. Herein lies the whole Oedipal mendacity of power. How the survivors rob the dead. In the case of Bernhard, this co-optation is carried to a caricature on stage. When Mrs. Dene pastes on a sickly swollen nose onto her face and begins to walk like Bernhard, we are dealing with a clear case of necrophilia. And it becomes clear, how this recuperation really operates: Instead of an interpretation that could bring the interesting subtexts of Bernhard's literature into clear view and thereby contribute to a political clarification of the cultural space, one resorts to slapstick comedy. The police officer himself starts slapping around. And everything remains the same. Had to remain the same so that a director of the Burgtheater would not run out of material for hatred and contempt. A hatred and contempt that uses in disconcerting fashion a vocabulary of discrimination and therein resembles the ridiculed enemies.

But well. Nothing has changed. The era Peymann will have passed unnoticed like those eras before him. They worked for the establishment. The establishment. These are the people who invent rules that cannot be kept. Those who simply want the opposite also belong to this group. For change. In order to not be forgotten, a different type of social imagination is necessary. Perhaps one contemporaneous with one's time and not always steeped in nostalgia for earlier, more radical years. And Thomas Bernhard. He did not succeed in withdrawing himself. But we will read him. And interpret. Regardless of anniversaries of his death. Or maybe not. And therein lies the difference. Reassuring. Somehow. — I will fulfill the final will of Thomas Bernhard and no longer attend any productions of his plays in this country. Final wills can be obeyed in this manner as well.

Translated by Matthias Konzett

Notes

[1] Marlene Streeruwitz, "My Latest Encounter with Bernhard," first published in *Falter* (February, 1999).

Works Cited

Adorno, Theodor W. et al. *The Authoritarian Personality.* New York: Harper, 1950.

Amann, Klaus. "Vorgeschichten: Kontinuitäten in der österreichischen Literatur von den dreißiger zu den fünfziger Jahren." *Literatur der Nachkriegszeit und der fünfziger Jahre in Österreich.* Eds. Friedrich Aspetsberger, Norbert Frei and Hubert Lengauer. Vienna: Österreichischer Bundesverlag, 1984.

Améry, Jean. *Jenseits von Schuld und Sühne.* Stuttgart: Klett-Cotta, 1977; first published 1966.

Anders, Günter. *Wir Eichmannssöhne. Offener Brief an Klaus Eichmann.* Munich: Beck, 1964.

Antonsen, Jan Erik. *Text-Inseln. Studien zum Motto in der deutschen Literatur vom 17. bis 20. Jahrhundert.* Würzburg: Königshausen & Neumann, 1998.

Arendt, Hannah. *Eichmann in Jerusalem.* Munich: Piper, 1964.

Artmann, Hans Carl. *med ana schwoazzn dintn.* Salzburg: Otto Müller, 1958.

Asbell, Bernard. "Glenn Gould." *Horizon* 4.3 (1962): 89.

Austin, John Langshaw. *How to Do Things with Words.* Oxford: Oxford UP, 1961.

Bachmann, Ingeborg. "[Thomas Bernhard:] Ein Versuch: Entwurf." *Werke,* vol IV. Eds. Christine Koschel, Inge von Weidenbaum, & Clemens Münster. Munich, Zurich: Piper, 1993.

———. "Unter Mördern und Irren." *Das dreißigste Jahr. Erzählungen.* Munich: dtv, 1995.

Barthes, Roland. "La mort de l'auteur." *Manteia* 5 (1968): 12–17.

———. *Mythologies.* Trans. Annette Laver. New York: Hill and Wang, 2000.

Barthofer, Alfred. "Berge schwarzer Qual: Zur thematischen Schwerpunktstruktur der Lyrik Thomas Bernhards." *Acta Germanica* 9 (1976): 187–211.

———. "Vorliebe für die Komödie: Todesangst." *Vierteljahresschrift des Adalbert-Stifter-Institut des Landes Oberösterreich* 31 (1982): 77–100.

Bartsch, Kurt. "Die österreichische Gegenwartsliteratur." *Die Geschichte der deutschen Literatur. Band 3.* Ed. Viktor Zmegac. Königstein: Athenäum, 1984.

Basil, Otto et al. *Das große Erbe.* Graz: Stiasny, 1962.

Baumgart, Reinhard. "Die vergrauste Komödie." *Frankfurter Allgemeine Zeitung* (14 September 1985).

Bayer, Konrad and Gerhard Rühm. "scheissen und brunzen." *Die wiener gruppe: a moment of modernity 1954–1960.* Ed. Peter Weibel. Vienna: Bundesverlag, 1997.

Bayer, Wolfram. "Das Gedruckte und das Tatsächliche: Realität und Fiktion in Bernhards Leserbriefen." *Thomas Bernhard: Beiträge zur Fiktion der Postmoderne. Londoner Symposion.* Ed. Wendelin Schmidt-Dengler, Adrian Stevens, and Fred Wagner. Frankfurt: Peter Lang, 1997.

Becker, Peter von. "Die Unvernünftigen sterben nicht aus: Über Thomas Bernhards *Vor dem Ruhestand.*" *Theater Heute* (1979).

Beckermann, Ruth. *Jenseits des Krieges. Ehemalige Wehrmachtssoldaten erinnern sich.* Vienna: Döcker, 1998.

———. *Unzugehörig.* Vienna: Döcker, 1989.

———. Director. *Jenseits des Krieges.* Vienna: filmladen, 1997.

Beller, Steven. *Vienna and the Jews 1867–1938: A Cultural History.* London, New York: Cambridge UP, 1993.

Benjamin, Walter. "Das Kunstwerk im Zeitalter seiner technischen Reproduzierbarkeit." *Illuminationen. Ausgewählte Schriften 1.* Frankfurt: Suhrkamp, 1977.

———. "Über den Begriff der Geschichte." *Illuminationen: Ausgewählte Schriften I.* Frankfurt: Suhrkamp, 1977.

Berg, Alban. "Schönberg als Lehrer." *Die Wiener Moderne. Literatur, Kunst und Musik zwischen 1890 und 1910.* Ed. Gotthart Wunberg and Johannes J. Braakenburg. Stuttgart: Reclam, 1981.

Berger, Albert. "Schwieriges Erwachen. Zur Lyrik der jungen Generation in den ersten Nachkriegsjahren (1945–1948)." *Literatur der Nachkriegszeit und der fünfziger Jahre in Österreich.* Eds. Friedbert Aspetsberger et al. Vienna: Österreichischer Bundesverlag, 1984.

Bernhard, Thomas. *Alte Meister. Komödie.* Frankfurt: Suhrkamp, 1988.

———. *Amras. Die Erzählungen.* Frankfurt: Suhrkamp, 1979.

———. "An der Baumgrenze." *An der Baumgrenze.* Salzburg: Residenz, 1969; Reinbek: Rowohlt Taschenbuch, 1980.

———. *Der Atem.* Salzburg: Residenz, 1978.

———. *Der Atem. Eine Entscheidung.* Munich: dtv, 1981.

———. *Auf der Erde und in der Hölle.* Salzburg: Müller, 1957.

———. *Auslöschung. Ein Zerfall.* Frankfurt: Suhrkamp, 1986.

———. *Die Berühmten.* Frankfurt: Suhrkamp, 1976.

———. *Beton*. Frankfurt: Suhrkamp, 1982.

———. *Claus Peymann kauft sich eine Hose und geht mit mir essen: Drei Dramolette*. Frankfurt: Suhrkamp, 1990.

———. *Concrete*. Trans. David McLintock. Chicago: U of Chicago P, 1986.

———. *Cutting Timber. An Irritation*. Trans. Ewald Osers. London, New York: Quartet Books, 1988.

———. *Elisabeth II. Keine Komödie*. Frankfurt: Suhrkamp, 1987.

———. *Die Erzählungen*. Frankfurt: Suhrkamp, 1979.

———. *Extinction*. Trans. David McLintock. New York: Alfred A. Knopf, 1995.

———. "Friedrich Torbergs 'brechtige Kunde,'" *Demokratisches Volksblatt* (29 August 1953).

———. *Frost*. Frankfurt: Suhrkamp, 1963.

———. *Gargoyles*. Trans. Richard and Clara Winston. Chicago: U of Chicago P, 1986.

———. *Gesammelte Gedichte*. Ed. Volker Bohn. Frankfurt: Suhrkamp, 1991.

———. "Großer, unbegreiflicher Hunger." *Stimmen der Gegenwart 1954*. Ed. Hans Weigel. Vienna: Albrecht Dürer, 1954.

———. *Heldenplatz*. Frankfurt: Suhrkamp, 1989.

———. *Heldenplatz*. Trans. Gitta Honegger. *Conjunctions* 33 (1999).

———. *Holzfällen*. Frankfurt: Suhrkamp, 1984.

———. "'Ich bin nur mehr kurz da.' Thomas Bernhard in seinem letzten Gespräch [mit Kurt Hofmann]." *Der Spiegel* 5 (1990): 168.

———. *In der Höhe/Rettungsversuch, Unsinn*. Frankfurt: Suhrkamp, 1990. First published 1989. Salzburg: Residenz Verlag.

———. *In hora mortis*. Salzburg: Müller, 1958.

———. "Interview." *Zeit-Magazin* 46 (1988): 40–50.

———. *Die Irren. Die Häftlinge*. Klagenfurt: Kleinmayr, 1962.

———. *Der Italiener*. Salzburg, Residenz, 1971.

———. *Das Kalkwerk*. Frankfurt: Suhrkamp, 1970.

———. *Die Kälte. Eine Isolation*. Salzburg: Residenz, 1981.

———. *Der Keller. Eine Entziehung*. Salzburg: Residenz, 1976.

———. *Korrektur*. Frankfurt: Suhrkamp, 1975.

———. "Die Landschaft der Mutter." *Handschreiben der Stifterbibliothek*, 13 (1954). Cited in *Thomas Bernhard Werkgeschichte*. Ed. Jens Dittmar. Frankfurt: Suhrkamp, 1990.

———. *Die Macht der Gewohnheit.* Frankfurt: Suhrkamp, 1974.

———. "Mein Weltenstück," *Münchner Merkur* (22 April 1952). *Demokratisches Volksblatt* (20 September 1952).

———. "Politische Morgenandacht," *Wort in der Zeit* 12/1 (1966): 11–13.

———. *Ritter, Dene, Voss.* Frankfurt: Suhrkamp, 1984.

———. "Der Schweinehüter." *Stimmen der Gegenwart 1956.* Ed. Hans Weigel. Vienna/Munich: Herold, 1956.

———. *Der Stimmenimitator.* Frankfurt: Suhrkamp, 1978.

———. *Stücke 1.* Frankfurt: Suhrkamp, 1998.

———. *Die Stücke 1969–1981.* Frankfurt: Suhrkamp, 1983.

———. *Der Theatermacher.* Frankfurt: Suhrkamp, 1984. Vienna: Burgtheater, Programmheft, 1986.

———. *Ungenach.* Frankfurt: Suhrkamp, 1968.

———. *Der Untergeher.* Frankfurt: Suhrkamp, 1983.

———. *Die Ursache. Eine Andeutung.* Munich: dtv, 1977.

———. *Verstörung.* Frankfurt: Insel, 1967.

———. *The Voice Imitator.* Trans. Kenneth J. Norton. Chicago and London: U of Chicago P, 1997.

———. *Watten. Ein Nachlaß.* Frankfurt: Suhrkamp, 1987.

———. *Der Weltverbesserer.* Frankfurt: Suhrkamp, 1979.

———. *Wittgensteins Neffe.* Frankfurt: Suhrkamp, 1982.

———. *Wittgenstein's Nephew.* Trans. David McLintock. New York: Alfred A. Knopf: 1989.

———. *Woodcutters.* Trans. David McClintock. New York: Alfred A. Knopf, 1987.

Betz, Uwe. *Polyphone Räume und karnevalisiertes Erbe. Analysen des Werks Thomas Bernhards aud der Basis Bachtinscher Theoreme.* Würzburg: Ergon, 1997.

Bloch, Ernst. *Gesamtausgabe 4: Erbschaft dieser Zeit.* Frankfurt: Suhrkamp, 1977.

Bodi, Leslie. *Tauwetter in Wien. Zur Prosa der österreichischen Aufklärung 1781–1795.* Frankfurt: Fischer, 1977.

Botond, Anneliese, ed. *Über Thomas Bernhard.* Frankfurt: Suhrkamp, 1970.

Botz, Gerhard. "Österreich und die NS-Vergangenheit: Verdrängung, Pflichterfüllung, Geschichtsklitterung." *Ist der Nationalsozialismus Geschichte? Zu Historisierung und Historikerstreit.* Ed. Dan Diner. Frankfurt: Fischer, 1987.

Bozzi, Paola. *Ästhetik des Leidens. Zur Lyrik Thomas Bernhards.* Frankfurt: Lang, 1997.

———. "'Das Wort des Todes.' Thomas Bernhard und Charles Péguy." *Thomas Bernhard. Traditionen und Trabanten.* Eds. Joachim Hoell, Kai Luehrs-Kaiser. Würzburg: Könighausen und Neumann, 1999.

———. "Nel freddo dei pensieri. La tragica 'Aufklärung' lirica di Thomas Bernhard." *Studia austriaca.* Vol. I. Ed. Fausto Cercignani. Milano: Edizioni dell'Arco, 1992.

Broder, Henryk M. "Diese Scheißbilder trage ich mit mir rum. Henryk Broder über die Reaktionen auf Niklas Franks 'Mein Vater, der Nazi-Mörder.'" *Der Spiegel* (6 July 1987).

Brodsky, Joseph. *Less Than One: Selected Essays.* New York: Farrar Straus Giroux, 1986.

———. *On Grief and Reason: Essays.* New York: Farrar Straus Giroux, 1995.

Butler, Judith. *Bodies That Matter: On the Discursive Limits of "Sex."* New York & London: Routledge, 1993.

Campbell, David K., ed. *Chaos / XAOC.* New York: AIP, 1990.

Craig, Gordon A. "The Waldheim File." *The New York Review of Books* (9 October 1986): 3–4; (26 February 1987): 44.

Crutchfield, James P. et al. "Chaos." *Scientific American* 255 (1986): 46–57.

Damerau, Burghard. *Selbstbehauptungen und Grenzen. Zu Thomas Bernhard.* Würzburg: Könighausen und Neumann, 1996.

Daviau, Donald G. "Preface," *Modern Austrian Literature* 21, no. 3/4 (1988): iii.

Demetz, Peter. "Der Anti-Jedermann." *Frankfurter Allgemeine Zeitung* (17 September 1983).

Dittberner, Hugo. "Der Dichter wird Kolorist: Thomas Bernhards Epochensprung." *Thomas Bernhard Text+Kritik.* Ed. Heinz Ludwig Arnold. Munich: text+kritik, 1991.

———. "Die heimliche Apologie der Macht: Kritisches zu Thomas Bernhards *Verstörung.*" *Thomas Bernhard Text+Kritik.* Ed. Heinz Ludwig Arnold. Munich: text+kritik, 1982.

Dittmar, Jens. *Sehr gescherte Reaktion: Leserbrief-Schlachten um Thomas Bernhard.* Vienna: Österreichische Staatsdruckerei, 1993.

———. *Thomas Bernhard: Werkgeschichte.* Frankfurt: Suhrkamp, 1990.

Doderer, Heimito von. *Die Dämonen.* Munich: Biederstein, 1956.

Donahue, William J. "Zu Thomas Bernhards *Die Ursache. Eine Andeutung.*" *Modern Austrian Literature* 21, no 3/4 (1988): 89–106.

Donnenberg, Josef. "Gehirnfähigkeit der Unfähigkeit der Natur." *Thomas Bernhard (und Österreich): Studien zu Werk und Wirkung 1970–1989.* Stuttgart: Heinz, 1997.

———. "War Thomas Bernhards Lyrik eine Sackgasse?" *In Sachen Thomas Bernhard.* Ed. Kurt Bartsch et al. Königstein: Athäneum, 1983.

Dowden, Stephen D. *Understanding Thomas Bernhard.* Columbia, SC: U of South Carolina P, 1991.

Dreissinger, Sepp. *Thomas Bernhard — Portraits — Bilder und Texte.* Weitra: Bibiliothek der Provinz, 1990.

Dusek, Peter, Anton Pelinka, and Erika Weinzierl. *Zeitgeschichte im Aufriß: Österreich seit 1918: 50 Jahre Zweite Republik.* Vienna: Jugend und Volk, 1995.

Endres, Ria. *Am Ende angekommen.* Frankfurt: Fischer, 1980.

Eybl, Franz M. "Thomas Bernhard's *Stimmenimitator* als Resonanz eigener und fremder Rede." *Kontinent Bernhard: Zur Thomas-Bernhard-Rezeption in Europa.* Ed. Wolfram Bayer. Vienna: Böhlau, 1995.

Felman, Shoshana. "Film as Witness: Claude Lanzmann's *Shoah.*" *Holocaust Remembrance: The Shapes of Memory.* Ed. Geoffrey H. Hartman. Oxford, UK: Blackwell, 1994.

Fetz, Gerald A. "Thomas Bernhard und die österreichische Literatur." *Österreichische Gegenwart. Die moderne Literatur und ihr Verhältnis zur Tradition.* Ed. Wolfgang Paulsen. Bern/ Munich: Francke, 1980.

Finkielkraut, Alain. *The Imaginary Jew.* Trans. Kevin O'Neill and David Suchoff. Lincoln and London: Nebraska UP, 1994.

Fitzmaurice, John. *Austrian Politics and Society Today: In Defense of Austria.* New York: St. Martin's P, 1990.

Frank, Niklas. "Ansichten eines unverbesserlichen Weltverbesserers." *Von einer Katastrophe in die andere. 13 Gespräche mit Thomas Bernhard.* Ed. Sepp Dreissinger. Weitra: publication PNo 1, 1992.

———. *Der Vater: Eine Abrechnung.* Munich: Bertelsmann, 1987.

Friedrich, Otto. *Glenn Gould: A Life and Variations.* New York: Random House, 1989.

Fueß, Renate. *Nicht fragen: Zum Double-bind in Interaktionsformen und Werkstruktur bei Thomas Bernhard.* Frankfurt: Lang, 1983.

Gamm, Gerhard. "Korrektur. Über Thomas Bernhard und die Melancholie der Moderne." *Lettre international* 56 (1999): 56–61.

Gamper, Herbert. "Theater machen oder Schluß machen." *Schauspiel. Staatstheater Stuttgart: Thomas Bernhard: Der Theatermacher* (1990).

Gehlen, Arnold. *Die Seele im technischen Zeitalter. Sozialpsychologische Probleme in der industriellen Gesellschaft.* Reinbek: Rowohlt, 1957.

———. "Thomas Bernhards philosophisches Theater." *Neue Zürcher Zeitung* (29 January 1988): 40.

Görner, Rüdiger. "Gespiegelte Wiederholungen. Zu einem Kunstgriff von Thomas Bernhard." *Thomas Bernhard. Beiträge zur Fiktion der Postmoderne. Londoner Symposion.* Eds. Wendelin Schmidt-Dengler, Adrian Stevens, Fred Wagner. Frankfurt: Suhrkamp, 1997.

Gößling, Andreas. *Die "Eisenbergrichtung": Versuch über Thomas Bernhards Auslöschung.* Münster: Kleinheinrich, 1988.

Gombrowicz, Witold. *A Kind of Testament.* Trans. Alistair Hamilton. Ed. Dominique de Roux. London: Calder and Boyars, 1973.

Gould, Glenn. *The Glenn Gould Reader.* Ed. Tim Page. New York: Knopf, 1984.

Greene, Malcolm. "Introduction." *Writings of the Vienna Actionists.* London: Atlas P, 1999.

Haider, Hans. "Sieben Worte im voraus: Gespräch mit Schindel." *Die Presse.* Literaricum (22 February 1992).

Hamann, Brigitte. *Hitler's Vienna: A Dictator's Apprenticeship.* Oxford: Oxford UP, 1999.

Hamm, Peter. "Auf der Erde und in der Hölle. Thomas Bernhard als Lyriker." *Die Zeit* (26 April 1991).

Handke, Peter. *Publikumsbeschimpfung.* Frankfurt: Suhrkamp, 1966.

———. *Wunschloses Unglück.* Frankfurt: Suhrkamp, 1972.

Hartman, Geoffrey H. "Introduction: Darkness Visible" *Holocaust Remembrance: The Shapes of Memory.* Ed. Geoffrey H. Hartman. Oxford, UK: Blackwell, 1994.

Haslinger, Adolf. "Mütze, Mantel, Wetterfleck: Kleiderthematik und poetisches Verfahren bei Thomas Bernhard." *Bernhard-Tage Ohlsdorf 1994: Materialien.* Ed. Franz Gebesmair & Alfred Pittertschatscher. Weitra: Bibliothek der Provinz, 1995.

Haslinger, Josef. *Die Politik der Gefühle.* Darmstadt: Luchterhand, 1987.

Hauptmann, Gerhart. *Sämtliche Werke. Band 7.* Ed. Hans-Egon Hass. Berlin: Ullstein, 1962.

Hayles, Katherine N. *Chaos Bound. Orderly Disorder in Contemporary Literature and Science.* Ithaca: Cornell UP, 1990.

Heidelberger-Leonard, Irene. "Auschwitz als Pflichtfach für Schriftsteller." *Anti-autobiografie. Thomas Bernhards Auslöschung.* Ed. Hans Höller and Irene Heidelberger-Leonard. Frankfurt: Suhrkamp, 1995.

Helms-Derfert, Hermann. *Die Last der Geschichte: Interpretationen zur Prosa von Thomas Bernhard.* Cologne: Böhlau, 1997.

Hens, Gregor. *Thomas Bernhards Trilogie der Künste: Der Untergeher, Holzfällen, Alte Meister.* Rochester, NY: Camden House, 1999.

Henscheid, Eckhard. "Der Krypto-Komiker: Wie der österreichische Schriftsteller Thomas Bernhard seine Bewunderer, seine Kritiker und wahrscheinlich sich selber an der Nase herumführt." *pardon* Heft 7 (1973): 21–23.

Höller, Hans. *Kritik einer literarischen Form: Versuch über Thomas Bernhard.* Stuttgart: Heinz, 1979.

———. "Menschen, Geschichte(n), Orte und Landschaften." *Antiautobiografie. Thomas Bernhards Auslöschung.* Ed. Hans Höller and Irene Heidelberger-Leonard. Frankfurt: Suhrkamp, 1995.

———. *Thomas Bernhard.* Reinbek: Rowohlt, 1993.

Hofer, Brigitte. "Das Ganze ist im Grunde ein Spass." *Von einer Katastrophe in die andere. 13 Gespräche mit Thomas Bernhard.* Ed. Sepp Dreissinger. Weitra: publication PNo 1, 1992.

Hofmann, Kurt. *Aus Gesprächen mit Thomas Bernhard.* Munich: dtv, 1991.

Holzer, Gabriele. *Verfreundete Nachbarn: Österreich/Deutschland, Ein Verhältnis.* Vienna: Kremayr und Scheriau, 1995.

Huntemann, Willi. *Artistik und Rollkenspiel. Das System Thomas Bernhard.* Würzburg: Königshausen & Neumann, 1990.

Jahraus, Oliver. *Die Wiederholung als werkkonstitutives Prinzip im Oeuvre Thomas Bernhards.* Frankfurt: Peter Lang, 1991.

Jameson, Frederic. *The Political Unconscious: Narrative as a Socially Symbolic Act.* London: Routledge, 1989.

Jankowitsch, Peter. "Die verschämte Republik." *Profil* (12 January 1987): 33.

Janz, Marlies. *Elfriede Jelinek.* Stuttgart: Metzler, 1995.

Jelavich, Barbara. *Austria: Empire and Republic 1800–1986.* Cambridge: Cambridge UP, 1987.

Jelinek, Elfriede. "Atemlos." *Die Zeit* (24 February 1989): 57. Reprinted in *Thomas Bernhard. Portraits.* Ed. Sepp Dreissinger. Weitra: Bibliothek der Provinz, 1992.

———. *Ein Sportstück.* Reinbek: Rowohlt, 1998.

———. *Stechen, Stab und Stangl / Raststätte / Wolken. Heim.* Reinbek: Rowohlt, 1997.

———. *Theaterstücke. Was geschah nachdem Nora ihren Mann verlassen hatte oder Stützen der Gesellschaft / Clara S. musikalische Tragòdie / Burgtheater / Krankheit oder moderne Frau.* Reinbek: Rowohlt, 1992.

———. *Totenauberg.* Reinbek: Rowohlt, 1991.

Kaindlstorfer, Günther. "Auf Wiederschaun, Herr Schindel." *Falter.* No. 32 (7–13 August 1992): 18.

Kazdin, Andrew. *Glenn Gould at Work: Creative Lying.* New York: Dutton, 1989.

Klinger, Kurt. "Flucht durch Europa: Thomas Bernhard." *Kindlers Literaturgeschichte der Gegenwart.* Vol. 6/II. Ed. Hilde Spiel. Frankfurt: Fischer, 1980.

Klug, Christian. "Thomas Bernhards Arbeiten für das Salzburger Demokratische Volksblatt 1952–54." *Modern Austrian Literature* 21, no. 3/4 (1988): 135–72.

———. *Thomas Bernhards Theaterstücke.* Stuttgart: Metzler, 1991.

Knight, Robert. "The Waldheim Context: Austrian and Nazism." *TLS* 13 (October 1986): 1083–84.

Knörrich, Otto. *Die deutsche Lyrik seit 1945.* Stuttgart: Kroener, 1978.

König, Josef. *Nichts als ein Totenmaskenball: Studien zum Verständnis der ästhetischen Intentionen im Werk Thomas Bernhards.* Frankfurt: Lang, 1983.

Köpnick, Lutz. "Leben in der Hölle. Thomas Bernhards *Heldenplatz*," *New German Review* 7 (1991): 15–25.

Konzett, Matthias. *The Rhetoric of National Dissent in Thomas Bernhard, Peter Handke and Elfriede Jelinek.* Rochester, NY; Woodbridge, UK: Camden House, 2000.

Langer, Norbert. "Die Schwierigkeit, mit Wolfsegg fertig zu werden: Thomas Bernhards *Auslöschung* im Kontext der osterreichischen Schloßromane nach 1945." *Antiautobiografie: Zu Thomas Bernhards Auslöschung.* Ed. Hans Höller and Irene Heidelberg-Leonard. Frankfurt: Suhrkamp, 1995.

Lavant, Christine. *Gedichte.* Ed. Thomas Bernhard. Frankfurt: Suhrkamp 1987.

Lindenmayr, Heinrich. *Totalität und Beschränkung: Eine Untersuchung zu Thomas Bernhards Roman Das Kalkwerk.* Königshausen: Athenäum, 1982.

Lorenz, Dagmar C. G. *Verfolgung bis zum Massenmord.* New York: Lang, 1992.

Lunzer, Heinz. "Der literarische Markt 1945 bis 1955." *Literatur der Nachkriegszeit und der fünfziger Jahre in Österreich.* Eds. Friedbert Aspetsberger et al. Wien: Österreichischer Bundesverlag, 1984.

Lyotard, Jean-François. *The Postmodern Condition: A Report on Knowledge.* Trans. Geoff Bennington and Brian Massumi. Minneapolis: U of Minnesota P, 1984.

Mádl, Antal. "Entwicklung der österreichischen Literatur." *helikon.* Sondernummer. Ed. Ilona T. Erdély (1979).

Mahler-Bungers, Annegret. "Die Antiautobiographie: Thomas Bernhard als 'Antiautobiograph?'" *Über sich selber reden. Zur Psychoanalyse autobiographischen Schreibens* (*Freiburger literaturpsychologische Gespräche* 11). Ed. Johannes Cremerius. Würzburg: Königshausen und Neumann, 1992.

Maier, Charles S. *The Unmasterable Past: History, Holocaust, and German National Identity*. Cambridge, Massachusetts: Harvard UP, 1987.

———. "Überaus bedenklich." *Profil* (15 December 1986): 16, 19.

Mandelbrot, Benoit B. *The Fractal Geometry of Nature*. New York: Freeman, 1983.

Matheis, Wera. *Glenn Gould: der Unheilige am Klavier*. Munich: scaneg, 1987.

Matt, Peter von. "Unbekannte Dichter. Thomas Bernhards poetische Paradiese." *Frankfurter Allgemeine Zeitung* (10 August 1991).

Menasse, Robert. *Überbau und Underground: Essays zum österreichischen Geist*. Frankfurt: Suhrkamp, 1996.

Meyerhofer, Nicholas J. *Thomas Bernhard*. Berlin: Colloquium, 1985.

Miller, Alice. *Am Anfang war die Erziehung*. Frankfurt: Suhrkamp, 1980.

Minetti, Bernhard. "Ein Autor namens Bernhard. Erinnerungen eines Schauspielers." *Thomas Bernhard. Portraits. Bilder & Texte*. Ed. Sepp Dreissinger. Weitra: Bibliothek der Provinz, 1991.

Mitchell, Michael. "Restoration or Renewal? Csokor, the Austrian PEN Club and the Re-establishment of Literary Life in Austria, 1945–55." *Austria 1945–1955: Studies in Political and Cultural Re-emergence*. Ed. Anthony Bushell. Cardiff: U of Wales P, 1996.

Mitscherlich, Alexander and Margarete. *Die Unfähigkeit zu trauern*. Munich: Piper, 1967.

Mittermayer, Manfred. *Thomas Bernhard*. Stuttgart: Metzler, 1995.

Mixner, Manfred. "Vom Leben zum Tode. Die Einleitung des Negationsprozesses im Frühwerk von Thomas Bernhard." *Bernhard. Annäherungen*. Ed. Manfred Jurgensen. Bern: Francke, 1981.

Moritz, Herbert. *Lehrjahre. Vom Journalisten zum Dichter*. Ed. Richard Pilz. Weitra: Bibliothek der Provinz, 1992.

Müller, Karl. *Zäsuren ohne Folgen. Das lange Leben der literarischen Antimoderne Österreichs seit den 30er Jahren*. Salzburg: Müller, 1990.

Neumann, Robert. *Der Tatbestand oder der gute Glaube der Deutschen*. Munich: Piper 1965.

Neumeister, Sebastian. *Der Dichter als Dandy: Kafka, Baudelaire, Thomas Bernhard*. Munich: Fink, 1973.

Nickel, Eckhart. *Flaneur. Die Ermöglichung der Lebenskunst im Spätwerk Thomas Bernhards*. Heidelberg: Manutius, 1997.

Palmer, Kurt. *Vom Boykott zur Anerkennung. Brecht und Österreich.* Vienna/Munich: Löcker, 1983.

Paslack, Rainer. "'...da stellt ein Wort zur rechten Zeit sich ein.' Die Karriere des Chaos zum Schlüsselbegriff." *Kursbuch* 98 (1989): 121–39.

Peitgen, Heinz-Otto and Peter H. Richter. *The Beauty of Fractals: Images of Complex Dynamical Systems.* Berlin: Springer, 1986.

Petersen, Jürgen. "Beschreibung einer sinnentleerten Welt: Erzählthematik und Erzählverfahren in Thomas Bernhards Romanen." *Bernhard: Annäherungen.* Ed. Manfred Jurgensen. Bern: Francke, 1981.

Petrasch, Ingrid. *Die Konstitution der Wirklichkeit in der Prosa Thomas Bernhards: Sinnbildlichkeit und groteske Überzeichnung.* Frankfurt: Lang, 1987.

Pfabigan, Alfred. *Thomas Bernhard. Ein österreichisches Weltexperiment.* Vienna: Zsolnay, 1999.

Porcell, Claude. "Théâtre: La scène obscure." *Thomas Bernhard: Ténèbres.* Ed. Claude Porcell. Paris: Nadeau, 1986.

Posner, Gerald L. Hitler's Children: Sons and Daughters of Leaders of the Third Reich Talk About Themselves and Their Fathers. New York: Random House, 1991.

Pulvirenti, Grazia. "'Con la morte negli occhi.' La produzione poetica di Thomas Bernhard: un apprendistato giovanile." *AION. Annali. Sezione Germanica.* N.S. 1 (1991) 1/2 (1992): 213–65.

Rabinovici, Doron. *Suche nach M.* Frankfurt: Suhrkamp, 1997.

Radax, Ferry. "Drei Tage." Published in Thomas Bernhard's *Der Italiener.* Salzburg: Residenz, 1971.

Rainer, Arnulf. "Malerei, um die Malerei zu verlassen." 1952. Reprinted in *Arnulf Rainer.* Ed. Rudi Fuchs. Vienna: Historisches Museum der Stadt Wien, 1987.

Rambures, Jean-Louis de. "Dans le labyrinthe." *Arcane* 17 (Nantes, 1987): 175.

Reich, Wilhelm. *Massenpsychologie des Faschismus.* Frankfurt am Main: Fischer, 1974.

Reiter, Andrea. "Die Bachmann . . . war halt eine gescheite Frau." *Die Rampe* (1992): 2, 17–43.

Rimbaud, Arthur. *Sämtliche Dichtungen. Französisch und Deutsch.* Ed. Walter Küchler. Heidelberg: Laubert Schneider, 1982.

Roeder, Anke, and Elfriede Jelinek. "Ich will kein Theater — Ich will ein anderes Theater." *Theater Heute* 8 (1989).

Rubel, Peter. "Wir sind schuldig!" *Plan* I/9 (1946): 781.

Rühmkorf, Peter. *Die Jahre, die ihr kennt. Abfälle und Erinnerungen.* Reinbek: Rowohlt, 1972.

Safranski, Rüdiger. *Martin Heidegger: Between Good and Evil.* Trans. Ewald Osers. Cambridge, MA: Harvard UP, 1998.

Scheib, Asta. "Von einer Katastrophe in die andere." *Von einer Katastrophe in die andere. 13 Gespräche mit Thomas Bernhard.* Ed. Sepp Dreissinger Weitra: publication PNo 1, 1992.

Schindel, Robert. "Erich Friedpreisrede." *Gott schütz uns vor den guten Menschen.* Frankfurt: Suhrkamp, 1995.

———. *Gebürtig.* Frankfurt: Suhrkamp, 1992.

Schlichtmann, Silke. *Das Erzählprinzip Auslöschung: Zum Umgang mit der Geschichte in Thomas Bernhards Roman Auslöschung. Ein Zerfall.* Frankfurt: Lang, 1996.

Schmid, Georg. "Die "Falschen' Fuffziger. Kulturpolitische Tendenzen der fünfziger Jahre." *Literatur der Nachkriegszeit und der fünfziger Jahre in Österreich.* Eds. Friedbert Aspetsberger et al. Vienna: Österreichischer Bundesverlag, 1984.

Schmidt-Dengler, Wendelin. *Bruchlinien. Vorlesungen zur österreichischen Literatur 1945 bis 1900.* Salzburg: Residenz, 1995.

———. "Komödientragödien: Zum dramatischen Spätwerk Bernhards." *Bernhard-Tage Ohlsdorf 1994: Materialien.* Ed. Franz Gebesmair & Alfred Pittertschatscher. Weitra: Bibliothek der Provinz, 1995.

———. *Der Übertreibungskünstler. Zu Thomas Bernhard.* Vienna: Sonderzahl, 1986.

———. "Zurück zum Text: Vorschläge für die Lektüre von Thomas Bernhards *Frost.*" *Thomas Bernhard: Beiträge zur Fiktion der Postmoderne. Londoner Symposion.* Eds. Wendelin Schmidt-Dengler, Adrian Stevens, and Fred Wagner. Frankfurt: Peter Lang, 1997.

Schorske, Carl E. *Thinking with History. Explorations in the Passage to Modernism.* Princeton: U of Princeton P, 1998.

———. *Fin-de-Siècle Vienna: Politics and Culture.* New York: Vintage, 1980.

Schuh, Franz. "Thomas Bernhard in Anekdote und Selbstzeugnis." *salz* 1, Heft 2 (1975/76): 8.

Schulz, Walter. *Wittgenstein. Die Negation der Philosophie.* Pfullingen: Neske, 1979.

Schutting, Jutta. *Der Vater.* Salzburg: Residenz, 1980.

Schwaiger, Brigitte. *Lange Abwesenheit.* Vienna: Zsolnay, 1980.

Seelich, Nadja. *Kieselsteine.* Dir. Lukas Stepanik. Cinéart. Filmverleih Hofmann, 1981.

Sorg, Bernhard. *Thomas Bernhard.* Munich: Beck, 1992.

Soyfer, Jura. *Das Gesamtwerk.* Ed. Horst Jarka. Vienna: Europa Verlag, 1980.

Spiel, Hilde. *Briefwechsel.* Ed. Hans A. Neunzig. Munich, Leipzig: List, 1995.

———. *Die Feder, Ein Schwert?* Ed. Harald Seuter. Graz: Leykam, 1981.

Streeruwitz, Marlene. "In der Gewohneit das Fürchterliche." *Und. Sonst. Noch. Aber. Texte. 1989–1996.* Vienna: edition selene, 1999.

———. "My Latest Encounter with Bernhard." First published in German in *Falter* (February, 1999).

Szyskowitz, Gerald. *Puntigam oder die Kunst des Vergessens.* Vienna: Zsolnay, 1988.

Theweleit, Klaus. *Männerphantasien.* Frankfurt: Rowohlt, 1980.

Thomas, Chantal. *Le Rire Tragique: Thomas Bernhard.* Paris: Seuil, 1990.

Töteberg, Michael. "Höhenflüge im Flachgau. Drei Anläufe, dreimal abgestürzt: die Vorgeschichte des Autors Thomas Bernhard." *Text und Kritik,* 43 (1991).

Vellusig, Robert. "Thomas Bernhards Gesprächs-Kunst." *Thomas Bernhard. Beiträge zur Fiktion der Postmoderne. Londoner Symposion.* Eds. Wendelin Schmidt-Dengler, Adrian Stevens, Fred Wagner. Frankfurt: Suhrkamp, 1997.

Wantoch, Erika. "Von '68 zu '38: Ein Gespräch mit Robert Schindel." *Profil* (21 December 1987): 62.

Weber, Albrecht. "Wittgensteins Gestalt und Theorie und ihre Wirkung im Werk Thomas Bernhards." *Österreich in Geschichte und Literatur* 25 (1981): 86–104.

Weibel, Peter. Ed. *die wiener gruppe: a moment of modernity 1954–1960.* Vienna: Bundesverlag, 1997.

Weininger, Otto. *Geschlecht und Charakter.* Vienna: Braumüller, 1906.

Weiss, Walter. "Österreichisches in der österreichischen Literatur seit 1945." *Literatur aus Österreich — Österreichische Literatur. Ein Bonner Symposion.* Ed. K. Pohlheim. Bonn: Bouvier, 1981.

Wiesenthal, Simon. *Doch die Mörder leben.* Munich: Droemer-Knaur, 1968.

———. *Ich jagte Eichmann.* Gütersloh: Mohn, 1961.

Wischenbart, Rüdiger. "Zur Auseinandersetzung um die Moderne. Literarischer 'Nachholbedarf' — Auflösung der Literatur." *Literatur der Nachkriegszeit und der fünfziger Jahre in Österreich.* Eds. Friedbert Aspetsberger et al. Vienna: Österreichischer Bundesverlag, 1984.

Wittgenstein, Ludwig. *Schriften: Tractatus logico-philosophicus, Tagebücher 1914–1916, Philosophische Untersuchungen.* Frankfurt: Suhrkamp, 1960.

Woodward, C. Vann. *The Burden of Southern History*. Baton Rouge: Louisiana State UP, 1960.

Wühr, Paul. *Wenn man mich so reden hört: Ein Selbstgespräch*. Graz: Droschl, 1993.

Young, James E. *Holocaust Memorials and Meaning*. New Haven: Yale UP, 1993.

Zech, Paul. *Rimbaud. Ein biographischer Essay und die szenische Ballade "Das trunkene Schiff."* Ed. Hermann Haarmann et al. Rudolstadt: Greifenverlag zu Rudolstadt, 1986.

Zweig, Stefan. *Die Welt von gestern. Erinnerungen eines Europäers*. Frankfurt: Suhrkamp, 1998. First published 1944.

Contributors

MARK M. ANDERSON is Professor in the Department of Germanic Languages and Literatures at Columbia University, New York. He is author of several books on Kafka (*Kafka's Clothes, Reading Kafka*), and the editor and translator of contemporary Austrian writers Ingeborg Bachmann and Thomas Bernhard. His most recent book publication (as editor) is *Hitler's Exiles: Personal Stories of the Flight from Nazi Germany to America* (2000).

PAOLA BOZZI is Assistant Professor of German at the University of Milano, Italy. She is the author of *Ästhetik des Leidens. Zur Lyrik Thomas Bernhards* (1997) and numerous essays on Bernhard.

STEPHEN D. DOWDEN is Professor of Germanic Languages, Chair at Brandeis University, Boston. He is author of *Understanding Thomas Bernhard* (1991) as well as book studies on Herman Broch and Kafka. His most recent publication (as editor) is *A Companion to Thomas Mann's Magic Mountain* (1999).

RÜDIGER GÖRNER is Professor of German Literature, School of Languages and European Studies at Aston University, Birmingham, United Kingdom. His work includes book publications on Rilke, Hölderlin and Goethe. His most recent publications are: *Goethe. Wissen und Entsagen — aus Kunst* (1995) and *Grenzgänger. Essays über Dichter und Denker im Dazwischen* (1995).

GITTA HONEGGER is Professor of German at Arizona State University. She is a director of numerous plays and is an author of essays on contemporary playwrights. She is also a translator of plays by Bernhard, Canetti, Handke, Kroetz, Jelinek, and Fleisser. She is the author of the biography *Thomas Bernhard: The Making of an Austrian* (2001).

MATTHIAS KONZETT is Associate Professor of Germanic Languages and Literatures at Yale University. He is author of *The Rhetoric of National Dissent in Thomas Bernhard, Peter Handke and Elfriede Jelinek* (2000) as well as numerous essays on contemporary German and Austrian literature. He is also the editor of *The Encyclopedia of German Literature* (2000).

JONATHAN LONG is Lecturer in German at University of Durham, United Kingdom. He is the author of essays on Bernhard, Hildesheimer, Schlink, Wilkomirski, and Lewis. He is the author of *The Novels of Thomas Bernhard* (2001).

DAGMAR LORENZ is Professor of German at University of Illinois, Chicago. She is editor of *German Quarterly*, and is the author of numerous books and essays, including *Keepers of the Motherland: German Texts by Jewish Women* (1997) and *Verfolgung bis zum Massenmord. Diskurse zum Holocaust in deutscher Sprache* (1992). Her most recent publication (as editor) is *Contemporary Jewish Writing in Austria* (1999).

WILLY RIEMER is Associate Professor of German Literature and Film at the University of Delaware. He has published numerous essays on Broch, Doderer, Bernhard, Strauss, Streeruwitz, and Handke. His most recent publication (as editor) is *After Postmodernism: Austrian Literature and Film in Transition* (2000).

WENDELIN SCHMIDT-DENGLER is Professor of German Literature, Chair at the University of Vienna, Austria and Director of the National Archive of Contemporary Austrian Literature. He is the author of numerous books, including works on Goethe, Jandl, Doderer, Mayröcker, and Serner. His most recent publications include *Bruchlinien: Vorlesungen zur österreichischen Literatur 1945 bis 1990* (1995). His publications on Bernhard include: *Der Übertreibungskünstler: Studien zu Thomas Bernhard* (1989) and *Statt Bernhard: Über Misanthropie im Werk Thomas Bernhards,* eds. Wendelin Schmidt-Dengler and Martin Huber.

MARLENE STREERUWITZ is an author and playwright in Vienna. Her plays have been performed on major stages in Germany, Austria, Sweden, Finland, the Netherlands, and the United States. She is the recipient of the National Prize for Literature from the Austrian government and the Hermann Hesse Prize (2001). Her most recent publications include *Majakowskiring. Erzählung* (2000), *Waikiki Beach und andere Orte. Die Theaterstücke* (1999), *Nachwelt.Ein Reisebericht. Roman* (1999), as well as the English translation of her novel *Verführungen* (1996) entitled *Seductions* (1998).

ANDREW WEBBER is Senior Lecturer in German at the University of Cambridge, United Kingdom. His works include *Sexuality and the Sense of Self in the Works of Georg Trakl and Robert Musil* (1990), *The Doppelgänger: Double Visions in German Literature* (1996), and numerous essays on Storm, Werfel, Kleist, and Brecht.

Index

Since the death of Thomas Bernhard in 1989, the literary reputation of this complex and unique writer has risen to the point that he is now regarded as a major European figure. Bernhard emerged in the 1960s as one of Austria's major writers, challenging the popularity of such established writers as Heinrich Böll and Günter Grass on the German literary scene. His idiosyncratic prose consists of a tragic-comic blend of themes such as suicide, madness, and isolation combined with highly satirical and histrionic invectives against culture, tradition, and society. As a skillful impresario of public scandals by means of verbal assaults upon Austrian elite culture, Bernhard also earned himself the epithet of *Übertreibungskünstler* (artist of exaggeration). In this art of cultural and political provocation he remains unmatched to the present day.

The present volume consists of new essays by well-known critics examining the most salient aspects of Bernhard's work. In four major categories — Bernhard in the public, Bernhard's poetics, Bernhard and drama, and Bernhard's social worlds — the authors flesh out the broad scope and impact of his innovative art. The volumeoffers insights into literary strategies and public themes that made Bernhard one of Europe's masters of modern prose and drama. Essays examine Bernhard's complex artistic sensibility, his impact on Austria's critical memory, his relation to the legacy of Austrian Jewish culture, his representative value as Austria's prime literary export, and his cosmopolitanism and its significance for the rapidly changing multicultural landscape of Europe.

MATTHIAS KONZETT is Associate Professor of German at Yale University. He is the author of *The Rhetoric of National Dissent in Thomas Bernhard, Peter Handke, and Elfriede Jelinek* (Camden House, 2000) and the editor of *The Encyclopedia of German Literature.*

Printed and bound by CPI Group (UK) Ltd, Croydon, CR0 4YY

07/07/2026

14916224-0004